History and Nature of Science [HNS]

CONTENT STANDARD G: As a result of the activities in grades K–4, all students should develop an understanding of

- Science as a human endeavor [HNS 1]

Content Standards: Grades 5–8

Science as Inquiry

CONTENT STANDARD A: As a result of their activities in grades 5–8, all students should develop

- Abilities necessary to do scientific inquiry
- Understanding about scientific inquiry

Physical Science [PS]

CONTENT STANDARD B: As a result of their activities in grades 5–8, all students should develop an understanding of

- Properties and changes of properties in matter [PS 4]
- Motion and forces [PS 5]
- Transfer of energy [PS 6]

Life Science [LS]

CONTENT STANDARD C: As a result of their activities in grades 5–8, all students should develop an understanding of

- Structure and function in living systems [LS 4]
- Reproduction and heredity [LS 5]
- Regulation and behavior [LS 6]
- Population and ecosystems [LS 7]
- Diversity and adaptations of organisms [LS 8]

Earth and Space Science

CONTENT STANDARD D: As a result of their activities in grades 5–8, all students should develop an understanding of

- Structure of the earth system [ESS 4]
- Earth's history [ESS 5]
- Earth in the solar system [ESS 6]

Science and Technology [S&T]

CONTENT STANDARD E: As a result of the activities in grades 5–8, all students should develop an understanding of

- Abilities of technological design [S&T 4]
- Understanding about science and technology [S&T 5]

Science in Personal and Social Perspectives [SPSP]

CONTENT STANDARD F: As a result of the activities in grades 5–8, all students should develop an understanding of

- Personal health [SPSP 6]
- Populations, resources, and environments [SPSP 7]
- Natural hazards [SPSP 8]
- Risks and benefits [SPSP 9]
- Changes in environments [SPSP 10]
- Science and technology in society [SPSP 11]

History and Nature of Science [HNS]

CONTENT STANDARD G: As a result of the activities in grades 5–8, all students should develop an understanding of

- Science as a human endeavor [HNS 2]
- Nature of science [HNS 3]
- History of science [HNS 4]

Teaching Children Science

*Discovery Methods for
the Elementary and Middle Grades*

Teaching Children Science

Discovery Methods for the Elementary and Middle Grades

SECOND EDITION

Joseph Abruscato

University of Vermont

PEARSON

Boston   New York   San Francisco
Mexico City   Montreal   Toronto   London   Madrid   Munich   Paris
Hong Kong   Singapore   Tokyo   Cape Town   Sydney

Series Editor: *Traci Mueller*
Editorial Assistant: *Krista E. Price*
Senior Marketing Manager: *Elizabeth Fogarty*
Editorial-Production Administrator: *Annette Joseph*
Editorial-Production Service: *Susan Freese, Communicáto, Ltd.*
Text Designer and Electronic Composition: *Denise Hoffman*
Composition Buyer: *Linda Cox*
Manufacturing Buyer: *Andrew Turso*
Cover Administrator: *Joel Gendron*
Cover Designer: *Suzanne Harbison*

For related titles and support materials, visit our online catalog at www.ablongman.com.

Between the time Website information is gathered and then published, it is not unusual for some sites to have closed. Also, the transcription of URLs can result in typographical errors. The publisher would appreciate notification where these errors occur so that they may be corrected in subsequent editions.

Many of the designations used by manufacturers and sellers to distinguish their products are claimed as trademarks. Where those designations appear in this book and Allyn and Bacon was aware of a trademark claim, the designations have been printed in caps or initial caps.

Library of Congress Cataloging-in-Publication Data

Abruscato, Joseph.
    Teaching children science : discovery methods for the elementary
and middle grades / Joseph Abruscato.—2nd ed.
      p. cm.
    Includes bibliographical references and index.
    ISBN 0–205–40261–5
    1. Science—Study and teaching (Elementary). 2. Science—Study
and teaching (Middle school). I. Title.

LB1585.A27 2004
372.3'5044—dc21

                                         2003052436

Printed in the United States of America

10 9 8 7 6 5 4 3   RRD-VA   08 07 06 05

See photo and permissions credits on page 199, which constitutes a continuation of the copyright page.

For my father
who came uneducated to a new and wonderful land
and taught his children that anyone willing to work hard,
live life fully, and make some sacrifices
could and would have a bright future

Contents

2 Constructing Knowledge and Discovering Meaning   23

How can I help children learn science?

3 The Inquiry Process Skills   43

How can I help children use the inquiry process skills to make discoveries?

4 Planning and Managing   61

How can I plan and manage inquiry-based, discovery-focused units and lessons?

5 Strategies and QuickChecks   81

How can I effectively use cooperative learning, questioning and wait-time strategies, active listening, demonstrations, and textbooks in my classroom?

6 Assessment of Understanding and Inquiry   99

How can I put the NSE Standards approach, along with traditional and authentic assessment techniques, to work in my classroom?

7 Integrating Science   121

*How can I integrate inquiry-based science
with other subjects in a child's school day?*

8 Science WebQuests   139

*How can I create inquiry-based, discovery-focused
Internet projects for children?*

9 Adapting the Science Curriculum   157

*How can I adapt the science curriculum for children from
diverse cultural backgrounds, children with special needs,
and children with special gifts and talents?*

Welcome to *Discovery Methods* for the Elementary and Middle Grades

Using this lively, streamlined, right-to-the-point book will help you become a great teacher! Its friendly style will deliver information to you that is both practical and immediately useful. Its pages will teach you how to apply all of these skills:

1. Provide children with *inquiry experiences* that lead to *discovery learning.*
2. Use the *National Science Education (NSE) Standards* to provide units and lessons with focus and direction.
3. Design units and lessons that recognize how children *construct knowledge and discover meaning.*
4. Use the *inquiry process skills* as the starting point for children's learning.
5. *Plan and manage* inquiry-based, discovery-focused units and lessons.
6. Plan and use *Internet-based WebQuests* to help children use the vast resources of the Internet in a meaningful way.
7. *Make effective use of strategies* such as cooperative learning, questioning, wait-time/think-time, and active listening.
8. Use observational tools called *QuickChecks* to assess your own teaching and the teaching you observe during field work or in-class peer teaching.
9. *Assess children's understanding and ability to conduct inquiry* using the NSE Standards approach as well as traditional and authentic assessment techniques.
10. *Integrate inquiry-based science* with other subjects in a child's school day.
11. *Adapt the science curriculum* for children who come from diverse backgrounds and who have special needs and talents.
12. Use the *Real Teachers Talking* feature in each chapter to gain insight into the challenges and opportunities faced by real teachers in real classrooms.

As you read and work with *Discovery Methods,* I hope that you will put all of these skills to work. I also hope that you will keep in mind the overarching ideas within this book that will help you make progress toward the goal of becoming a great teacher. Let me point out some of these "big ideas":

1. *A constructivist approach.* Consider how children construct knowledge and create meaning as you plan and teach. There is little question that we create much of our own reality. One way of looking at how we integrate life experiences into our mental processes is provided by the theory of *constructivism.* When applied in the

classroom, this theory guides teachers in thinking about what they are doing to help children get beyond scientific misconceptions and acquire more appropriate knowledge, skills, and values. Constructivism is introduced in Chapter 1, discussed in more detail in Chapter 2, and then used as a guiding principle throughout the rest of the book.

2. *References to standards.* "If you don't know where you're going, you'll end up someplace else" are the words of a character in one of the vignettes in this book. All of us who teach children science need some direction, and the best current direction is provided by the National Science Education (NSE) Standards. The NSE Standards for grades K–8 are addressed at relevant points throughout the book, as indicated by the icon shown in the margin, and the full text of the standards is provided just inside the front cover for handy reference. Another set of standards, known as Project 2061, is also addressed in the text through a series of boxes.

3. *Productive use of the Internet.* As incredible as it may seem, teachers and students today have almost instant access to much of the recorded information of humankind. The Internet is now ubiquitous in U.S. classrooms, from kindergartens through the primary grades and on up. But applying this technology in useful and productive ways remains a challenge for many teachers. This text will provide guidance for doing so in three primary ways:

- Each chapter ends with a section called *Resources for Discovery Learning,* which includes a section of valuable websites that pertain to the topic at hand. A brief description is given of each site as well as the URL (uniform resource locator).

- Chapter 8, Science WebQuests, is still the only chapter in any science methods text to teach future teachers how to plan specific Internet-based, science-related experiences for children. A master WebQuest is provided along with several completed examples.

- Internet-related content is identified throughout the text using the icon shown in the margin.

To help focus your reading and discussion, I'd like you to keep in mind that each chapter has a consistent format, which includes these components:

- *A Look Ahead:* A list of the topics discussed in the chapter
- *Text:* A discussion of specific content-related topics
- *Real Teachers Talking:* Excerpts from conversations between teachers that will stimulate your own thinking and discussions with others
- *Make the Case:* A thought-provoking challenge for you to complete individually or as a member of a cooperative learning group
- *Summary:* A review of the main ideas in the chapter
- *Going Further:* Learning activities that you may do on your own or in a cooperative learning group
- *Resources for Discovery Learning:* A list of content-related Internet sites and a list of books and articles that will help extend your study of the chapter's main points

Finally, I hope you take full advantage of the special section at the end of the book called *For the Teacher's Desk.* The materials in this section are provided as a resource for your use now and in the future. The first part, *Your Classroom Enrichment Handbook,* includes guidelines for ensuring safety and curriculum planning, among other things. And a new section provides position statements from the National Science Teachers Association (NSTA) on these subjects: women in science education; multicultural science education; substance use and abuse; and science competitions. Reviewing these statements should stimulate your thinking about some of the very important issues that teachers face today. The second part, *Your Science Source Address Book,* provides contact information for a variety of materials suppliers and professional organizations. All of this information has been reviewed and updated for this new edition.

I'm sure that you will enjoy reading *Discovery Methods for the Elementary and Middle Grades* and that you will learn much from it. Use it to help create a classroom in which children look forward to science time as a wonderful opportunity to learn from and be with *you!*

Acknowledgments

Many people have shaped the content of this book, directly and indirectly. First, let me thank the "real teachers" who were kind enough to take the time to participate in conversations about the topics in each chapter.

I would also like to thank a few of my dearest friends and colleagues for their continued support and encouragement: Lowell J. Bethel at the University of Texas; Jack Hassard at Georgia State University; Russell Agne, Susan Baker, and Joyce Morris at the University of Vermont; Rod Peturson of the Windsor Schools, Ontario, Canada; Marlene Nachbar Hapai at the University of Hawaii, Manoa; William Ritz at California State University, Long Beach; Larry Schaeffer at Syracuse University; and the public school teachers I work with every week at Orchard Elementary School and Malletts Bay School.

J. A.

Strategies and Techniques

The whoosh and locomotive roar of a powerful tornado, tossing about cars and flattening houses; the careful maneuvering of a brightly colored lady bug, making its way through branches and leaves, touching, smelling, and tasting all in its path; and the first dark, belching breaths of a volcano coming to life after being dormant—all are parts of the natural world in which we live.

Wanting to make sense of that world is a powerful drive that leads we humans to inquire, to discover, and, ultimately, to understand. And to empower children to be able to inquire, discover, and understand—not just now but throughout their lives—is the greatest challenge we teachers face. To teach children *science* is to meet that challenge head on.

This book will help prepare you to meet that challenge. To be sure, there is *much* to know! First of all, you need to know your children. How do children learn, and what can you do to enhance their learning? How can you help them learn the inquiry process skills and construct their own scientific knowledge?

You also need to know what to teach and how to teach it. What are the recommendations of the National Science Education (NSE) Standards and other curriculum guideposts that your school district or state might have? How can you plan meaningful lessons and units and manage an inquiry-based classroom? How can you make good use of the valuable resources of the Internet? How can you integrate science with other subject areas? What specific strategies and techniques will help you foster discovery learning? And what can you do to adapt science activities for children who come from diverse cultural backgrounds and who have special needs and abilities?

Finally, you need to know how and when to assess children's progress in meaningful ways. What are the different approaches to assessment, and how successful are they? Again, what do the NSE Standards recommend? How can children best show what they have learned in terms of both understanding and inquiry? .

This book will answer these questions and more, and in reading it, you will build a foundation of general knowledge about teaching children science. Once that foundation is firmly in place, you can add the specific knowledge and skills related to the earth/space, life, and physical sciences.

Yes, it's a lot to learn! And I encourage you to learn it well, so that you will get off to a good start as a teacher. Mastering this information is essential to developing your own approach to teaching children science.

The truth is, becoming an OK teacher isn't too difficult. But becoming a truly excellent teacher—one who broadens children's horizons, gives them a knowledge base upon which they can build, and raises their hopes and dreams to unexpected heights— takes focus and determination. *That's* what you and I will be working toward throughout this book!

1

Inquiry: The Path, Discovery: The Destination

How will I create my inquiry-based, discovery-focused classroom?

A New Day Begins

Most of the passengers are sleeping quietly—but not all.

A tiny infant begins to stir, but his mother shushes him back to unknown dreams. A bellowing snore shakes an older man awake; he looks around and then falls back into a deep sleep. Except for these disturbances, it has been a long, dark, and quiet night.

Then, an early riser opens her sleepy eyes, picks a little "night sand" from her eyelids, and looks upward and outward to the vast black darkness of space. Her eyes slowly focus on the diamond sparkling of distant stars. She wonders. She wonders where she is going.

As she wonders, she begins to notice a glow slowly emerging low in the eastern sky. Light begins to steadily consume the darkness. Then, with a burst, the star paints the eastern horizon with bold, bright, orange strokes. A new day begins.

Our early rising space traveler rides the most extraordinary spaceship of all time. It spins as it travels a high-speed path around the sun, bringing forth day and night with each rotation. And each day brings to every woman and man, every girl and boy, enormous possibilities. It brings those possibilities to you and to me, as well!

A Chance to Touch Tomorrow

All of the flowers
Of all of the future
Are in the seeds of today
   —Source unknown

As you awake and start your new day, I'd like you to think of these three short lines as your gentle alarm. I want them to remind you of the enormous potential that lies in the hearts and minds of children. You are their temporary mindstretcher and caretaker. You are the overseer of the seeds and the creator of the rich soil that will nurture these seeds of new tomorrows to grow. *What* and *how* you teach children will race ahead of you to a time you will never know. The responsibility is enormous. It will take dedication, energy, and the unwavering belief that what you do and how you do it will actually change lives.

What and *how* you teach will touch tomorrow. *You* will touch tomorrow.

You: Science-Teaching Fears, Hopes, and Dreams

You don't know me, but I think I know you. You are fairly confident of your ability to teach children to write, to do mathematics, and to learn social studies. You grew up with e-mail, MP3 players, and DVDs, and you are comfortable using the Internet as an endless library shelf.

Now I might be wrong, but my guess is that you are not *that* confident about teaching children science. You may fear that science will be difficult for children to understand and that it will provoke questions that will be hard for you to answer. You may also think that science time will be a period of utter chaos and confusion, as liquids bubble out of beakers and chemicals flash, pop, and bang. Of course, there is also the possibility that a child will bring you, the science teacher, a slightly bloodied, injured bird to heal.

I also know that deep down, you would really like science time to become the favorite time of day for your students. You would like to help them get the critical knowledge and skills that will carry them to a happy, productive, and prosperous adulthood.

I would like to help you start your personal and professional journey toward that future—a journey in which you will overcome your fears, expand your hopes, and fulfill your dreams. This book is a tool that will help you do that. Preparing every page is my way of stretching out a helping hand. Let's begin the journey by considering the children who will be in your classroom.

Your Children: Curious, Small Scientists Who Need Guidance and Direction

Children love to touch! At least, most children do. They also like to look at things, to smell them, to move them about and twist and turn them. Children want to know how things work, and like squirrels, they sometimes horde papers, science materials, and wildlife in their desks for more detailed inspection later.

At the heart of science is this natural human desire to explore the world that is directly reachable as well as those worlds that are hard to reach. The children in your classroom are, in this respect, very much like scientists. In fact, some would say that *they* are more like scientists than are teenagers or even college students!

Your children will tend to have boundless energy and curiosity. Your job will be to make sure you deliver a curriculum that capitalizes on both. Let's turn to the general types of direction you will give to the curriculum and classroom in order to ensure that children will fulfill their potential while they are in your care.

Constructivism: Their Natural Way of Learning

The children you teach are not "blank slates" that you can write on. They come to you with some knowledge, including both conceptions and misconceptions about the world. It is critical that you prepare a classroom in which you draw upon their previous knowledge and engage them in hands-on experiences in which they explore, inquire, and discover. You will correct faulty knowledge, add new knowledge, and create accurate conceptions about the natural world.

A term you will see emphasized as you work with *Teaching Children Science* is *constructivism.* It will be at the heart of much of what you do in teaching in the modern classroom and in creating and using curriculum materials. Constructivism is dealt with in detail in Chapter 2, Constructing Knowledge and Discovering Meaning.

By providing children with hands-on experiences, you will help them correct faulty knowledge, add new knowledge, and create accurate conceptions about the natural world.

Child Development: Your Science Teaching Will Affect It

Developing Thinking Skills

"Young man, you should know that an empty wagon makes the most rattle."

One of my teachers used to tell me this often. (However, I won't tell you *how* often!) In her own quaint, repetitive way, she was saying that if I was ever going to get anywhere, I had better gain some knowledge before voicing an opinion. She wanted me to use my full range of mental capacities. She was trying to get me ready for an unknown future.

Science time is a wonderful opportunity for you to help your children gain the knowledge they need to become better thinkers. Experts in human thinking and learning have identified six levels of thinking, from simple to more complex:

1. Knowledge
2. Comprehension
3. Application
4. Analysis
5. Synthesis
6. Evaluation

As you design your science units and lessons, be mindful of these levels of thinking so that you will provide children with opportunities to develop their full range of thinking skills.

Developing Positive Affect

For many teachers, a lesson about a caterpillar becoming a butterfly will only be about a caterpillar and a butterfly. But the same lesson in the hands of a master teacher—a great teacher, an extraordinary teacher, a truly gifted teacher—will be an experience in which the children are thunderstruck with the realization that *one living thing has become a completely different living thing right before their eyes.*

The day of that lesson will be one on which those children's lives will be changed forever. They will leave school filled with a sense of wonder that was sparked by the acquisition of brand-new knowledge that is as extraordinary as anything they will see on television that night. They will leave school wanting to know more—curious about what may lie around the corner. They will also leave school with new attitudes and values that will shape who they are and who they will become.

This change in attitudes and values signals the development of *positive affect.* The science experiences you deliver to children will do much to create positive affect about science, school, and the wonders of the natural world. It is the classroom environment that will help children grow toward the positive goals presented so beautifully in Dorothy Law Nolte's "Children Learn What They Live" (see Figure 1.1, page 8).

Developing Psychomotor Skills

You might not think of your classroom as a place where children learn to coordinate what their minds *will* with what their bodies *perform*—but it is. Children need to develop gross motor abilities as well as fine motor skills, and well-planned science experiences can help them do so.

Gross motor skills can be developed through inquiry-based activities such as assembling and using simple machines, hoeing and raking a class vegetable garden, and carefully shaping sand on a table to make various land forms. Examples of experiences that develop *fine motor skills* include cutting out leaf shapes with scissors, drawing charts and graphs, and sorting seeds on the basis of physical characteristics. So, in addition to gaining knowledge and understanding and developing positive affect, science time can be a time to improve a child's physical skills.

Developing Responsible Citizens

When your children look at you during science time, they aren't thinking about issues such as raising taxes to pay for a park's underground sprinkler system and eliminating the smells and fumes issuing from a local factory without causing unemployment for some citizens. However, at some time in their lives, they will be concerned about societal issues. And to be responsible citizens, they will need to address such issues with wisdom—wisdom based on a foundation of knowledge constructed many years earlier. Perhaps some of that knowledge will be gained in your classroom.

With your guidance, children will learn that real inquiry requires gathering facts before reaching a conclusion. Hopefully, learning to gather knowledge systematically and to reach carefully thought out conclusions will be skills they apply as they confront societal issues in the future. If you do your job, then today's children will make positive contributions to the civic decision-making processes that will lead to a better life for us all.

FIGURE 1.1
A child's environment has
a powerful impact on his or
her affective development.

Children Learn What They Live
Dorothy Law Nolte

If a child lives with criticism,
  he learns to condemn.
If a child lives with hostility,
  he learns to fight.
If a child lives with fear,
  he learns to be apprehensive.
If a child lives with pity,
  he learns to feel sorry for himself.
If a child lives with ridicule,
  he learns to be shy.
If a child lives with shame,
  he learns to feel guilty.
If a child lives with encouragement,
  he learns to be confident.
If a child lives with praise,
  he learns to be patient.
If a child lives with praise,
  he learns to be appreciative.
If a child lives with acceptance,
  he learns to love.
If a child lives with approval,
  he learns to like himself.
If a child lives with recognition,
  he learns that it is good to have a goal.
If a child lives with sharing,
  he learns generosity.
If a child lives with honesty and fairness,
  he learns what truth and justice are.
If a child lives with security,
  he learns to have faith in himself and in those about him.
If a child lives with friendliness,
  he learns that the world is a nice place in which to live.
If you live with serenity,
  your child will live with peace of mind.

With what is your child living?

Scientific Literacy: Your Science Teaching Will Create It

Add *STS* to the list of acronyms you carry in your brain. It stands for *science, technology, and society,* a catchphrase that represents what average citizens should know about two things that affect them and their society constantly: science and technology. In short, STS is related to creating citizens who are scientifically literate.

To create citizens who understand the implications of developments in science and technology is an enormous task. But the task for you, as a teacher, is more specific and reachable: teaching children to become scientifically literate.

To help you in this effort, the *National Science Education (NSE) Standards* identify what it means to be scientifically literate and specify what should be taught at various grade levels to reach this goal. The NSE Standards also deal with a variety of other issues, including what knowledge teachers should have, how students should be assessed, and how schools should implement curriculum changes that will result in greater scientific literacy.

Later in this book, in Chapter 4, you will learn what content the NSE Standards suggest for your classroom. You will discover that much of the content suggested has, as its focus, the creation of citizens who have a good understanding of new developments in science and technology and what implications those developments have for their lives.

Gender and Equity Issues: Your Science Teaching Will Help Resolve Them

> The scientist is a brain. He spends his days indoors, sitting in a laboratory, pouring things from one test tube into another. . . . He can only eat, breathe, and sleep science. . . . He has no social life, no other intellectual interests, no hobbies or relaxations. . . . He is always reading a book. He brings home work and also brings home creepy things.[1]

Although students made these observations almost 50 years ago, their attitudes reflect, to a large degree, the views of society today. The students' choice of pronoun does not seem to reflect the purposeful use of *he* for *she* but rather the strength of the stereotype of the scientist as male.

One of my favorite activities with children (and also with adults) is to ask each of them to draw a scientist (see Figure 1.2, page 10). In most cases, the scientist is presented as a bespectacled white man with a slightly mad glint in his eyes and a crop of straggly hair. While it may seem amusing, the real harm of this stereotype lies in the fact that it may discourage children from considering science or science-related careers. Also, girls learn that science is not for females, and boys learn that girls don't like science. Hopefully, you'll be able to create a classroom environment that helps to overcome these stereotypes.

The science classroom can also provide you with a wonderful opportunity to assist children from cultural minorities and for whom English is not their home language. When children are encouraged to explore phenomena that are real to them, to learn and use inquiry skills, and ultimately to make their own discoveries, the power of these experiences will do much to integrate *all* children into the task at hand.

Just think of how fortunate you are to teach children science, a subject whose natural allure for children will draw them into learning experiences irrespective of gender, language, and cultural barriers. By having a classroom that respects cultural and linguistic diversity and addresses gender inequities, you can make a real difference in the lives of children. That's right! *You* can and will make a difference.

FIGURE 1.2   A sampling of "Draw a Scientist" illustrations by *college* students.

Science: What Is It, Really?

Science is the body of knowledge people build when they use a group of processes to make discoveries about the natural world. The people who produce this particular body of knowledge carry out work that is characterized by certain values and attitudes. We call these people *scientists.*

As a science teacher, you will teach children how to use this special group of processes to make their own discoveries and gather new knowledge. You will do this by creating an environment in which children discover and learn and then discover some more.

Rick: You really look frustrated today. What's up?

Jodie: Well, I *am* frustrated! I was just watching my student teacher doing a science activity with groups, and two of the girls were sitting back and letting the boys do all of the work. What is aggravating me is that I've pushed the idea of *everyone* being responsible all year long, but it just doesn't seem to happen.

Rick: Oh, it's definitely a problem for my class, too. But I've been trying something a little different that *is* working—at least for now.

Jodie: What's that?

Rick: I've been purposefully pairing them so the groups are boy/boy or girl/girl, with the idea being that in the girl/girl groups, there won't be a boy who tries to dominate. The kids are not completely happy about it—particularly, the social butterflies—but it is working.

Jodie: Well, anything different is worth a try. Let me run another idea by you: What if I kept the children in mixed groups but assigned specific roles? You know, if I made specific girls "team captains" and specific boys "data takers." Then I'd sprinkle the other jobs among the other group members.

Rick: That would certainly make it easier to step in when you saw the domination begin.

Jodie: Right. If they are doing things that are not part of their role, I could intervene immediately and remind them about what they are *supposed* to be doing.

Rick: Well, that would be a big change from the way we *have* been doing things. If we assign roles, we can make sure that each child gets a chance to be leader or whatever. You know, that would not only help with this equity problem for the girls, but it would also help a few of the more laid-back boys who seem to get "run over." We would definitely have to change the roles on a regular basis to be fair.

Jodie: Of course we would! How strict do you think I want to be? I don't want you to think that I don't like boys, but they just seem to take over. Nothing personal! Guys are great, but some of them get really pushy when we put things in front of them like magnets and magnifying glasses. That's what happened today when we brought out the pulleys, strings, and weights.

Rick: Don't be so hard on the guys just because you've had a tough day. Sometimes, we are completely innocent! Guys just have more experience taking things apart and putting them back together, so when you put good stuff out, we want to be the first ones to get our hands on it. I think the temptation is so great that the boys don't even realize they are "running over" their classmates.

Jodie: Oh, no. I'm not going to let you get off the hook with that one! The boys should know better.

Rick: I give up! Yes, of course, the boys should know better. We just have to *help* them know better!

▶ **POINT TO PONDER:** *You may have had personal experiences in science classes that reflect some of the issues raised in Rick and Jodie's conversation. What do you think motivates the behavior of males versus females when they are in mixed groups doing inquiry-based, discovery-focused science? From your perspective, what steps can teachers take to make such science group work a more positive experience for boys and for girls?*

Science as Inquiry Process Skills That Lead to Discovery

Just as a newborn reaches out to touch the new world, we continually explore the world around us. As humans, we wonder and discover, trying very hard to make sense of our surroundings.

In an effort to make sense of *their* surroundings, scientists use one or more *inquiry process skills:* observing, using space/time relationships, using numbers, classifying, measuring, communicating, predicting, inferring, controlling variables, interpreting data, formulating hypotheses, defining operationally, and experimenting. These skills are explained in greater detail in Chapter 3 (see also Figure 1.3).

If you are going to teach children science, however, I hope that your curiosity drives you to ask why, what, when, and how, because you will be surrounded by children who ask those questions constantly. Your challenge will be to mesh your curiosity with theirs as they make discoveries about their world. The challenge is not that difficult because children bring tremendous energy and enthusiasm to their quest for answers. *All* children seem to be scientists at heart; they want to discover.

Science as Knowledge

The processes of science produce a body of knowledge that we usually call *content*. This body of knowledge includes the facts gathered, the generalizations or concepts that unify these facts, and a set of principles that can be used to make predictions. To a very large measure, science is a search for underlying principles, or *laws*, that predict how objects and organisms behave.

FIGURE 1.3
While these sample concepts and principles relate to the physical sciences, the sample science processes shown here also apply to the earth/space and life sciences.

Concepts
- Energy can be changed in form.
- Matter can be changed in form.
- The total amount of matter and energy in the universe never changes but is just changed in form.

Principles
- Objects that are dropped increase in velocity as they approach the earth's surface.
- Like poles of magnets will repel each other. Unlike poles of magnets will attract each other.
- For every action, there is an equal and opposite reaction.

Processes
- Observing
- Using space/time relationships
- Using numbers
- Classifying
- Measuring
- Communicating
- Predicting
- Inferring
- Controlling variables
- Interpreting data
- Formulating hypotheses
- Defining operationally
- Experimenting

What do children think science is? Figure 1.4 offers the ideas of some fourth-graders. Most show some enthusiasm for science—it's fun! How can you nurture that feeling?

If, as a teacher, you only emphasize the facts of science, children will learn that science is an accumulation of factual knowledge. If you only emphasize the concepts of science, children will learn that science is a set of generalizations. If you only emphasize the principles of science, children will learn that science is a set of predictions. But science consists of more than process skills and more than content. Science manifests a set of *values*.

Science as a Set of Values

While there are many values you can emphasize as you help children experience science processes and learn content, there are six that you will find particularly useful:

1. Truth
2. Freedom
3. Skepticism
4. Order
5. Originality
6. Communication

FIGURE 1.4
A few fourth-grade children offer their definitions of *science*.

"Science is a class that we go to and learn about important things we have to know. I think science is the funnest class I've ever been to." —Jennifer

"Science is . . . I think that science is neat, fun. It is interesting you learn all kinds of neat stuff." —Renee

"Science is fun and it can be really hard to do. It is very hard to do some of the worksheets." —Mark

"Science is . . . Alot of fun we study Whales. We work in books and get more homework but science is fun learning experiment. We make maps and we blow them up." —Alan

"Science is the explanation for the way the things on Earth work." —Nico

"Science is important to me. I will be an vet or animal scientist. I love science and when I'm sad or up set I try to be scietific and it cheers me up. It makes me happy when I make a dedution. Once I start trying to think up the answer to a problem and I won't I mean won't stop even for eating and sleeping even reading! So I love science a lot." —Mary Catherine

"Science is important to me couse we have alot of pages we have to do. I think it is easy to do." —Robbie

"Science is fun. I liked it when we used salt and flour to mold a map. Salt and flour is sticky. I like science." —Erik

Since science seeks to make sense out of our natural world, it has as its most basic value the search for *truth*. The scientist seeks to discover not what should be but what *is*. The high value placed on truth applies not only to the discovery of facts, concepts, and principles but also to the recording and reporting of such knowledge.

The search for truth relies on another important value: *freedom*. Real science can only occur when a scientist is able to operate in an environment that provides him or her with the freedom to follow paths wherever they lead. Fortunately, free societies rarely limit the work of scientists. When scientists are *not* allowed to act freely, the reason is not so much from the fear of what they may discover than the fear that freedom will cultivate another dangerous value: *skepticism*.

Skepticism—the unwillingness to accept many things at face value—moves scientists to ask difficult questions about the natural world, society, and even each other. Scientists value skepticism, and skepticism sometimes causes nonscientists to doubt the results of scientific enterprise. In an article entitled "Uh-Oh, Here Comes the Mailman," James Gleick, a well-known science writer, describes excerpts from some of the letters he has received:

> Here is a lengthy single-spaced essay (painstakingly tied up with what looks like tooth floss) titled "Chaos and Rays." Apparently, one of these rays "impregnates the chaos" and "fructifies the forces."

> A Canadian reader has discovered (he encloses the calculations) that all spheres, including the Earth, are 20 percent larger than geometers have thought—"Perhaps the reason missiles keep crashing short of their course."[2]

While Professor Gleick may smile at these letters, he also makes this observation:

> It's hard to remember, but it's surely true, that the instinct bubbling to the surface in these letters is the same instinct driving real scientists. There is a human curiosity about nature, a desire to peer through the chaos and find the order.[3]

There is, then, an underlying *order* to the processes and content of science. In their search for truth, scientists gather information and then organize it. It is this order that allows scientists to discover patterns in the natural world. Children need to develop this ability to organize information, which is why you will be helping them learn how to organize and keep track of their observations.

For all its order, however, science also values *originality*. Although some may view science as a linear activity—one in which people plod along, acquiring more and more detailed explanations of phenomena—in reality, science is fueled by original ideas and creative thinking. It is this kind of thinking that leads to discoveries.

Children love to talk with each other; so do scientists. The talk of scientists includes reports, articles, speeches, and lectures, as well as casual conversations. The ability to communicate results is vital if knowledge is to grow. Without extensive *communication,* progress would be greatly limited.

As a teacher, you will need to help children understand that science is more than a collection of facts and a group of processes. Science is a human activity that has as its framework a set of values that are important in day-to-day life.

Technology: It's Changing Your Life and Their Lives

What do these terms have in common? Prescription drugs, hip-replacement surgery, instant hair dye, "squeeze cheese" (orange/yellow, putty-like cheese product primarily used by busy college students that is squeezed directly from tube to bread and crackers of uncertain vintage), soft contact lenses, electric cars, CAT scans, X-ray treatment for cancer, and ramen noodles (noodle-like material that can be reconstituted through the addition of tap water). The answer, of course, is *technology.* They all are products or procedures that apply science to the solution of human problems—real or imagined.

The crunch of traffic, the lack of parking spaces, and the need for more pollution-free vehicles were a few of the problems that a group of scientists and inventors headed by Dean Kamen decided to solve by creating a personal transportation vehicle called the *Segway Human Transporter (HT).* The technology behind the Segway permits it to travel as fast as 12 miles per hour (or 20 km per hour), and it can almost read your mind in deciding to go forward or backward or to turn or stop. It doesn't *actually* read your mind, of course, but sensors are able to detect the tiny changes in muscle pressure transmitted by your body and then make adjustments accordingly. Another important "plus" is that the Segway is powered by batteries, so no pollution is released as it travels along. The initial cost of the Segway is about $5,000, but over time, that will likely come down. And when it does, expect to see mail carriers, park police officers, delivery persons, and workers in large warehouses and airplane hangars riding Segways. And someday, teachers and children will be arriving at school riding Segways! Now that would be a sight, wouldn't it?

One of your obligations in teaching children science is to pay attention to how technology-based products and procedures work. You will find this goal referred to in any list of curriculum objectives as *technological design.* The NSE Standards point out that children should be able to do these things:

1. Identify a problem.
2. Design a solution.
3. Implement their solution.
4. Critically examine how well their solution worked.
5. Communicate with others about their design and the strengths and weaknesses of their solution.[4]

Meet the Segway: a personal transportation vehicle that uses the technology of computers, small electric motors, gyroscopes, and much more to move people from place to place.

How might teaching about technological design be translated into your own real-world classroom? Children could design any of the following:

1. A dog-walking machine
2. A machine for removing and sorting garbage and trash from lunch trays
3. A car seatbelt system that's easier to get into
4. A backpack with a self-contained umbrella that automatically opens during a rainstorm

The point is that new and emerging technology impacts virtually every minute of a child's day. In order for children to lead lives in which technology is used intelligently, with minimal negative side effects, they need to understand what technology is, how new products and procedures are designed, what resources are needed, and what deleterious consequences may occur, such as allergic reactions, environmental pollution, and safety hazards. Students need to fully understand the larger impact of new technologies within the context of how those technologies affect their communities—and themselves.

MAKE THE CASE   *An Individual or Group Challenge*

■ **The Problem**   The children in your classroom may be unaware of the many ways in which science and technology affect their daily lives.

■ **Assess Your Prior Knowledge and Beliefs**   To what extent are each of the following aspects of your life affected by science and technology?

Health	very little	little	somewhat	a great deal
Safety	very little	little	somewhat	a great deal
Nutrition	very little	little	somewhat	a great deal
Personal security	very little	little	somewhat	a great deal
Communication	very little	little	somewhat	a great deal
Transportation	very little	little	somewhat	a great deal
Recreation	very little	little	somewhat	a great deal

■ **The Challenge**   Your principal has asked you to give a five-minute talk at the next meeting of the Parents/Teachers Organization to encourage parents to cultivate their children's interest in science and technology. Identify five key points you would make in your presentation.

Discovery: Your Destination

"How do we know what we know?"

It certainly seems like a simple question when you look at. I could even develop a rather complicated answer for it, if I was so disposed—but I won't! I suggest that we know what we know because we have made discoveries, and we have made those discoveries through inquiry. You made discoveries yesterday, you will make discoveries today, and you will make discoveries tomorrow. In fact, you are making discoveries as you read the printed words on these pages.

Every bit of knowledge in your brain—every concept, every attitude, every value, and every motor skill that you possess—exists because you made a discovery. Your brain didn't come fully loaded. Rather, you have acquired each piece of new information and every attitude, value, and motor skill through some sort of discovery. You may have built on previous knowledge or experience, but the discovery was brand new at the moment you made it.

Discovery, which is part of the subtitle of this book (*A Discovery Approach*), is your destination as a teacher. It is where you will lead your students. It is our discoveries that make us what we are. They underlie what we think, feel, and do.

Now the question is, How do you make those discoveries? Although there are many paths to discovery, this book is based on the path called *inquiry.* In fact, the paths of inquiry are different for bakers, accountants, cosmetologists, auto mechanics, and shepherds. We will focus on the way *scientists* inquire because we want children to make their science-related discoveries in the same way that real scientists do. (Shepherds do it very differently.)

Inquiry: The Path Children Will Take toward Discovery

"Do chickens have teeth?"
"Why does a light bulb get hot?"
"Why are there holes in cheese?"
"Why can't we send the new baby back?"

Questions, questions, and more questions! Asking questions is what makes we humans what we are. We seem to have a genetic urge to make sense of our surroundings, and this constant questioning is our most powerful tool. When you teach science, that is the tool all children will bring to you—the urge to question their surroundings—and so it will provide the foundation for much of your teaching.

Although the focus of what we do as teachers should be to create an environment in which children make discoveries, it is *inquiry*—the systematic search for answers—that will get them there. Think about it like this: The overarching goal for your children is to make discoveries. And while they will make their discoveries in many ways, the hands-on experiences you provide will incorporate the inquiry process skills.

As you get more deeply into *Teaching Children Science,* you will learn that what science teachers try to accomplish involves a three-step sequence:

1. *Exploration:* Children interact with materials somewhat informally so that questions emerge or become clarified.
2. *Inquiry and acquisition:* Children attack problems or questions using the inquiry process skills and get information.
3. *Discovery and application:* Children ultimately resolve problems and questions by organizing their new knowledge, concepts, and skills to gain new insights that serve as the starting points for new explorations.

This sequence is called the *learning cycle.* You'll learn much more about it later in this book (see Chapter 3).

National, State, and Local Standards: They Will Light Your Way

Have you ever dreamt that you were lost in a forest and had no idea of how to get out? You may remember such a dream as an overpowering nightmare from which you awoke filled with dread and hopelessness.

The thought of teaching children science may be similarly overwhelming, but it should not leave you feeling hopeless. You should feel uplifted! In the bad dream, you were alone. In the real world of teaching children science, you are not. Many people have spent their entire professional lives developing goals, objectives, procedures, and materials for science teaching. You will have access to the fruits of all of their labor. For now, think about just one aspect of all of this: the goals and objectives of your science teaching.

Again, you will not have to invent them all yourself! A group of scientists have created the *National Science Education Standards,* which outline what the point of your science teaching should be. (You may recall that we discussed the NSE Standards with respect to technology earlier in the chapter.) The NSE Standards are readily available to you in print form and on the Internet, and an important portion of those standards related to the content you should be teaching or at least considering is reprinted inside the front cover of this book.

The NSE Standards give real direction to science teaching, so you will not feel lost and alone as you plan science units and lessons. In fact, the NSE Standards are not your only resource for science teaching. Individual states, provinces, and local communities also have developed curriculum guides based on their own standards, and they provide even more direction. Sometimes called *frameworks,* they often provide sample units and lessons that are excellent resources.

Rest assured that you are not lost and alone in the forest. The path you will take as you lead children to discovery is well marked. You will have many resources as you guide children to explore, inquire, and discover. You are definitely not alone. Sleep well, and then awake and seize the day!

Project 2061: Implications for Your Inquiry-Based, Discovery-Focused Classroom

To develop an inquiry-based, discovery-focused classroom, you'll need to draw on a wide range of resources. One resource that may prove useful is the curriculum development effort known as *Project 2061.* Developed by scientists and educators, and with the sponsorship of the American Association for the Advancement of Science, this project is intended to help reform K–12 science, mathematics, and technology education. Its basic reference document, *Science for All Americans,* offers recommendations called *benchmarks* in many areas, which will be important to you as you plan and teach.

Project 2061 has twelve benchmarks that you may wish to study in some detail:

- The nature of science
- The nature of mathematics
- The nature of technology
- The physical setting
- The living environment
- The human organism
- Human society
- The designed world
- The mathematical world
- Historical perspectives
- Common themes
- Habits of mind

To find helpful information about any of these benchmarks, visit the Project 2061 website at <www.project2061.org/>.

Yes, You Can Do It! Science for All Children, Every Day in Every Way

This book is full of resources that will help you create wonderful classroom experiences for children—experiences in which they explore, inquire, and discover. In Part One of this book (which includes this and the next eight chapters), you will learn basic science-teaching methods that will also help you create that wonderful classroom! And beyond Part One, you will find three very specific parts of the book that deal with teaching the earth/space sciences, the life sciences, and the physical sciences. In the chapters in those parts, you will find unit and lesson "starter ideas," activities and demonstrations, and even basic science content for your reference as you prepare to teach children science.

I am confident that you will be successful if you are motivated to use your talent to its fullest and the available resources to the maximum. If you do, each day in your classroom will be a day when every child has the opportunity to explore, inquire, and discover. So, get started on your journey to discover how children actually learn science.

Summary

You will be teaching children science by creating a classroom environment in which inquiry is carried out for the purpose of making discoveries. You can think of *inquiry* as the path and *discovery,* the destination. You will guide children along the path of inquiry by teaching them to use the inquiry process skills to gain new knowledge and understanding, to learn and enhance their psychomotor skills, and to use the attitudes and values that undergird science.

Science is both a body of knowledge about the natural world and a systematic way of gathering knowledge. In other words, it is a *product* (an organized set of facts, concepts, and principles) as well as a *process* (a method of obtaining and extending that knowledge). Technology is the application of that knowledge or the systematic ways of getting knowledge to solve human problems.

The general approaches you will use in the classroom will incorporate aspects of a three-step learning cycle: (1) exploration, (2) inquiry and acquisition, and (3) discovery and application. You will also use constructivist techniques to help children improve their thinking skills, gain scientific literacy, and become aware of and understand science- and technology-related issues of gender and equity.

The challenges of teaching children science will require you to use a variety of resources, including units and lessons that you plan yourself, science resource books, and the Internet. The NSE Standards, along with regional and local science standards and frameworks, will also guide you as you plan a learning environment in which children inquire and make discoveries.

GOING FURTHER

On Your Own

1. Think about when you have observed children in elementary, middle, or high school exploring, doing inquiry, and making discoveries, or recall your own experiences in science. Provide any examples that you can, including examples of students using the inquiry process skills (e.g., observing, interpreting data, etc.).

2. Consider your present feelings about teaching children science, and identify the factors that have influenced your attitudes.

3. If possible, interview an elementary school teacher to find out how he or she would answer such questions as these: How do you feel about teaching children inquiry-based, discovery-focused science? What do children think science is? What materials for learning science are available in your classroom or school? Do you feel well prepared to teach science? Why or why not?

4. Do some research to determine the role that science and technology have played in shaping present-day society. Consider such questions as these: Would society be better served if science were pursued only for the sake of the technology that results from it? Does the scientist occupy a prestigious position in modern society? What responsibility do scientists have for communicating the results of their work in a way that is understandable to the public?

On Your Own or in a Cooperative Learning Group

5. Discuss the role models that your parents, teachers, textbooks, and the media offered you in elementary school. Can you recall your level of career awareness as an elementary student? What did you want to become? Why? If you are a woman, what factors tended to turn you toward or away from a scientific career? If you are a man, what stereotypes, if any, did you have about women and careers in science and technology?

6. Review the NSE Standards inside the front cover of this book, and then have members of your group offer examples of learning experiences from their own elementary, middle grade, high school, and college schooling that could be appropriately placed under each standard.

RESOURCES FOR DISCOVERY LEARNING

Internet Resources
Websites for Inquiry-Based, Discovery-Focused Classrooms

Key Science Concepts

www.sasked.gov.sk.ca/docs/elemsci/menu_ksc.html

The authors identify 26 concepts that should be part of a science curriculum. As a person who teaches children science, you should be aware of the range of concepts that teaching units and plans should cover. Science content examples are linked to each concept shown.

The Values That Underlie Science

www.sasked.gov.sk.ca/docs/elemsci/menu_val.html

This site identifies seven values that should be part of any science curriculum. Each is linked to resource materials that provide specific examples of how that value can be fostered in the classroom.

NSE Standards Online

www.nap.edu/readingroom/books/nses/html

This is the complete text of the *National Science Education Standards*. Since it is in hypertext format, you will find it easy to navigate from one part of the standards to another.

LatinoWeb

www.latinoweb.com

As you browse through this site, you will discover information related to strategies and techniques for encouraging youths from minority groups to pursue careers in science and engineering. You should be able to apply some of these ideas in developing career awareness activities for elementary-age children.

Society for the Advancement of Chicanos and Native Americans in Science (SACNAS)

www.sacnas.org/

This page has an extremely useful link to a resource you should find helpful in working to overcome scientist stereotypes. Search for the link to the "Biography Project," and then explore the helpful information included within the "By Scientist," "By Subject," "By Grade Level," and "Women Scientists" categories.

African Americans in the Sciences

afroamhistory.com/cs/blacksinscience

This site profiles African Americans who have made important contributions to the sciences and engineering. It is extremely well organized and lists individuals by category (e.g., biologists, chemists, physicists, inventors, etc.). Each name listed also serves as a link to biographical information. This site is another excellent resource for teachers who wish to demolish the scientist stereotype.

African American Scientists and Inventors

www.princeton.edu/~mcbrown/display/faces.html

This site is an excellent resource for elementary- and middle-level teachers who wish to expand their curricula by including the accomplishments of African American scientists and inventors. Many links are provided to other helpful Internet resources.

Women in Science and Technology

www.feminist.org/gateway/science.html

This site contains numerous links to Internet resources that provide examples of science and technology contributions made by women. It is also an excellent source of biographical information on well-known female scientists and females in technology-related careers. This site is very easy to use efficiently, since every link is accompanied by a brief description of the resource you will find at that destination.

4,000 Years of Women in Science

www.astr.ua.edu/4000WS/4000WS.html

This is a "must see" Internet site. It is a truly extraordinary collection of biographies, photographs, and graphics about women scientists and the contributions they have made. There are approximately 150 separate, detailed entries.

Print Resources
Suggested Readings

Bodzin, Alec, and Mike Gehringer. "Breaking Science Stereotypes." *Science and Children* 25, no. 5 (January 2001): 36–41.

Coverdale, Gregory. "Science Is for the Birds: Promoting Standards-Based Learning through Backyard Birdwatching." *Science Scope* 26, no. 4 (January 2003): 32–37.

Davis, Elizabeth A., and Doug Fitzpatrick. "It's All the News: Critiquing Evidence and Claims." *Science Scope* 25, no. 5 (February 2002): 32–37.

Demers, Chris. "Analyzing the Standards." *Science and Children* 37, no. 4 (January 2000): 22–25.

Dillon, Nancy. "Sowing the Seeds of the Standards." *Science and Children* 37, no. 4 (January 2000): 18–21.

Ferrell, Kathy. "Keeping the Joy in Teaching." *Science Scope* 24, no. 6 (March 2001): 50–52.

Fitzner, Kenneth. "Issues-Oriented Science." *Science Scope* 25, no. 6 (March 2002): 16–18.

Goodnough, Karen. "Humble Advice for New Science Teachers." *Science Scope* 23, no.6 (March 2000): 20–24.

Houtz, Lynne E., and Thomas H. Quinn. "Give Me Some Skin: A Hands-On Science Activity Integrating Racial Sensitivity." *Science Scope* 26, no. 5 (February 2003): 18–22.

Jesky-Smith, Romaine. "Me, Teach Science." *Science and Children* 39, no. 6 (March 2002): 26–30.

Kelly, Catherine A. "Reaching the Standards." *Science and Children* 37, no. 4 (January 2000): 30–32.

Koenig, Maureen. "Debating Real-World Issues." *Science Scope* 24, no. 5 (February 2001): 18–24.

Lee, Suzie. "Achieving Gender Equity in Middle School Science Classrooms." *Science Scope* 26, no. 5 (February 2003): 42–43.

Lightbody, Mary. "Countering Gender Bias in the Media." *Science Scope* 25, no. 6 (March 2002): 40–42.

Lowery, Lawrence F. (Ed.). *NSTA Pathways to the Science Standards: Guidelines for Moving the Vision into Practice*. Arlington, VA: National Science Teachers Association, 1997.

Lucking, Robert A., and Edwin P. Christmann. "Tech Trek: Technology in the Classroom." *Science Scope* 26, no. 4 (January 2003): 54–57.

McDuffie, Thomas E., Jr. "Scientists—Geeks and Nerds." *Science and Children* 38, no. 8 (May 2001): 16–19.

National Research Council. *National Science Education Standards*. Washington, DC: National Academy Press, 1996.

Ostlund, Karen, and Sheryl Mercier. *Rising to the Challenge of the National Science Education Standards: Grades 4–8*. Arlington, VA: National Science Teachers Association, 1996.

Ostlund, Karen, and Sheryl Mercier. *Rising to the Challenge of the National Science Education Standards: Grades K–6*. Arlington, VA: National Science Teachers Association, 1999.

Timmerman, Barbara. "Keeping Science Current." *Science Scope* 25, no. 6 (March 2002): 12–15.

N O T E S

1. M. Mead and R. Metraux, "Image of the Scientist among High School Students," *Science* 126, no. 3270 (August 30, 1957): 384–390.

2. James Gleick, "Uh-Oh, Here Comes the Mailman," *The New York Times Review of Books* 4 (March 1990): 32.

3. Ibid.

4. Based on Lawrence F. Lowery (ed.), *NSTA Pathways to the Science Standards: Guidelines for Moving the Vision into Practice* (Arlington, VA: National Science Teachers Association, 1997), p. 84.

2

Constructing Knowledge and Discovering Meaning

How can I help children learn science?

What Is Learning, Really?

My last visit to the dairy section of a local market yielded a precious trophy: a brand-new, lowfat version of my favorite double-chocolate fudge ice cream. Ah, the unimaginable and unreachable dream of low calories plus delectable chocolate fudge would soon go from the icy-cold container into me! The pressures, tensions, frustrations, and excitement of my professional work would all vanish as I inhaled the silky-smooth chocolateness of this cherished find.

But it was not to be! A careful reading of the too-fine print on the container gave me unsettling information. The fat content of this product had been lowered by adding corn syrup, sugar, brown sugar, and syrup solids (whatever they are). Sadly, the new calorie count for this lowfat version was remarkably close to the calorie count for the full-fat version!

When my newly acquired knowledge was added to my previous knowledge, an entirely new meaning of the term *lowfat ice cream* was constructed in my mind. I had learned something new.

So, learning doesn't happen only for children, and it doesn't happen only in school. Learning is an ongoing process, in which the learner integrates new knowledge with previous knowledge and discovers new ways of thinking, acting, and feeling. We are *always* constructing new meanings in this way. I am always learning, you are always learning, and right now, somewhere a child is learning that it doesn't matter whether a corn seed is planted upside down or rightside up. That child is learning what even teachers who have overdosed on high-calorie ice cream have always known: In the proper environment, new shoots, like young children, grow toward the light.

Project 2061: Implications for Helping Children Construct Knowledge and Discover Meaning

Project 2061 addresses the thinking skills you may wish to consider as you teach children science. Namely, they are outlined in the benchmark "Habits of mind":

- Values and attitudes
- Computation and estimation
- Manipulation and observation
- Communication skills
- Critical-response skills

Note that the item "Critical-response skills" is intended to help children separate sense from nonsense, which is crucial to helping them become scientifically literate citizens.

You'll find specific benchmarks (or recommendations) for the skills of most interest to you at the Project 2061 website: <www.project2061.org/>.

Traditional Views about How Children Learn Science

There are two traditional and very broad ways of thinking about how children learn. One is known as *behavioral theory,* and the other is known as *cognitive theory.* If you wish to be successful in teaching children science, you will need to use elements of both and integrate these ideas with *constructivism:* a modern, emerging view of learning that you will learn about later in this chapter.

Behavioral Theory

The behavioral approach suggests that what a child does, and consequently what a child learns, depends on what happens as a result of the child's behavior. From this perspective, your job as a teacher is to create a classroom in which good things happen when children work with science materials, interact with one another in cooperative group work, and complete science projects. If children enjoy these experiences, receive praise from peers and the teacher, and are successful, they will be learning and developing a positive attitude. In order to have more experiences and receive more praise, they will continue to work hard.

From the behavioral perspective, the teacher's job is to create a science-learning environment in which certain behaviors and the acquisition of knowledge, concepts, and skills are increased and reinforced. *Tangible reinforcers* include receiving good grades, winning certificates and prizes in science fairs, earning points for free time, earning the privilege of taking care of the classroom animals for a week, and so forth. *Intangible reinforcers* include recognition of good work and praise from the teacher and the child's peers and parents. Figure 2.1 (page 26) offers a list of some practical applications of behavioral principles.

Cognitive Theory

Cognitive theorists believe that what children learn depends on their mental processes and what they perceive about the world around them. In other words, learning depends on how children think and how their perceptions and thought patterns interact.

To understand the cognitivist view, try this: Look at the drawing on the right. What does it look like? Now ask other people to look at the drawing. What do they believe it is? If you ask a few people, you will soon discover that people perceive the world differently and that their solutions to questions depend on what they see and how they think. According to cognitive learning theorists, a teacher should try to understand what a child perceives and how a child thinks and then plan experiences that will capitalize on these.

Many learning theories have evolved from cognitivism. In the sections that follow, you will read about two of the most important of these theories.

Piaget's Theories

Jean Piaget spent his professional life searching for an understanding of how children view the world and make sense of it. His work led him to propose that children progress through stages of cognitive development. The list that follows gives the stages and a few examples of the characteristics of each stage:

1. *Sensorimotor knowledge (0 to 2 years).* Objects and people exist only if the child can see, feel, hear, touch, or taste their presence. Anything outside the child's perceptual field does not exist.

2. *Preoperational (representational) knowledge (2 to 7 years).* The ability to use symbols begins. Although the child is still focused on the "here and now" early in this stage, the child can use language to refer to objects and events that are not in his or her perceptual field. The child has difficulty understanding that objects have multiple properties. For instance, he or she is not completely aware that a block of wood has color, weight, height, and depth all at once. Concepts of space and time are difficult to grasp. The child does not *conserve* attributes such as mass, weight, and number. For example, the child views a drink placed in a tall, narrow glass as more than the same amount of drink placed in a short, wide glass.

3. *Concrete operations (7 to 11 years).* The child can group objects into classes and arrange the objects in a class into some appropriate order. The child understands

FIGURE 2.1   You can find many ways to apply behavioral principles in your science classroom.

Practical Applications

Behavioral Principles for Your Science Classroom

1. *Reinforce positive behavior.*

   EXAMPLES   ▪ Praise children when they complete projects well.

   ▪ Tell children who do a particularly good job of cleaning up after a messy science activity that you appreciate their efforts.

2. *Reinforce effort.*

   EXAMPLES   ▪ Thank children for trying to answer questions during class discussions.

   ▪ Praise children whose behavior improves with each field trip.

3. *After a behavior has been established, reinforce the behavior at irregular intervals.*

   EXAMPLES   ▪ Surprise the class with special visitors or field trips during particularly challenging units.

   ▪ Take individual photographs of children at work on long-term (multiweek) science projects, and present them unannounced at various times during the project.

that mass, weight, volume, area, and length are conserved. The child has some difficulty isolating the variables in a situation and determining their relationships. The concepts of space and time become clearer.

4. *Formal operations (12 years through adulthood).* The child is able to think in abstract terms, is able to isolate the variables in a situation, and is able to understand their relationship to one another. The child's ability to solve complex verbal and mathematical problems emerges as a consequence of being able to manipulate the meanings represented by symbols.

Figure 2.2 (page 28) offers some practical applications of this theory.

Bruner's Theories

Jerome Bruner's research revealed that teachers need to provide children with experiences to help them discover underlying ideas, concepts, and patterns. Bruner is a proponent of *inductive* thinking, or going from the specific to the general. You are using inductive thinking when you get an idea from one experience that you use in another situation. Bruner believes that children are able to grasp any concept, provided it is approached in a manner appropriate for their particular grade level. Therefore, teachers should encourage children to handle increasingly complex challenges. See Figure 2.3 (page 29) for some practical applications of Bruner's work.

Constructivism: A Modern View of How Children Learn Science

What Is Constructivism?

Constructivism is a theory of human learning that is rooted in cognitive psychology and, to a lesser extent, behavioral psychology. It provides modern science teachers invaluable guidance. In fact, if you grasp the essential principles of constructivism, you will find it much easier to answer the two questions that will always be running through your mind as you approach a topic: *What should I teach?* and *How should I teach?*

Three Constructivist Principles to Guide Your Planning and Teaching

Three fundamental principles underlie the theory of constructivism:

1. *Naive conceptions.* A person never really knows the world as it is. Each person constructs beliefs about what is real.
2. *Assimilation.* What a person already believes, what a person brings to new situations, filters out or changes the information delivered by his or her senses.
3. *Accommodation.* A person creates a reality based on his or her previous beliefs, ability to reason, and desire to reconcile what he or she believes and actually observes.

FIGURE 2.2   Piaget's ideas have many practical
classroom applications.

Piaget's Ideas for
Your Science Classroom

1. *Infants in the sensorimotor stage (0 to 2 years)*

   EXAMPLES
   - Provide a stimulating environment that includes eye-catching displays, pleasant sounds, human voices, and plenty of tender, loving care so the infant becomes motivated to interact with the people and things in his or her perceptual field.
   - Provide stuffed animals and other safe, pliable objects that the child can manipulate in order to acquire the psychomotor skills necessary for future cognitive development.

2. *Preschoolers and children in the primary grades (2 to 7 years)*

   EXAMPLES
   - Provide natural objects such as leaves, stones, and twigs for the child to manipulate.
   - Toward the end of this stage, provide opportunities for the child to begin grouping things into classes—that is, living/nonliving, animal/plant.
   - Toward the end of this stage, provide experiences that give children an opportunity to transcend some of their egocentricism. For example, have them listen to other children's stories about what they observed on a trip to the zoo.

3. *Children in the elementary grades (7 to 11 years)*

   EXAMPLES
   - Early in this stage, offer children many experiences to use their acquired abilities with respect to the observation, classification, and arrangement of objects according to some property. Any science activities that include observing, collecting, and sorting objects should be able to be done with some ease.
   - As this stage continues, you should be able to successfully introduce many physical science activities that include more abstract concepts such as space, time, and number. For example, children could measure the length, width, height, and weight of objects or count the number of swings of a pendulum in a given time.

4. *Children in middle school and beyond (12 years through adulthood)*

   EXAMPLES
   - Emphasize the general concepts and laws that govern observed phenomena. Possible projects and activities include predicting the characteristics of an object's motion based on Newton's laws and making generalizations about the outcomes of a potential imbalance among the producers, consumers, and decomposers in a natural community.
   - Encourage children to make hypotheses about the outcomes of experiments in the absence of actively doing them. A key part of the process of doing activities might appropriately be pre-lab sessions, in which the children write down hypotheses about outcomes.

FIGURE 2.3   Bruner's ideas can be used to encourage children to make their own science discoveries.

Practical Applications

Bruner's Ideas for Your Science Classroom

1. *Emphasize the basic structure of new material.*

   EXAMPLES
   - Use demonstrations that reveal basic principles. For example, demonstrate the laws of magnetism by using similar and opposite poles of a set of bar magnets.
   - Encourage children to make outlines of basic points made in textbooks or discovered in activities.

2. *Present many examples of a concept.*

   EXAMPLES
   - When presenting an explanation of the phases of the moon, have the children observe the phases in a variety of ways, such as direct observations of the changing shape of the moon in the evenings, demonstrations of the changes using a flashlight and sphere, and diagrams.
   - Using magazine pictures to show the stages in a space shuttle mission, have the class make models that show the stages and list the stages on the chalkboard.

3. *Help children construct coding systems.*

   EXAMPLES
   - Invent a game that requires children to classify rocks.
   - Have children maintain scrapbooks in which they keep collected leaf specimens that are grouped according to observed characteristics.

4. *Apply new learnings to many different situations and kinds of problems.*

   EXAMPLE
   - Learn how scientists estimate the sizes of populations by having children count the number in a sample and then estimate the numbers of grasshoppers in a lawn and in a meadow.

5. *Pose a problem to the children, and let them find the answer.*

   EXAMPLES
   - Ask questions that will lead naturally to activities—Why should we wear seatbelts? and What are some ingredients that most junk foods have?
   - Do a demonstration that raises a question in the children's minds. For example, levitate a washer using magnets or mix two colored solutions to produce a third color.

6. *Encourage children to make intuitive guesses.*

   EXAMPLES
   - Ask children to guess the amount of water that goes down the drain each time someone gets a drink of water from a water fountain.
   - Give children magazine photographs of the evening sky, and have them guess the locations of some major constellations.

Naive Conceptions

The first of these three principles is very important to teachers. Your experience with children probably has already taught you that not everything a child believes or knows is true. For example, Tom may believe that sweaters keep him warm because sweaters are warm. Uncle Harry, who lives with Tom's family, has told him many times to wear a warm sweater on a cool day. The belief that a sweater is warm is an example of a *naive conception:* an idea that does not fit reality when its validity is checked. Children and adults have many naive conceptions, and it is extremely difficult for a teacher to help a child construct new understandings if the child's naive conceptions filter out new experiences.

Assimilating and Accommodating New Learnings

The last two principles come into play when planning hands-on experiences for children. What happens when you provide a child with a hands-on experience in which he or she learns something that fits into ideas that the child already has about how the natural world works? Suppose, for example, that Susie already believes that sunlight and plant growth are related and her teacher provides an experience in which she observes firsthand that depriving plants of light is detrimental to their health. Cognitive psychologists use a term that aptly describes this situation: *assimilation.* Susie assimilates, or absorbs, her new learning easily.

Suppose, however, that Susie's teacher has the class plant seeds in two containers. One container is exposed to sunlight and one is kept in darkness. What sense will Susie make of her observation when she sees that both sets of seeds have produced tiny, healthy plants with small, green leaves? With help from the teacher, she can *accommodate* this strange observation by broadening her beliefs about plant growth to include the possibility that in its earliest stages of development, a plant is not dependent on light for food production but rather on food stored in the seed.

Giving children opportunities to assimilate and accommodate new learning is basic to the theory of constructivism.

Constructivism focuses on the interplay between what the child already knows and the experiences the teacher provides. The conceptions and naive conceptions that the child has before an experiment make a very real difference in what the child will learn. Figure 2.4 identifies some practical applications of constructivism.

Ways to Support Your Constructivist Teaching

The NSE Standards

Here is a question for you: Do you know what *re-bar* is? Oh, you don't. Before I reveal its meaning, you must answer another question: Have you ever thought of becoming a construction worker instead of a science teacher? Perhaps you haven't.

FIGURE 2.4   When used in the classroom, the principles of constructivism will lead you to discover what children know and believe before beginning a new unit.

Practical Applications

Constructivism for Your Science Classroom

1. *A person never really knows the world as it is. Each person constructs beliefs about what is real.*

   EXAMPLE   ▪ When beginning a unit of study, have children write or talk about what they already know or believe about that topic. For example, if you are starting a unit on space, give children a chance to write or talk about whether the terms *solar system* and *universe* are the same or different.

2. *What a person believes filters out or changes the information delivered by his or her senses.*

   EXAMPLE   ▪ After children have had an opportunity to tell what they know and believe, ask them if they would be willing to change some of their ideas if a discovery activity gave them new information. For example, ask the children who think a seed will grow properly if it is planted upside down if they will be able to change their minds if the activity gives a result that is different from what they expect.

3. *Each person creates a reality based on his or her previous beliefs, ability to reason, and desire to reconcile what he or she believes and actually observes.*

   EXAMPLE   ▪ Early in the year and perhaps early in each unit, discuss with children how they learn science. Share and discuss ideas about the importance of making careful predictions and hypotheses before an activity and the importance of reporting actual results, not results that fit their earlier ideas.

Surprisingly, teaching children science has elements of the construction industry in it. For one thing, you want to build a foundation that will give your children the knowledge, skills, and attitudes to keep them interested and constantly learning about science and technology. Without that foundation, children will find it difficult, if not impossible, to add new layers of learning.

That's where re-bar comes in. It is a thick strand of steel that runs within the concrete slabs of a foundation. You probably have seen re-bar sticking out from chunks of broken concrete. The re-bar strengthens the concrete so that foundation is durable and can stand the test of time.

The specific science content identified in the National Science Education (NSE) Standards is our teaching "re-bar." Content from the standards must cross and recross the plans you create and the lessons you teach. That content will strengthen the foundation on which children will construct knowledge and discover meaning.

Let's be more specific about how the NSE Standards will support and reinforce your constructivist teaching. I'll discuss this support within the three guiding principles of constructivism presented earlier in this section:

1. **Naive conceptions.** *A person never really knows the world as it is.*
   Each person constructs beliefs about what is real.

   The most basic support for this principle comes from the existence of the NSE Standards themselves. Since we finally have science standards, you, as a teacher, have something against which to compare students' prior knowledge and beliefs. If you listen carefully to children, you'll hear some amazing things about how they think the world works. Unfortunately, some of those beliefs are simply wrong!

   What you need to do is first carefully study the standards to ascertain within which standard children's inaccurate knowledge and misconceptions lie. Then, you can take guidance from the A and B chapters of this book and other resources to properly address the deficiencies.

   Here are two examples:

   A child says: "I think that the moon followed us when my mom walked me to Janet's house for a sleepover."

   This misconception can be dealt with by providing content and experiences related to Earth and Space Sciences Standards ESS 2 and ESS 3—"Objects in the sky" and "Changes in earth and sky."

   A child says: "My dad said Becky caught a cold because she played outside without her jacket on."

   This misconception can be dealt with by providing content and experiences related to Science in Personal and Social Perspectives Standard SPSP 1—"Personal health."

M A K E   T H E   C A S E   *An Individual or Group Challenge*

■ **The Problem**

Providing a rich learning environment for children may require the teacher to take them out of the traditional classroom occasionally and into the real world. Sometimes, it is difficult for new teachers to identify real-world experiences that will really improve children's achievement in science.

■ **Assess Your Prior Knowledge and Beliefs**

What do you presently believe about the way in which children learn both in and out of the classroom?

1. Children learn best from direct experience with natural objects and phenomena.

    _____ agree   _____ disagree

    Your evidence: _____

2. Hands-on science experiences automatically reinforce children's learning.

    _____ agree   _____ disagree

    Your evidence: _____

3. A child's prior knowledge and beliefs should be assessed before new experiences are introduced to ensure that the experiences will be meaningful.

    _____ agree   _____ disagree

    Your evidence: _____

4. Children have few misconceptions about the natural world.

    _____ agree   _____ disagree

    Your evidence: _____

5. For highly able children, it probably makes little difference whether direct or hands-on instruction is used in the classroom.

    _____ agree   _____ disagree

    Your evidence: _____

6. Because children progress through identifiable stages of development, teachers should provide only experiences that fit the stage of development indicated by the children's age.

    _____ agree   _____ disagree

    Your reasoning: _____

■ **The Challenge**

Integrate your knowledge of how children learn into one paragraph that will provide a rationale for taking the children to locations beyond the school grounds. Your intention is to use this paragraph in a letter you will send (with your principal's permission) to community leaders who may be willing to donate funds for this curriculum enrichment project.

2. **Assimilation.** *What a person already believes filters out or changes the information delivered by his or her senses.*

The NSE Standards clearly state that children should both have the ability to do scientific inquiry and to understand scientific inquiry (see Content Standard A). By creating science unit and lesson plans for children that are consistent with the methods advocated in this book, you will be infusing the curriculum with discovery experiences and activities that are based on careful inquiry. Children will learn to confront the differences between what they believe and what they discover with their own senses. Your challenge is to teach them that firsthand, personally gathered knowledge must override incorrect beliefs.

Here are two examples:

A young child might say: "Magnets pull on everything."

This misconception can be countered and replaced by having children actually do magnet activities in which they make discoveries to the contrary.

An older child might say: "It's starting to get hot. The earth must be getting closer to the sun."

This misconception can be countered by doing an activity in which children use models to discover that the inclination of the earth as it proceeds in orbit varies the surface area upon which a given amount of sunlight falls. In other words, when the earth is in a position in orbit in which the Northern Hemisphere is inclined away from the sun, a given amount of sunlight is spread over a larger surface area and people in the Northern Hemisphere have winter. The warming of the earth doesn't have much to do with how close the earth is to the sun.

3. **Accommodation.** *Each person creates a reality based on his or her previous beliefs, ability to reason, and desire to reconcile what he or she believes and actually observes.*

By helping children learn about *and* practice the scientific methods of inquiry—as expressed in the Science and Technology Standards S&T 2 and S&T 5, "Understanding about science and technology," and in History and Nature of Science Standards HNS 1 and HNS 2, "Science as a human endeavor"—children will learn that some ways of getting knowledge are better than others.

Children's lives and future success will be greatly enhanced if they learn to appreciate the importance of stating hypotheses, gathering information systematically, and withholding the drawing of conclusions until all the facts are in. If you emphasize the nature of careful scientific inquiry as children make discoveries, they will construct new and more complete understandings about the world in which they live.

Gardner's Multiple Intelligences

If you intend to create a discovery-focused, inquiry-based classroom, in which children construct knowledge and discover meaning, you will need to consider a "raw material" that is more important than any aquarium, ant colony, or microscope in the room. That raw material is the intelligence of children.

Introductory psychology books tell us that intelligence is measured by IQ tests, which is a less than satisfying answer. At the very minimum, *intelligence* relates to a capacity to learn as well as an ability to apply that learning. It is usually reported as a number called an *intelligence quotient,* or *IQ.* Someone of normal or average intelligence has an IQ of 100.

REAL TEACHERS TALKING   *A Starting Point for Thinking, Talking, and Writing*

Robin: I've been reading a lot about Gardner's ideas in teacher magazines and discussing them in teacher workshops. I must admit that they have really caught my attention. They've broadened my vision of what we can accomplish with children.

Angela: Do you think they have actually affected your planning or your teaching or how you assess the children? I think his ideas could really affect all of them.

Robin: Oh, they really have affected all three. The idea that really stands out is that children have a wide variety of abilities beyond just the academic. So Gardner's ideas are affecting how I plan, teach, and assess. He is saying that we may be missing opportunities to capitalize on these multiple intelligences, and that really bothers me.

Angela: For me, the most important thing is that you use the theory in your actual teaching. Of course, some parts of his theory fit some people's teaching style better than others. Personally, I think most of it fits for me.

Robin: Even though teachers sometimes complain that their preservice or in-service courses are too theoretical, as professionals we need to have some framework to support what we do. Teaching is not incidental. We need to have a reason for doing what we do. Gardner's ideas about human abilities can help us clean up and straighten out basic assumptions and bring what we actually do with children in science more in line with what we believe about how all of us learn.

Angela: Especially if it's a theory that has such an optimistic view about the range of abilities that each child has. The flip side of all this is that I'm not sure that the general public is ready for the idea that we want to change the curriculum in ways that take it pretty far beyond the traditional academics they want us to teach.

▶ **POINT TO PONDER:** *If you were asked to present some of Gardner's ideas to a meeting of 50 elementary- and middle-grade teachers who were working on a rationale for a new science curriculum, what would you emphasize?*

How will knowing that number for each of your students help you create a classroom in which all children can construct knowledge and discover meaning? For instance, would knowing that Maria has an IQ of 135 and Ricky has an IQ of 110 change how you teach Maria and Ricky? Probably not. In fact, this traditional way of measuring and reporting a child's theoretical capacity to learn will be of little help as you plan science experiences that are responsive to individual differences.

Gardner's Original Theory

Howard Gardner has suggested a radically new way of thinking about intelligence. Early in his work, he discovered seven different intelligences that he believes each of us has to various degrees:

1. Logical-mathematical
2. Linguistic
3. Musical
4. Spatial
5. Bodily-kinesthetic
6. Interpersonal
7. Intrapersonal[1]

According to Gardner's theory, each child can be viewed as having a greater or lesser capacity to learn in each specific area. This means, in turn, that you as a teacher can focus on particular intelligences as you create science-learning experiences. You can teach to each child's strengths and find appropriate ways to help him or her grow in weak areas.

Gardner's Addition: Naturalist Intelligence

In more recent years, Gardner's work has led to what he describes as *naturalist intelligence:* the ability to discern subtle characteristics and patterns and then easily group objects or events in appropriate categories.[2]

As a science teacher, the possibility that this intelligence exists could be very important, since you might be able to identify how much individuals are "science prone" based on their measured naturalist intelligence. Knowing this could help you adjust your teaching to build on the abilities of children who have strong naturalist intelligence and to develop ways to be more responsive to children who have a more modest level of naturalist intelligence. Adjustments might include providing some children with more sophisticated observation and classification challenges and others with more time to complete work that requires high levels of naturalist intelligence. Making adjustments like these is at the heart of constructivist teaching, as doing so helps you capitalize on the wide range of intelligences a child might have.

See Figure 2.5 for a few real-world examples of how you can help children grow in all eight of Gardner's multiple intelligences.

FIGURE 2.5   Gardner's theory of multiple intelligences has exciting implications and many practical applications for the classroom.

Practical Applications

Gardner's Theory of Multiple Intelligences for Your Science Classroom

1. *Logical-mathematical*

   EXAMPLES
   - Emphasize the underlying patterns children observe in science activities.
   - Have children list the steps they undertook in an activity and what they thought at each step.

2. *Linguistic*

   EXAMPLES
   - Emphasize writing down predictions, observations, and so on in science journals and the importance of using appropriate descriptive words and new terminology.
   - Encourage children to maintain their own science dictionaries, which will include new science terms and drawings to illustrate word meanings.

3. *Musical*

   EXAMPLES
   - Whenever possible, use vocal and instrumental music selections to accompany the introduction of new concepts. For example, use songs related to the seasons when carrying out a unit on climate.
   - When teaching a unit on sound, emphasize the connections to music, such as the effect of changing the thickness of a string or the length of the air column of an instrument.

4. *Spatial*

   EXAMPLE
   - Have children express what they have learned through drawings and models.

5. *Bodily-kinesthetic*

   EXAMPLES
   - Encourage children to use equipment that builds upon coordination skills, such as the microscope, balance, and hand lens.
   - Wherever possible, have children demonstrate new learnings through movement and dance. For example, children might create a dance to illustrate the expansion of a balloon resulting from increasing the energy of motion of the molecules contained within it.

6. *Interpersonal*

   EXAMPLES
   - Have children create simulated television advertising on issues investigated in class, such as the environment or proper nutrition.
   - When doing cooperative group work, provide time for children to process how well their group has worked on a science project.

7. *Intrapersonal*

   EXAMPLE
   - Provide opportunities for children to informally assess their interest in science, how well they are learning, and how they feel about matters related to science and technology.

8. *Naturalist*

   EXAMPLE
   - Early in the school year, give children sets of natural objects or pictures of natural objects or events they have not previously seen (e.g., rocks, leaves, pictures of various cloud types). Then ask them to observe and group members of each set.

Alternative Learning Styles

Think about what's the best way for you to learn. Is it enough to read the material and perhaps highlight key points here and there? Do you take notes, as well? Or does your best learning come from discussing the ideas with others or from doing a project or activity? And what about the person sitting next to you in a class? Does he or she learn in the same way that you do?

Constructivism is based on the idea that we are unique as a result of our different life experiences and that these experiences result in our individual knowledge and beliefs. It is these differences in knowledge and beliefs that make us different from one another. And since we are all fundamentally different in this sense, we will learn all differently, too. We have individual *learning styles*. And for you as a science teacher, the implications of this are enormous.

FIGURE 2.6   An understanding of individual learning styles can help you prepare science experiences that all children can learn from and enjoy.

Practical Applications

Learning Styles for Your Science Classroom

1. *It is likely that children prefer to learn in different ways.*

   EXAMPLE   ▪ Study curriculum materials to ascertain whether they will accommodate differences in learning styles, and then develop some alternative teaching techniques. For example, if children are expected to name and describe the functions of the organs of the digestive system, study the unit carefully and try to come up with two or three different ways for children to learn this information.

2. *You can tell a great deal about how children learn by observing how they deal with new learning experiences.*

   EXAMPLE   ▪ Early in the year, provide activities that include studying a section in a reference book, doing hands-on activities, doing library research, and working with a computer program. Observe how various children approach each task and their relative success with each.

3. *Provide a range of experiences in the classroom so that all children have opportunities to put their preferred learning styles to use as often as possible.*

   EXAMPLE   ▪ Think about the extent to which the activities for each unit are the same or different in terms of what children actually do, and consider how you could build in variations in approach. For example, suppose you realize that all the activities for a unit on sound require the children to do the activity first, observe phenomena, and then report results. To accommodate children who have trouble with this approach, adapt a few of the activities so that early in the unit, children have the option of reading and talking about a concept before beginning an activity.

If you are an experienced teacher who has attended many in-service workshops or courses or you are a preservice teacher who has had a variety of courses concerning how to teach, you may have heard and learned about learning styles. This is an interesting area of study because so many experts have their own ideas about the learning styles that people may have. Some expound about convergent and divergent thinkers; some emphasize the idea that some people prefer concrete experiences and others prefer abstract discussions of ideas and principles; some suggest that people can be grouped on the basis of whether they respond quickly (impulsive) or think first and talk or act later (reflective). See Figure 2.6 for some practical applications of this theory.

Summary

Constructivism, a useful theory about how children learn, has evolved from classical learning theories such as behaviorism and cognitivism. The challenge for you as a teacher is to help children replace naive conceptions or lack of knowledge about the natural world by constructing more accurate and complete understandings. This chapter suggests three guiding principles as you approach the challenge of teaching from a constructivist viewpoint.

Additional interesting insights about teaching and learning come from the NSE Standards, from Gardner's work on multiple intelligences, and from the idea that each of us has a preferred style of learning. Modern teachers formally and informally assess children's capabilities with respect to the diverse multiple intelligences and to preferred learning styles, and they tailor science experiences based on those assessments and the content guidelines set by the standards.

GOING FURTHER

On Your Own

1. Informally assess the extent to which you can apply your knowledge of the NSE Standards, multiple intelligences theory, and learning styles to support constructivist teaching in an actual science classroom. Do this by interviewing a primary-, elementary-, or middle-grade teacher to determine what factors he or she believes affect how well a child learns science and what types of science experiences happen in the classroom. Gather as much information as you can without guiding the interview toward any of the ideas from this chapter. After the interview, make a list that summarizes the key points made by the teacher. Categorize the items with respect to their relevance to constructivism, the standards, multiple intelligences, and learning styles. (Be mindful of preserving the confidentiality of your interviewee in any summary report you prepare.)

2. Interview a school principal to determine what he or she believes are the key factors that affect the quality of science instruction in the school. After the interview, prepare a chart that relates key phrases from the interview to the major ideas of this chapter.

3. Based on your personal experiences as a student or teacher, to what extent are behavioral principles applied when children have science experiences? Provide as many firsthand examples as you can.

4. Based on your personal experiences as a student or teacher, to what extent are cognitivist principles applied when children have science experiences? Provide as many firsthand examples as you can.

5. Based on your personal experiences as a student in science classrooms, would you say that you have a preferred style of learning that leads to success in such environments? If you would, identify the factors that contribute to your preference.

On Your Own or in a Cooperative Learning Group

6. Have each member of the group reflect on Gardner's theory of multiple intelligences, and then identify which intelligences each member feels he or she would score the highest and lowest in if they could be measured. Have members of the group comment on the nature of their science experiences in primary, elementary, or middle school and the extent to which these intelligences were applied.

7. Have each member of the group interview at least one child to find out about his or her knowledge or beliefs about a key concept from the life, earth/space, or physical sciences and technology. In the course of each interview, be sure to encourage the child to respond to questions that might reveal some naive conceptions. Use questions such as these: Why doesn't the moon fall to the earth? Are whales fish? Does the sun move across the sky? Is a sweater warm?

8. As a group, reflect on the difference between *assimilation* and *accommodation*. Have group members identify one or two naive conceptions that they once had about the life, earth/space, or physical sciences and technology. Have individuals indicate whether it was difficult or easy for them to revise these conceptions when they learned facts to the contrary or had direct experiences that produced results in conflict with their conceptions. Based on this group work, prepare a list of implications for teachers who wish to create science classroom environments in which children have experiences that reveal naive conceptions and lead to new learnings.

RESOURCES FOR DISCOVERY LEARNING

Internet Resources
Websites for Constructing Knowledge and Discovering Meaning

Behaviorist versus Cognitivist Theory

psych.fullerton.edu/navarick/behavcog.ppt

When you reach this site, you will be able to download a PowerPoint presentation that gives you a very quick and clever overview of the different ways in which behaviorists and cognitivists view human learning. The graphics in the presentation make the included explanations quite clear.

Constructivism in Elementary Education

www.ericse.org/

This is the national ERIC (Educational Resources Information Center) site for Science, Mathematics, and Environmental Education and as such is a vast repository of information on a variety of useful topics. To get the most recent information on constructivism do the following when you reach the opening page:

Type in the term *constructivist* at the search location for searching just the ERIC site. The full texts of selected articles will appear. Additionally, you may wish to select "Science Education" from the home page to see the full array of resources available to you at this ERIC site.

Constructivism

library.trinity.wa.edu.au/teaching/construct.htm

This is an excellent site if you wish to quickly survey the views of a wide variety of educators about the nature of constructivism and how it can be applied in your classroom. This site provides many examples of how teachers have integrated constructivism into their curricula along with the results of some research done on the impact of constructivist teaching on children and schooling.

Science Myths

www.amasci.com/miscon/miscon.html

This is a rather amazing site in that it identifies common science misconceptions found in textbooks and related articles. It includes many specifics as well as articles written by others detailing "science myths." The possible impact of these errors on students' and teachers' own conceptions about the natural world makes constructivist teaching more of a challenge.

Multiple Intelligences Links Pages

ss.uno.edu/SS/Theory/MultiIntelLks.html

This site provides links to a variety of Internet resources dealing with Howard Gardner's theory of multiple intelligences. Some of the articles are practical in nature and offer specific suggestions for assessing and teaching individuals with particular intelligences. One category of links will even take you to schools that have made a schoolwide commitment to trying to use multiple intelligences as the basis for developing curriculum and instruction. You'll need to search within the links to the particular schools to see the practical application of multiple intelligences theory to science teaching.

Multiple Intelligences Presented by Surf Aquarium

surfaquarium.com/intelligences.htm

This lively, graphics-intensive site presents very specific ideas for implementing your knowledge of multiple intelligences in the classroom. In particular, the creator of the site links other sites to each of the multiple intelligences. You will likely find all the subtopics and links on this page fascinating, but pay close attention to the links that support naturalist intelligence. To refresh your knowledge of the theory of multiple intelligences or to take an online multiple intelligences inventory and self-assess your own strengths, go to the related page <surfaquarium. com/mi_overview.htm>.

Online Learning Styles Inventory

www.metamath.com/lsweb/dvclearn.htm

You may be curious as to whether you have a preferred learning style. The Learning Style Survey at this site will help you identify that style as well as learning strategies that will help you match your study skills to that style. If you want further background on the characteristics of the various styles, go to the following page at the site: <www.metamath. com/lsweb/fourls.htm>.

 **Print Resources**
Suggested Readings

Aram, Roberta J., and Brenda Bradshaw. "How Do Children Know What They Know?" *Science and Children* 39, no. 2 (October 2001): 28–33.

Bransford, Jon, Rodney Cocking, and Ann Brown. *How People Learn: Brain, Mind, Experience, and School.* Washington, DC: National Academy Press, 2000.

Buck, Gloria A., and Patricia Meduna. "Exploring Alternative Conceptions." *Science Scope* 25, no. 1 (September 2001): 41–45.

Farenga, Stephen J., et al. "Balancing the Equity Equation: The Importance of Experience and Culture in Science Learning." *Science Scope* 26, no. 5 (February 2003): 12–15.

Fetters, Marcia, et al. " Making Science Accessible: Strategies to Meet the Needs of a Diverse Student Population." *Science Scope* 26, no. 5 (February 2003): 26–29.

Frazier, Richard. "Rethinking Models." *Science Scope* 26, no. 4 (January 2003): 29–33.

Pusey, Douglas. "Accessible Reading Assignments." *Science Scope* 26, no. 5 (February 2003): 44–46.

Science Scope 26, no. 4 (January 2003). (Entire issue emphasizes how to address misconceptions about science.)

Searson, Robert, and Rita Dunn. "The Learning-Style Teaching Model." *Science and Children* 38, no. 5 (February 2001): 22–26.

Van Klaveren, Karen, et al. "How Do Your Students Learn?" *Science Scope* 25 no. 7 (April 2002): 24–29.

NOTES

1. Thomas Armstrong, *Multiple Intelligences in the Classroom* (Washington, DC: Association for Supervision and Curriculum Development, 1994), pp. 2–3.

2. Kathy Checkley, "The First Seven . . . and the Eighth: A Conversation with Howard Gardner," *Educational Leadership* 55, no. 1 (September 1997): 8, 9.

3

The Inquiry Process Skills

How can I help children use the inquiry process skills to make discoveries?

Digging to Discover

Her lips are starting to swell and crack under the broiling desert sun. Hot dry air has been relentlessly attacking since daybreak. She stops for a moment, lifts the bandana covering her mouth and nose, and shakes out her stringy hair. Incredibly, with that headshake, something catches her attention. To her left, a tiny, gray fossil bone fragment sticks out from the soil. The last gust of wind must have revealed it. Now, she doesn't feel the sun or the heat or the dust at all! Her full attention is focused on the fragment.

A series of images flashes through her mind as she compares what she can tell about this fragment to what she already knows. Her mental pictures are of dinosaur skeletons, and none has the anatomical structure into which this tiny bone would fit. It is a toe bone, for sure—but one she has never seen before. Her heart starts to race at the thought of this.

From her grimy tool pack, she carefully pulls several tiny dental picks and small brushes and gently works away the material around the bone. With each gentle poke and sweep of the brush, she grasps more clearly what has just been revealed to her eyes alone: A brand-new dinosaur has stuck its toe into her world and ours. Her careful inquiry has led to an extraordinary discovery.

She will draw the fossil, photograph it, plot its location, and then ever so slowly search the surrounding area for more fragments. Eventually, she will pull from the reluctant earth a creature that so far has only been imagined. A wonderful discovery has been made—and she made it!

Discovery: The Destination

When we discover, we find or gain knowledge, usually for the first time. And while the act of discovery may only take an instant, getting there can take a long, long time.

When we teach science with the focus on discovery, we prepare children to make their personal discoveries with our strong guidance. We give them their very own "tool packs." And with any luck at all, they will use those tools in a variety of contexts all through their lives. Only a few children will find brand-new dinosaurs, but all of them will use the tools of scientific inquiry to unearth the facts and develop the concepts, principles, attitudes, and values that will help them lead full and productive lives.

It's now time to focus on how you can make discovery learning a central feature of every class you teach. First, we'll look at a formal definition of *discovery learning* that will give direction to the science units and lessons you plan and teach.

What Is Discovery?

"Discovery simply means coming to know something you didn't know before."

Discovery learning happens when a child uncovers new information or gleans new insight about how to approach a problem or task and then completes the task or solves the problem on her or his own. It is an individual and personal experience. *Classrooms don't discover; individual children do.*

Considering some common synonyms for *discover* will help you comprehend the active, individual nature of discovery learning: *detect, discern, disclose, expose, unearth, find, invent, realize,* and *learn.* If your classroom is truly one in which discovery is the destination, any or all of these synonyms should be swirling through your mind as you plan units and lessons.

How Do I Teach So Discovery Learning Happens?

To teach for discovery learning, you must, wherever possible, provide hands-on, mind-stretching experiences that will enable children to use their knowledge and skills to make discoveries. Your challenge is to provide the physical and intellectual context that ensures that these new discoveries are related to what learning has come before and to what learning will follow. Discovery learning does not happen in a vacuum. It is connected to the past and to the future. It is your job to be sure that these connections are made.

Is Discovery Time Really "Circus Time"?

OK, it's true: Some science classrooms *do* become accidental "circuses." It happens from time to time when teachers make the naive assumption that if they just provide a super-rich context of science "stuff," then good things will automatically happen. Well, sometimes they do, and sometimes they don't.

I know of no elementary- or middle-grade teachers who, as their total approach to discovery learning, dump a box of leaves, shells, or magnets on the front desk and cheerfully announce "Come on up, get some stuff, have some fun, and discover!"

That is not discovery learning. It's an invitation to a circus.

Inquiry: The Path

By now, you should understand that the point of your science experiences with children is to foster discovery learning. Remember to think of discovery learning as a *destination.*

You must also be firm in your conviction that discovery learning does not happen by accident. It must be clearly guided—by you. In fact, some educators use the term *guided discovery* to describe learning experiences for children.

The obvious question at this point (which I really hope is running through your mind) is, How do I guide children so they really get on the path to discovery and then actually make their own discoveries? Recall from earlier chapters that that path is *inquiry.*

What Is Inquiry?

Within the current educational scene, the term *inquiry* has far too many definitions, and that's unfortunate. I will explain it as clearly as I can, beginning with this straightforward definition:

> *"Inquiry is a very careful and systematic method of exploring the unknown so that discoveries are made."*

To further enhance your understanding of the term, let me share this detailed definition proposed by the National Science Education (NSE) Standards:

Scientific inquiry refers to the diverse ways in which scientists study the natural world and propose explanations based on the evidence derived from their work. Inquiry also refers to the activities of students in which they develop knowledge and understanding of scientific ideas, as well as an understanding of how scientists study the natural world.[1]

Of course, as a teacher, you should have a fairly clear understanding of what discoveries will be made and how to guide children's inquiry in fruitful ways. The information in the following section will help you with that.

Examples of Inquiry Methods

In describing *inquiry* in further detail, the NSE Standards give examples of activities that children or scientists would do if they were engaged in inquiry:

1. Making observations
2. Posing questions
3. Examining books and other sources of information to see what is already known
4. Planning investigations
5. Reviewing what is already known based on experimental evidence
6. Using tools to gather, analyze, and interpret data
7. Proposing answers, explanations, and predictions and communicating the results
8. Identifying assumptions, using critical and logical thinking, and considering alternative explanations[2]

This is an overwhelming range of activities! Fortunately, over the years, these ideas have been transformed into much more useful forms. Educators have identified the specific classroom skills that children need in order to actively participate in the activities listed above. They are commonly called the *inquiry process skills* or *skills of inquiry.*

Jodie: It looks like you're on clean-up duty. I thought you'd be all done by now. Dismissal was a half hour ago.

Rick: Just a few more minutes, and I think I'll have everything back in the kits. I think we might be missing a few plastic pieces for the robots.

Jodie: I sure hope not! I'm starting that unit tomorrow. Oh, are all the computers working that run the robots?

Rick: Most of them are fine. Only one is a little flaky. It works most of the time. I think you'll do OK. Now, where is that little yellow gear?

Jodie: There—it's under the table. Anyway, I don't want too many surprises. I'm really feeling pressed for time. The investigations are taking a lot longer than I thought they would. I think this robot lab is going to be a long one. Aren't you burning up your prep time getting ready?

Rick: Of course not. I'm a veteran now! This is my second year using the robot kit, and the get-ready time is actually less this time around. Of course, I've got a secret that you don't know about: I appointed a few kids as special helpers. Boys *and* girls, of course! Together, we can get the kits opened and the materials out pretty quickly now. Another plus is that the students are much better at moving through the activities. They seem to work much faster in these inquiry labs than they do with traditional work. I think it's the high motivation that comes with doing science this way. There is actually much more on-task behavior.

Jodie: You know, I started to see that today with the kit I was finishing. I noticed that the kids are getting better at organizing their information. They immediately put it into different types of tables and charts, which is something that used to take forever.

Rick: These kits are creating such a high level of interest and engagement that the students are not only doing the fun part but they are also doing the "nuts and bolts" stuff— writing down their observations and making labeled diagrams. Oh, here is something else I noticed: They are becoming little "watchdogs."

Jodie: Watchdogs?

Rick: Absolutely. Now, every time I do a demonstration, they start complaining that I didn't control all the variables or that I forgot to write down our predictions on the whiteboard.

Jodie: Serves you right!

▶ **POINT TO PONDER:** *It seems that inquiry-based, discovery-focused learning has brought several positive developments to Rick and Jodie's classrooms but certain problems, as well. Based on their conversation, produce a list of the challenges that will likely come about as you bring inquiry-based, discovery-focused units and lessons to your classroom.*

A little later in this chapter, we will learn what these skills are. (See the section titled "The Inquiry Process Skills," on pages 51–57.) But for now, I want to turn your attention to a topic that will help you grasp how to incorporate discovery-focused, inquiry-based science in your classroom. Educators have devised a way for you to think about this "big picture" in a simple and effective way. It's called the *learning cycle*.

The Learning Cycle

Tying Together Inquiry and Discovery

Over the years, various individuals have developed the learning cycle as a general structure that can be followed to institute discovery-oriented experiences in the classroom. So, it has taken various forms over the years. The generally accepted form of the learning cycle, which I use in this book, identifies these three stages:

1. Exploration
2. Inquiry and acquisition
3. Discovery and application

In the next few sections, we'll consider the learning cycle from your perspective as a teacher and from your children's perspective, as well.

At some point, you should direct your attention to the work of two of my friends and colleagues as it relates to inquiry and the learning cycle: Charles Barman's discussion of the learning cycle in a carefully prepared monograph[3] and Alan Colburn's article dealing with various definitions of inquiry as well as the learning cycle.[4] Both are identified specifically in the Notes section of this chapter.

The Learning Cycle from Your Perspective

Since the implications of the learning cycle for your planning and teaching are profound, let's consider each of the stages in detail from your perspective as a teacher:

1. Exploration

During this phase, you present materials and situations and pose questions, problems, and challenges that will get students thinking about the work at hand. The children make their first try at manipulating materials and equipment, using resource books, accessing the Internet, discussing, and just beginning to think about the challenge you have provided. This stage typically lasts just a few minutes; however, for some units and lessons, you might wish to allow more time.

2. Inquiry and Acquisition

Now, you assume a somewhat more traditional role and provide more guidance to the children. For instance, you may do a demonstration, present information, or introduce a new concept. This is your chance to explain, if explaining is necessary. This is also your chance to focus the children more immediately and clearly on the challenge and get them moving forward.

Most important of all, this is your opportunity to review the inquiry process skills, which are the basic tools children will use. (Again, they are presented in detail in the next section of this chapter.) This is the time to present the appropriate skills and help children use them as they inquire and acquire new knowledge.

3. Discovery and Application

You have set the stage for children to make discoveries, so now, let them really get to work! Your job at this point is to provide additional information and direction as they carry out their work. Coach and guide children as needed so they will be able to successfully complete the challenge you have set out for them. In doing so, they will discover new concepts and principles and even develop positive affect about doing science and other activities.

When you feel that the children are on the verge of completing their discovery work, it is time to take the next step—the step that really makes the learning cycle a *cycle*. That step is to pose new challenges or situations so children can *apply* what they have just discovered. These new challenges will lead naturally to brand-new opportunities to explore, to inquire and acquire, and to discover and apply. And so the cycle goes!

You can use the three stages of the learning cycle to organize your thinking about how to teach and how to provide a good environment for discovery learning. This is not to suggest that you should always follow these three stages but that you should reflect upon the stages as you think through your approach to planning and teaching science lessons. What you actually do with the children will depend on a number of variables unique to you and your teaching environment.

The Learning Cycle from Your Children's Perspective

Let's switch desks now and think about what the learning cycle looks like from the children's point of view:

1. I explore.
2. I inquire and acquire knowledge, skills, and attitudes.
3. I make discoveries and then use them.

As noted earlier, you should think of children's role in discovery learning as that of *scientist*—say, the archaeologist we met at the beginning of this chapter. What would that scientist do during each stage of the learning cycle?

1. **Exploration**
   - Study the work that previous archaelogists have done.
   - Survey the area.
   - Look at rock layers.
   - Gather samples.

2. **Inquiry and Acquisition**

- Carefully map the location of the discovery.
- Locate, study, and remove the fossil.
- Keep careful notes and labeled drawings.
- Search reference material for matches to the fossil.

3. **Discovery and Application**

- Identify the fossil as being previously unknown to science.
- Use the fossil to begin construction of the anatomy of a new dinosaur.
- Make a presentation to other archaelogists about the discovery.
- Plan an expedition to uncover more of the dinosaur, identifying the appropriate tools and software needed and selecting assistants with the appropriate qualifications.

Now, consider each phase of the learning cycle in the context of a science unit on ocean creatures. And the "scientists" are the children in your classroom:

1. **Exploration**

- Observe a collection of fresh fish, shrimp, clams, and the like from a local fish market, which the teacher has prepared.
- Observe an indoor saltwater aquarium, containing appropriate sea life bought at a pet store, which the teacher has created.

2. **Inquiry and Acquisition**

- Use inquiry process skills to observe and classify the living things observed.
- Use resource books and Internet sites to acquire additional information about each classification of sea life.
- Keep careful notes, journals, and labeled drawings of the sea life.

3. **Discovery and Application**

- Identify common traits among the organisms that have been classified into groups, and make drawings to show the probable characteristics of the natural environment for each creature.
- Share their knowledge about sea life with parents by creating posters that will be displayed on Back-to-School Night.
- Use their new knowledge and skills as they begin a unit of study on how humans adapt to the earth's environment.

This review of an actual science unit should make it clear what kinds of activities children do during each phase of the learning cycle. Next, let's look at the specific skills involved in doing these activities: the inquiry process skills.

The Inquiry Process Skills

The discoveries that scientists like our archaeologist friend make come from their ability to use the *inquiry process skills.* They are important skills that teachers can use to develop a classroom learning environment that has discovery learning as its central focus.

The Basic Inquiry Process Skills

Observing

■ *What Does It Mean?*

Observing means using the senses to obtain information, or *data,* about objects and events. It is the most basic process of science. Casual observations spark almost every inquiry we make about our environment. Organized observations form the basis for more structured investigations. Acquiring the ability to make careful observations will create a foundation for making inferences or hypotheses that can be tested by further observations.

Project 2061: Implications for Including the Inquiry Process Skills in Your Teaching

Project 2061 has a very strong emphasis on teaching inquiry process skills to students. It suggests that teachers should help students look at the world in a more scientific or objective manner, that students should be actively involved in exploration, and that everyone should be aware that scientific exploration is an important enterprise of modern society. Project 2061 addresses these three areas within the benchmark "The nature of science":

- ■ The scientific world view
- ■ Scientific inquiry
- ■ The scientific enterprise

To find specific recommendations for each area, visit the Project 2061 website at <www.project2061.org/>.

Observing is the most basic of all the inquiry process skills.

Sample Activity

Children can observe that different animals have very different solutions to the problem of getting from place to place. By directly observing animals outdoors or displayed in the classroom, children can describe whether each animal walks, swims, or flies. You may wish to challenge children to identify animals that can do all three—for example, ducks.

Using Space/Time Relationships

■ *What Does It Mean?*

All objects occupy a place in space. The process skill *using space/time relationships* involves the ability to discern and describe directions, spatial arrangements, motion and speed, symmetry, and rate of change.

Sample Activity

Provide each child or group of children with a small metal mirror (metal instead of glass as a safety precaution) and half an apple or a pear made by a lengthwise cut through the fruit. Ask children to discover if the right and left sides of the half are symmetrical. They can put the mirror lengthwise down the middle of the fruit section to see if they can observe the image of a complete fruit.

Using Numbers

■ *What Does It Mean?*

We need numbers to manipulate measurements, order objects, and classify objects. The amount of time spent on the activities devoted to *using numbers* should depend largely on the school's mathematics program. It is important for children to realize that the ability to use numbers is also a fundamental process of science.

Sample Activity

Help young children learn to compare sets with the use of natural objects such as rocks. Place a collection of rocks on a table. Pick out a set of six rocks, and ask various children to come to the collection and make a set containing one more element than your set. Encourage children to use language such as the following to describe their set: "My set has seven, which is more than your set of six rocks." Do this with other sets of rocks.

Classifying

■ *What Does It Mean?*

Classifying is the process scientists use to impose order on collections of objects or events. Classification schemes are used in science and other disciplines to identify objects or events and to show similarities, differences, and interrelationships.

Sample Activity

Ask children to bring pictures of plants and animals to school. Use the pictures from all the children to develop entries for a classification system.

Measuring

■ *What Does It Mean?*

Measuring is the way observations are quantified. Skill in measuring requires not only the ability to use measuring instruments properly but also the ability to carry out calculations with these instruments. The process involves judgment about which instrument to use and when approximate rather than precise measurements are acceptable. Children can learn to measure length, area, volume, mass, temperature, force, and speed as they work on this process skill.

Sample Activity

Have children estimate the linear dimensions of classroom objects using centimeters, decimeters, or meters, and then use metersticks to measure the objects.

Communicating

■ *What Does It Mean?*

Clear, precise communication is essential to all human endeavors and fundamental to all scientific work, which makes *communicating* skills valuable. Scientists communicate orally, with written words, and through the use of diagrams, maps, graphs, mathematical equations, and other visual demonstrations.

Sample Activity

Display a small animal such as a gerbil, hamster, or water snail. Ask children to write descriptions of the organism, emphasizing the need to include details such as size, shape, color, texture, and method of locomotion.

Predicting

■ *What Does It Mean?*

A *prediction* is a specific forecast of a future observation or event. Predictions are based on observations, measurements, and inferences about relationships between observed variables. A prediction that is not based on observation is only a guess. Accurate predictions result from careful observations and precise measurements.

Sample Activity

Have children construct a questionnaire about breakfast cereal preference and gather data from all the classrooms in the school except one. Have students analyze their data and make a prediction about the outcome of the survey of the children in the last room before polling those children.

Inferring

■ *What Does It Mean?*

Inferring is using logic to draw conclusions from what we observe. Nothing is more fundamental to clear thinking than the ability to distinguish between an observation and an inference. An *observation* is an experience that is obtained through one of the senses. An *inference* is an explanation of an observation. The thought involved in making an inference can occur in a fraction of a second and is often strongly affected by past experiences.

Sample Activity

Take children on a mini–field trip to a tree on school property, and have them prepare a list of observations about the ground at the base of the tree, the tree bark, and the leaves. Ask children to make inferences from their observations about the animals that may live in or near the tree (e.g., birds, insects, squirrels).

The Integrated Inquiry Process Skills

Controlling Variables

■ *What Does It Mean?*

Controlling variables means managing the conditions of an investigation. A *variable* is an object or quantity that can change. In an investigation, the best results are achieved when the variables are identified and carefully controlled. Students can develop skills in identifying variables and in describing how they have controlled variables during science activities.

Sample Activity

Children can identify the variable that causes roots to grow downward in the following manner. Have them plant the same number and type of bean seeds at the sides of three sealed, clear containers. This will allow them to see the root systems develop. After the roots have grown about 2 centimeters, have children turn one container upside down and one sideways. They will observe over a few days that the roots of seeds in the two turned containers have changed their direction of growth and are now growing downward. Children should be able to identify the one variable that might have caused the roots to change direction: gravity.

Interpreting Data

■ *What Does It Mean?*

The process of *interpreting data* involves making predictions, inferences, and hypotheses from the data collected in an investigation. We are constantly interpreting data when we read weather maps, watch the news on television, and look at photographs in newspapers and magazines. Students should have had previous experience in observing, classifying, and measuring before the process of interpreting data is approached.

Sample Activity

Through extended study of a population of mealworms, children can participate in many activities emphasizing the interpretation of data. Mealworms, the larvae stage of a common cereal beetle, can be easily maintained in a classroom. Students

---

MAKE THE CASE *An Individual or Group Challenge*

■ **The Problem**

Children in discovery-focused, inquiry-based classrooms may become so involved in their explorations that they spend too much time *doing* and too little time *thinking*.

■ **Assess Your Prior Knowledge and Beliefs**

What are your present beliefs about each of the following?

1. Before engaging in an activity, children should establish a hypothesis.

    _____ agree   _____ disagree

    Your reasoning: _____

2. Even if there is an official recorder, all the children in a group should record their personal observations.

    _____ agree   _____ disagree

    Your reasoning: _____

3. As long as children have hands-on, inquiry-based experiences, they will learn the inquiry process skills.

    _____ agree   _____ disagree

    Your reasoning: _____

■ **The Challenge**

Your state or province has awarded you a $500 grant for a single discovery-focused science project that involves a simulation of life in a space colony on Mars. At the end of the year, you must write a report describing what the children have learned. Describe how you would incorporate the children's mastery of the basic inquiry process skills as central elements of your report.

can count the number of mealworms that are in the culture each week and graph their data. The interpretation of these data can focus on such questions as What reasons could explain an increase in population? and What reasons could explain a decrease in population?

Formulating Hypotheses

■ *What Does It Mean?*

A *hypothesis* is an "educated guess." *Formulating hypotheses* should be based on observations or inferences. For example, you may observe that a cube of sugar dissolves faster in hot water than in cold water. From this observation, you might formulate the hypothesis that all substances soluble in water dissolve faster in hot water than in cold water. A hypothesis may also be generalized from an inference. For example, if you invert a glass jar over a burning candle, the candle will go out in a short time. You might infer from this observation that the candle goes out because all of the oxygen in the jar is used up. You might then formulate the hypothesis that all burning candles covered with glass jars go out when the oxygen in the jar is used up.

Sample Activity

Provide children with the materials needed to make a simple lever. After they have made a lever, identify the fulcrum (the turning point) and explain that the force we apply to move an object is called *effort.* The object moved is the *load.* Have children make hypotheses about the amounts of effort needed to move various loads. Then move the fulcrum closer and farther away from the load and have children make hypotheses about how these changes will affect the effort needed to move the load.

Defining Operationally

■ *What Does It Mean?*

When students use the *defining operationally* process, they define terms in the context of their own experiences. That is, they work with a definition instead of memorizing it. A definition that limits the number of things to be considered and is experiential is more useful than one that encompasses all possible variations that might be encountered. In the physical sciences, an operational definition is based on what is done and what is observed. In the biological sciences, an operational definition is often descriptive.

Sample Activity

Have students invent operational definitions for plant parts based on the functions of the parts they observe. For example, part of an operational definition for a *stem* is that "water moves up it." This definition might be derived by observing that a carnation stem placed in colored water serves to conduct the coloring to the petals. Part of the operational definition for a *bud* might include a reference to it as a site where they have observed a flower or a leaf emerge.

Experimenting encompasses all of the basic and integrated inquiry process skills.

Experimenting

■ *What Does It Mean?*

Experimenting is the process that encompasses all of the basic and integrated processes. An exercise in experimenting usually begins with observations that suggest questions to be answered. Sometimes the student formulates a hypothesis from a question or questions. The succeeding steps in experimenting involve identifying the variables to be controlled, making operational definitions, constructing a test, carrying out the test, collecting and interpreting data, and sometimes modifying the hypothesis that was being tested.

Sample Activity

Children can invent an experiment to test the effects of light on the growth of plants. Provide children with an assortment of sprouted corn and bean plants. Ask them to describe an experiment that would see how the availability of light affects how fast plants grow. Be sure to ask children to indicate what tools they may need to complete the experiment (e.g., lamp, meterstick, graph paper).

Summary

The science knowledge, concepts, skills, attitudes, and values that are the fabric of your curriculum are all the result of discoveries made over many years of scientific inquiry. One important approach to teaching children science is to create a classroom environment in which they make their own discoveries through careful inquiry about various aspects of the natural world.

While there are many ways to foster discovery-focused, inquiry-based learning in the science classroom, one important strategy involves a three-stage learning cycle, in which children (1) explore; (2) inquire and acquire knowledge; and (3) discover and apply what they have learned. As children progress through these stages, they use a number of investigative tools commonly known as the *inquiry process skills*.

GOING FURTHER

On Your Own

1. This chapter described a three-stage learning cycle that can be useful as you think about fostering discovery learning in the classroom. Pick a science topic that you might teach a group of children, and provide examples of specific things you might do to involve students in each stage of the cycle.

2. Some of the inquiry process skills discussed in this chapter are also used in the nonscience portions of the elementary/middle school (e.g., social studies, language arts, and so on) curriculum. Select three inquiry process skills, and discuss how each might be used to integrate at least one other subject with science.

3. This chapter discussed the importance of using the inquiry process skills in doing hands-on science. What potential is there for an elemen-tary- or middle-grade teacher to teach some of these skills through classroom demonstrations? Explain your response.

4. This book identifies the content domains of science as the life, earth/space, and physical sciences. Would you foresee a teacher having problems incorporating particular inquiry process skills in any of the content fields? If so, which skills might pose difficulty with which content fields? Why?

5. Some resistance to including the inquiry process skills comes from teachers who have not had much personal experience with science activities or experiments in college. To what extent did your college-level experience include opportunities to utilize the inquiry process skills?

On Your Own or in a Cooperative Learning Group

6. Draw a line on a sheet of paper or a whiteboard to represent the continuum from content-based science to process-based science. Challenge others to identify positions on the continuum that represent (1) the degree to which their own science experiences in elementary-/middle-grade science emphasized the inquiry process skills; (2) the extent to which their secondary school science experiences emphasized these skills; (3) the extent to which their college-level science experiences emphasized these skills; and (4) the extent to which they believe their own teaching of elementary-/middle-grade science will emphasize the inquiry process skills.

7. How might a week of classroom time (30 minutes per day) early in the school year be used to teach children in primary, elementary, or middle school that science is a way of doing things as well as an organizational collection of facts, concepts, and principles? Illustrate your idea with specific examples.

8. Select either a commercially available school science textbook series or a science curriculum prepared by a school district, and determine which inquiry process skills are emphasized. Note whether particular skills are intended to be stressed at particular grade levels. Using examples from these materials, prepare a chart that illustrates the relationships between the inquiry process skills and the stages of the learning cycle, both discussed in this chapter.

RESOURCES FOR DISCOVERY LEARNING

 Internet Resources

Websites for Inquiry Process Skills

The Annenberg Project—Frequently Asked Questions about Inquiry

www.learner.org/channel/workshops/inquiry/faq.html

This very comprehensive site answers many of the questions teachers might have about how to teach science using inquiry as the principal method by which children make discoveries. The questions are really focused on teachers' needs as they approach planning units and lessons—for example: What is inquiry and why do it? What is my role in an inquiry classroom? How can teachers keep all students involved in an inquiry classroom? The framework for this part of the site is a list of workshops on inquiry-related topics, with each linked to important resource materials.

State of Texas—Why Teach Science?

www.tenet.edu/teks/science

This is a portion of a very well-designed site that brings together important resources for teachers who wish to emphasize inquiry as the method through which children learn science. On this particular page, you will find articles dealing with inquiry, the inquiry process skills, and the relationship of the inquiry process skills to national standards.

Washington Virtual Classroom

www.wavcc.org/wvc/cadre/WaterQuality/science

This site offers a structured way of looking at a science unit in terms of the content, concepts, and inquiry process skills to be taught and assessed. The site's "Water Quality Project" is the unit of study that reflects all these elements. As you study this project,

note how it relates to inquiry science and the number and kinds of discovery-focused experiences that it includes.

Growing the Scientific Method

www.unc.edu/depts/cmse/curriculum/growing.html

This site begins with a brief introduction to the inquiry process skills, which is followed by an identification of resources that relate these skills to environmental education and gardening.

Greenwood School District 50 Kindergarten Science

www.gwd50.k12.sc.us/exp-web/Exp9801/ExprPage.htm

If you have a special interest in teaching young children, you should become aware of which inquiry process skills and manipulative skills children of this age are expected to learn. This site presents an overview of the skills that one school district believes should be emphasized at the kindergarten level.

Intended Learning Outcomes

www.usoe.k12.ut.us/curr/science/ele_out.htm

Various states have prepared lists of expected outcomes for children's work in science. At this site, you will find Utah's state curriculum expectations for both the basic and integrated inquiry process skills. You will also find a list of outcomes related to affective development and the social and historical impact of science as well as other key components of the science curriculum.

Print Resources
Suggested Readings

Barman, Charles. *A Procedure for Helping Prospective Elementary Teachers Integrate the Learning Cycle into Science Textbooks.* Monograph 4. Arlington, VA: Council for Elementary Science International, an affiliate of the National Science Teachers Association, n.d.

Colburn, Alan. "An Inquiry Primer." *Science Scope* 23, no. 6 (March 2000): 42–44.

Delisle, Robert. *How to Use Problem Based Learning in the Classroom.* Alexandria, VA: Association for Supervision and Curriculum Development, 1997.

Denniston, Erin. "What a Puzzle!" *Science and Children* 39, no. 8 (May 2002): 14–18.

Hall, Sue, and Dori Hall. "Packing Peanut Properties." *Science and Children* 39, no. 5 (February 2002): 31–35.

Hammrich, Penny L., and Kathleen Fadigan. "Investigations in the Science of Sports." *Science Scope* 26, no. 5 (February 2003): 30–35.

Koschmann, Mark, and Dan Shepardson. "A Pond Investigation." *Science and Children* 39, no. 8 (May 2002): 20–23.

McWilliams, Susan. "Journey into the Five Senses." *Science and Children* 40, no. 5 (February 2003): 38–43.

Shaw, Mike. "A Dastardly Density Deed." *Science Scope* 26, no. 4 (January 2003): 18–21.

Sitzman, Daniel. "Bread Making: Classic Biotechnology and Experimental Design." *Science Scope* 26, no. 4 (January 2003): 27–31.

Waffler, Elizabeth Sumner. "Inspired Inquiry." *Science and Children* 38, no. 4 (January 2001): 28–31.

Wittrock, Cathy A., and Lloyd H. Barrow. "Blow-by-Blow Inquiry." *Science and Children* 37, no. 5 (February 2000): 34–38.

NOTES

1. National Research Council, *National Science Education Standards* (Washington, DC: National Academy Press, 1996), p. 23.

2. Ibid.

3. Charles Barman, *A Procedure for Helping Prospective Elementary Teachers Integrate the Learning Cycle into Science Textbooks*, Monograph 4 (Arlington, VA: Council for Elementary Science International, an affiliate of the National Science Teachers Association, n.d.).

4. Alan Coburn, "An Inquiry Primer," *Science Scope* 23, no. 6 (March 2000): 42–44.

4

Planning and Managing

How can I plan and manage inquiry-based, discovery-focused units and lessons?

The Water Rat and the Sea Horse

How will you plan your teaching so that the children you teach will learn? One way to develop your response to this fundamental question is first to consider the extremes of planning styles that may be used. To show you these extremes, I would like to have two very interesting animals present their approaches to the teaching and learning process: the Water Rat and the Sea Horse. The Water Rat, who is explaining the joys of boating to his friend the Mole, will speak first:

"Believe me, my young friend, there is nothing—absolutely nothing—half so much worth doing as simply messing about in boats. Simply messing," he went on dreamily: "messing—about—in—boats; messing—."

"Look ahead, Rat!" cried the Mole suddenly.

It was too late. The boat struck the bank full tilt. The dreamer, the joyous oarsman, lay on his back at the bottom of the boat, his heels in the air.

"—about in boats—or with boats," the Rat went on composedly, picking himself up with a pleasant laugh. "In or out of 'em, it doesn't matter. Nothing seems really to matter, that's the charm of it. Whether you get away, or whether you don't; whether you arrive at your destination or whether you reach somewhere else, or whether you never get anywhere at all, you're always busy, and you never do anything in particular; and when you've done it there's always something else to do, and you can do it if you like, but you'd much better not. Look here! If you've really nothing else on hand this morning, supposing we drop down the river together, and have a long day of it?"

The Mole waggled his toes from sheer happiness, spread his chest with a sigh of full contentment, and leaned back blissfully into the soft cushions. "What a day I'm having!" he said. "Let us start at once!"[1]

Now, the Sea Horse:

Once upon a time a Sea Horse gathered up his seven pieces of eight and cantered out to find his fortune. Before he had traveled very far he met an Eel, who said,

"Pssst. Hey, bud. Where ya' going?"

"I'm going out to find my fortune," replied the Sea Horse, proudly.

"You're in luck," said the Eel. "For four pieces of eight you can have this speedy flipper, and then you'll be able to get there a lot faster."

"Gee, that's swell," said the Sea Horse, and paid the money and put on the flipper and slithered off at twice the speed. Soon he came upon a Sponge, who said,

"Pssst. Hey, bud. Where ya' going?"

"I'm going out to find my fortune," replied the Sea Horse.

"You're in luck," said the Sponge. "For a small fee I will let you have this jet-propelled scooter so that you will be able to travel a lot faster."

So the Sea Horse bought the scooter with his remaining money and went zooming through the sea five times as fast. Soon he came upon a shark, who said,

"Pssst. Hey, bud. Where ya' going?"

"I'm going out to find my fortune," replied the Sea Horse.

"You're in luck. If you'll take this short cut," said the Shark, pointing to his open mouth, "you'll save yourself a lot of time."

"Gee, thanks," said the Sea Horse, and zoomed off into the interior of the Shark, there to be devoured.

The moral of this fable is that if you're not sure where you're going, you're liable to end up someplace else—and not even know it.[2]

As a teacher, you will face the same important choices—to rush ahead, to putter, to go in one direction only, or to let the stream carry you—that these animals faced, but your environment will not be a stream or an ocean. Instead, your environment will be a classroom overflowing with hopes and dreams for the future.

As you begin the planning process, you will undoubtedly develop some learning experiences that are very open, informal, and consistent with the Water Rat's approach to life. You probably will also develop some learning experiences that are more directed. Finding the balance between structure and balance comes with experience. Discovery learning and planning go hand in hand. They are not a contradiction in terms. Expert teachers plan in ways that foster discovery within a context that helps children acquire the knowledge, attitudes, and skills needed for success in school and in life.

The Scope of the Science Curriculum

Imagine observing a tiny gnat walking across a pebble as lightning flashes in the sky. How does each component of this scene fit into the area of knowledge we call *science?* The gnat is understood through biology, the science of living things. The origin and

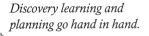
Discovery learning and planning go hand in hand.

characteristics of the pebble are understood through the earth/space sciences. The energy of the lightning flash and the atoms and molecules that make up the gnat and the pebble are understood through the physical sciences. Each component of the scene represents one part of the *scope,* or breadth of content, of science.

Determining the Scope of Your Curriculum

The *earth/space sciences* represent our knowledge of the origins of the universe and of our Earth in particular. They include astronomy, geology, meteorology, and other areas of study. The earth/space science topics commonly taught in elementary school include the following:

1. The stars, sun, and planets
2. The soil, rocks, and mountains
3. The weather

The *life sciences* include botany, zoology, and ecology. These disciplines are usually represented in the elementary science curriculum as the following topics:

1. The study of plants
2. The study of animals
3. The study of the relationship between plants and animals
4. The study of the relationship between living things and the environment

The *physical sciences* include physics and chemistry. Physics is concerned with the relationship between matter and energy. Chemistry is concerned with the manner through which various types of matter combine and change. In the elementary school, the following topics would be considered part of the physical sciences component of a science curriculum:

1. The study of matter and energy
2. The study of the chemical changes that matter undergoes

Although these three areas of content would seem to be more than enough, there is another area of study not usually listed as a major content component: technology. As noted in Chapter 1, *technology* is the use of science to solve human problems. An infusion of technology into the three central areas of the curriculum can offer you many opportunities to raise and consider questions of great societal import with children.

Science, technology, and society (STS) is not a "cold" curriculum area to be dealt with reluctantly. It can, without question, be an important and relevant part of science instruction that touches the lives of children and helps them grow as people and as scientifically literate citizens.

The NSE Standards:
Implications for Appropriate Scope

As noted in earlier chapters, the National Science Education (NSE) Standards provide guidance for teachers and others on a variety of aspects of science education. The area of the standards that will probably be of most interest to you will be that dealing with what you should be teaching. If you wish to teach content that is sensitive to the NSE recommendations, then its scope should at least range across the following eight topics, or *standards:*

1. Unifying concepts and processes in science
2. Science as inquiry
3. Physical science
4. Life science
5. Earth and space sciences
6. Science and technology
7. Science in personal and social perspectives
8. History and nature of science[3]

The first standard—"Unifying concepts and processes in science"—identifies broad science concepts that are needed to tie the other content areas together:

1. Systems, order, and organization
2. Evidence, models, and explanation
3. Change, constancy, and measurement
4. Evolution and equilibrium
5. Form and function[4]

If you presently lack a strong science content background, you will need to study the explanations and examples of these unifying concepts presented in the full NSE report.

The second standard—"Science as inquiry"—essentially states that children should be expected to ask questions about objects, organisms, and events; plan and carry out investigations; gather data; explain what they have learned; and communicate what they have learned. Teachers are expected to help children understand that scientists continually engage in these aspects of inquiry themselves.[5]

Standards 3 through 8 are more straightforward than the first two. Study Figure 4.1 (pages 67–68) to get a clear picture of the intended scope for units and lessons based on the NSE Standards. Also use this figure as a reference as you consider the appropriate sequence of topics for children. As you use these lists, however, please bear in mind that they are *recommendations* and should be treated as such.

FIGURE 4.1   The *National Science Education Standards, Grades K–8*

Unifying Concepts and Processes

Standard: As a result of activities in grades K–12, all students should develop understandings and abilities aligned with the following concepts and processes.

Systems, order, and organization

Evidence, models, and explanation

Constancy, change, and measurement

Evolution and equilibrium

Form and function

Content Standards Grades K–4

SCIENCE AS INQUIRY*

Content Standard A: As a result of activities in grades K–4, all students should develop
- Abilities necessary to do scientific inquiry
- Understanding about scientific inquiry

PHYSICAL SCIENCE [PS]**

Content Standard B: As a result of the activities in grades K–4, all students should develop an understanding of
- Properties of objects and materials [PS 1]
- Position and motion of objects [PS 2]
- Light, heat, electricity, and magnetism [PS 3]

LIFE SCIENCE [LS]

Content Standard C: As a result of the activities in grades K–4, all students should develop an understanding of
- The characteristics of organisms [LS 1]
- Life cycles of organisms [LS 2]
- Organisms and environments [LS 3]

EARTH AND SPACE SCIENCES [ESS]

Content Standard D: As a result of the activities in grades K–4, all students should develop an understanding of
- Properties of earth materials [ESS 1]
- Objects in the sky [ESS 2]
- Changes in earth and sky [ESS 3]

SCIENCE AND TECHNOLOGY [S&T]

Content Standard E: As a result of the activities in grades K–4, all students should develop an understanding of
- Abilities of technological design [S&T 1]
- Understanding about science and technology [S&T 2]
- Ability to distinguish between natural objects and objects made by humans [S&T 3]

SCIENCE IN PERSONAL AND SOCIAL PERSPECTIVES [SPSP]

Content Standard F: As a result of the activities in grades K–4, all students should develop an understanding of
- Personal health [SPSP 1]
- Characteristics and changes in populations [SPSP 2]
- Types of resources [SPSP 3]
- Changes in environments [SPSP 4]
- Science and technology in local challenges [SPSP 5]

*This general standard is the foundation of all the NSE Standards. Since it is emphasized in all *Teaching Children Science* activities, it is not identified for each experience.

**The bracketed symbol to the right of each standard was prepared for this book by this author.

HISTORY AND NATURE OF SCIENCE [HNS]

> **Content Standard G:** As a result of the activities in grades K–4, all students should develop an understanding of
> - Science as a human endeavor [HNS 1]

Content Standards Grades 5–8

SCIENCE AS INQUIRY

> **Content Standard A:** As a result of their activities in grades 5–8, all students should develop
> - Abilities necessary to do scientific inquiry
> - Understandings about scientific inquiry

PHYSICAL SCIENCE [PS]

> **Content Standard B:** As a result of their activities in grades 5–8, all students should develop an understanding of
> - Properties and changes of properties in matter [PS 4]
> - Motion and forces [PS 5]
> - Transfer of energy [PS 6]

LIFE SCIENCE [LS]

> **Content Standard C:** As a result of their activities in grades 5–8, all students should develop an understanding of
> - Structure and function in living systems [LS 4]
> - Reproduction and heredity [LS 5]
> - Regulation and behavior [LS 6]
> - Population and ecosystems [LS 7]
> - Diversity and adaptations of organisms [LS 8]

EARTH AND SPACE SCIENCES [ESS]

> **Content Standard D:** As a result of their activities in grades 5–8, all students should develop an understanding of
> - Structure of the earth system [ESS 4]
> - Earth's history [ESS 5]
> - Earth in the solar system [ESS 6]

SCIENCE AND TECHNOLOGY [S&T]

> **Content Standard E:** As a result of the activities in grades 5–8, all students should develop an understanding of
> - Abilities of technological design [S&T 4]
> - Understanding about science and technology [S&T 5]

SCIENCE IN PERSONAL AND SOCIAL PERSPECTIVES [SPSP]

> **Content Standard F:** As a result of the activities in grades 5–8, all students should develop an understanding of
> - Personal health [SPSP 6]
> - Populations, resources, and environments [SPSP 7]
> - Natural hazards [SPSP 8]
> - Risks and benefits [SPSP 9]
> - Changes in environments [SPSP 10]
> - Science and technology in society [SPSP 11]

HISTORY AND NATURE OF SCIENCE [HNS]

> **Content Standard G:** As a result of the activities in grades 5–8, all students should develop an understanding of
> - Science as a human endeavor [HNS 2]
> - Nature of science [HNS 3]
> - History of science [HNS 4]

The Sequence of the Science Curriculum

A knowledge of the scope of science will help you decide what topics can be reasonably included within the body of science experiences you present to children. However, one important question still remains: In what order should these topics be presented? For example, should children learn about the earth they live on before they learn about the structure and function of their bodies, or should the sequence be reversed?

Determining the Sequence of Your Curriculum

There is no definitive answer to the question of sequence. However, these three guidelines may help you consider the place of science in a child's school experience:

1. Since no learning can occur if the learner is inattentive to the experience, any decision you make should favor those topics that will generate the most learner involvement and interest.

2. As a general rule, organize learning experiences from the child outward. That is, select experiences that relate first to the child and then to the science content. In teaching electricity, for example, have children consider how they use electricity before they study its source.

3. In general, when deciding to expose children to a concept that can be considered concretely or abstractly, use the concrete approach first.

The NSE Standards: Implications for Appropriate Sequence

One of the very best ways of starting a spirited discussion in a teachers meeting is to say something like "The butterfly life cycle is too complicated for second-graders." If you are silly enough to make such a statement, you should be prepared to immediately weave your own protective chrysalis!

Too often, interested parties tell us that first-graders should learn X, second-graders should learn Y, and so on. That approach is much too specific and assumes that children in certain grades are homogeneous in terms of their present knowledge of science as well as their interest and ability to pursue science concepts. They are not. What children are able to do at a given grade level largely depends on the particular children, the teacher, and the resources available.

The NSE Standards take a more sensible and flexible approach to recommending the sequence in which science topics should be introduced. They identify the recommended content for grades K–4 and 5–8, as shown in Figure 4.1.

Unit Planning

What Makes a Good Unit Plan?

When full-time teachers lack a sense of the "big picture," their students have, in effect, a substitute teacher every day of the school year. Each school day that children have learning experiences that are not part of any larger context is a day that relates neither to the past nor to the future.

Children need appropriate learning experiences in school—activities that will reflect their teacher's concern with goals and that will involve them cognitively, affectively, and physically. To accomplish this, teachers must plan their science units. Unit plans can take a variety of forms. The list of possible components in Figure 4.2 may prove useful when you develop your own unit plans.

FIGURE 4.2
A science unit may have many components, but each component has a specific purpose.

Component	Purpose
■ Rationale	Helps you think through the reasons for doing a unit on a particular topic
■ Instructional objectives*	Help you focus on the intended outcomes of the unit
■ Listing of science concepts and processes to be emphasized	Helps you focus on the major ideas and methods of science that should be stressed
■ Content outline (for teachers)	Helps you review the content that will provide the foundation for the learning experience
■ Daily lesson plans*	Help you think through learning activities and their relationship to exploration, concept acquisition, and concept application
■ Materials list	Helps you make certain that you have all the materials needed for science activities that occur in daily lessons
■ Audiovisual materials and list	Help you make certain that you have such things as computer hardware and software, videotapes, and other required equipment
■ Assessment strategies	Help you consider informal and formal ways to assess the extent to which children have achieved cognitive, psychomotor, and affective growth during the unit

*Considered in greater detail later in this chapter.

Project 2061: Implications for Your Planning and Managing

Clearly, Project 2061 tells you much about what you *should* teach, but it also provides some direction about *how* you should go about it. It draws on research about how children learn as well as what methods effective teachers tend to use with children. This latter area is referred to as *craft knowledge*.

Project 2061 presents its recommendations for what you should actually do in the classroom in the benchmark "Effective learning and teaching." There are two key ideas within this benchmark:

- Principles of learning
- Teaching science, mathematics, and technology

You'll find specific recommendations for these ideas at the Project 2061 website: <www.project2061.org/>.

Will Unit Plans Work in Schools That Use Science Textbooks?

Many schools use textbooks or curriculum guides as organizing elements for the curriculum. With some creative planning on your part, such materials can offer a starting point for the development of meaningful science experiences for children. After diagnosing student needs and interests, you can use a portion of a textbook or curriculum guide as a basis for a unit plan. Indeed, the teachers' editions of many recent science textbooks can be important planning resources. Many contain lists of concepts to show scope and sequence; lists of emphasized inquiry process skills; ideas for beginning units and lessons; lesson plans; lists of science materials needed; science content for the teacher; lesson enrichment ideas; bulletin board and field trip ideas; lists of related children's books and websites; and computer software and audiovisual aids.

Although a teacher's edition can be an important resource, it is not a recipe book and should not be used in place of your own planning. After all, you are the only one who knows the children in your class.

Lesson Planning

What Makes a Good Learning Objective?

The central characteristic of a learning objective is the specification of the behavior that the child is likely to exhibit as a result of the learning process. When you write an objective, be sure to specify the action you wish the child to perform. Attempt to answer this question: What will the child be able to do?

Here are some key performance words that appear in instructional objectives. Notice how some of these are used in the sample objectives that follow this list:

Write	Plan	Explain orally	Select	Measure	Label
Bake	List	Construct (make)	Define	Solve	Name
Sing					

Unit Title	**Sample Objective**
1. Force and Motion	Measure how high a tennis ball bounces when dropped from different heights.
2. Using Electrical Energy	List five safety rules for using electrical appliances.
3. The Nervous System	Name the five senses.
4. Good Nutrition	Bake a batch of cookies that do not require sugar.
5. Protecting Our Environment	Write a poem about preventing pollution.
6. The Changing Earth	Construct a model of a volcano.

The science activities presented in this book include learning objectives that specify expected student behaviors. These objectives will probably be specific enough for most schools. However, some school systems require teachers to establish objectives that are even more specific.

What Makes a Good Lesson Plan?

If you were to lock three teachers in a room and ask them (under pain of losing their parking spaces) to reach a consensus about the best format for a lesson plan, you would probably end up with four formats (and three teachers walking to school). The fact is, there are many approaches to lesson planning, and it is difficult to know in advance which one will work best for you.

Be that as it may, you *do* need a starting point for lesson planning. The following key elements—enhanced with additional components suggested by veteran teachers, school administrators, and others—will serve you well:

1. Objectives
2. Process Skills Emphasized
3. Materials
4. Learning Cycle Procedures
5. Assessment
6. Assignment

Terry: I think most of us feel that planning is much easier than management. Good management is what makes it work. It really is what creates success or failure with your lessons.

Marie: But it's good planning that leads to good management, and the key to planning is to try the lesson yourself beforehand. That is what really helps you get the steps in the best sequence and the timing right, especially if you are going to be doing a lot of hands-on science with children. It's only when I try each activity myself that I get the sequence and timing down. That's what makes the actual class management of everything easier.

Terry: But there is more to it than just getting the science activities worked out. You have to think about other things, also. Something as simple as allocating space in the classroom for cooperative groups working on science projects can make a real difference. Working and reworking the directions you are going to give to groups also seems like a small matter, but it makes all the difference in the world.

Marie: Sometimes when new teachers observe experienced teachers, it almost looks too easy. People shouldn't think a classroom, especially a science classroom, runs smoothly by accident. There is a lot to it, and most of the work that makes it happen is done before class even starts!

Terry: Well, there is a lot that happens during class, as well. I am always changing my plans during a lesson. I've noticed that I am making changes even in my cooperative group work.

Marie: What do you mean?

Terry: Sometimes you think that a science project might be too hard for a group, but as soon as the group gets started, you realize it's going to be too easy. As soon as you see this happening, you've got to intervene, to make changes right on the spot. If you don't, a management disaster is just a few minutes away.

Marie: I think the trick with cooperative group work is to be ready with alternatives so that each group gets projects that are so challenging that the group has to come up with alternative ways of working things out. If you can do this, you get the children a lot more focused. I think that is what makes the idea of assigning roles to different children in a group really work. If the project is too easy, the roles lose their meaning.

Terry: Nothing ties a group together like a real challenge—one where they really depend on each other for success.

➤ **POINT TO PONDER:** *These teachers stressed the ability to take quick remedial action during class time as a critical component of good management. They also emphasized the need for challenging science projects to keep groups focused. What do you see as the possible management consequences of giving groups science projects that are too challenging? What could you do to be ready to deal with the management problems that might result from such a situation?*

Sample Lesson Plans

Figures 4.3, 4.4, and 4.5 (pages 74–76) are sample lesson plans that all have a strong discovery emphasis. This should be evident as you note, in particular, the Learning Cycle Procedures component that is the foundation for each.

As you review these plans, notice what they have in common and how they are different. Also note that each plan follows the three phases of the learning cycle (as discussed in Chapter 3).

Classroom Organization and Management

I'm not going to provide an elaborate treatise on maintaining appropriate classroom behavior. The fact is, I have seen more *teachers* produce discipline problems than I have seen *children* cause them. If you are able to maintain appropriate behavior when you teach social studies, reading, math, or any other subject, you will be able to do so when you teach science. If you have problems with classroom control, science activities will neither solve your problems nor make them worse. Even so, you can take some steps that will help things go more smoothly for everyone. Appropriate classroom behavior is not hard to achieve; it just requires attention to a few common-sense matters.

Distributing Materials

The attack of a school of piranha on a drowning monkey is a model of tranquility when compared with a group of 20 children trying to acquire a magnet from a tote tray containing 10 of them.

In order to distribute materials effectively, you need to devise techniques that are appropriate for your setting. In some settings, for example, two or three children can distribute materials to all the groups. Another technique is to have one child from each group come forward to acquire needed materials. Regardless of the procedure you employ, try to avoid having all the children get what they need simultaneously.

Providing Work Space

"Please make him (her) stop bugging us, or I will wring his (her) neck."

This is a rather common classroom request (threat) among children involved in science activities. One way to diminish this type of problem is to give your learning groups some work space. This may be difficult if you have a small room, but you should try anyway. Movable bookcases, room dividers, and similar objects should be pressed into service to give groups of children semiprivate work spaces. Since science activities provide ample opportunities for social interaction among group members, there is little need for groups to interact with one another. Such contact is often counterproductive.

FIGURE 4.3   A sample discovery-based lesson for grade K or 1

Lesson
Plan

Will It Sink or Will It Float?

OBJECTIVES   Observe that some objects sink and some float.
Predict whether various small objects will sink or float.
Classify objects as "sinkers" and "floaters."

PROCESS SKILLS   Observing, predicting, classifying
EMPHASIZED

MATERIALS   Easel paper and marker
Empty aquarium
Plastic water jugs (filled)
Shell, pine cone, leaf, marble, coin, buttons, clothespin, cork, and spoon
Bath soap that floats and bath soap that doesn't
One paper bag containing assortment of different objects that sink or float,
including a rubber duck (put a question mark on the bag)
Second paper bag containing additional three objects

LEARNING   1. *Exploration.* Ask children, "Do you play with toys when you take a bath?
CYCLE   If you do, what toys do you play with?" As they answer, list their bath toys on
PROCEDURES   the easel paper. Ask, "Do your toys sink or float on the water?" Write an "S"
in front of each item that sinks and an "F" in front of each that floats. Display
the collection of objects. Invite children to come to the front of the room or
center of the learning circle to select an object and tell whether he or she
thinks it will sink or float.

2. *Inquiry and Acquisition.* After all predictions have been made, ask children to
classify the objects according to the predictions. Have a child help you pour
water into the aquarium. Now have various children act as assistants and
gently place each object in the water. Have the children reclassify the objects
based on the results.

3. *Discovery and Application.* Display the bag with the question mark. Tell the
children that when they have free time, they can work at the table to classify
the objects in the bag as to whether they will sink or float and then experiment to test their predictions.

ASSESSMENT   Observe whether any children offer to bring in objects from home to test. Note
whether their predictions about sinking and floating are correct. Listen for children to bring experiences with floating objects into classroom conversations.

ASSIGNMENT   Display the second paper bag. Show the objects and have children practice
remembering what the objects are by putting them back in the bag and removing
them again. Finally, tell the children to think about each object tonight and predict whether it will sink or float when tested tomorrow.

FIGURE 4.4   A sample discovery-based lesson for grade 2 or 3

Lesson
Plan

Planting Popcorn

OBJECTIVES   Make careful observations of a popcorn kernel and pebble without using sight.

List the conditions needed for the kernel to become a plant and then plant the kernel.

Write a story telling how one of the twins in Tomie dePaola's *The Popcorn Book* gets into trouble by mixing a jar full of popcorn kernels into a gardener's flower seeds.

Develop a positive attitude about caring for living things, as demonstrated by the children's follow through on plant care responsibilities.

PROCESS SKILLS EMPHASIZED   Observing, measuring, inferring

MATERIALS   Bag of popcorn kernels and bag of equal-sized pebbles

Paper cups, potting soil, and small sandwich bags

The Popcorn Book, by Tomie dePaola (Holiday House, 1978)

Access to water

LEARNING CYCLE PROCEDURES   Keep the seeds and pebbles out of the children's sight. Soak enough kernels in water for two days so each child can trade his or her dry kernel for a soaked one.

1. *Exploration.* Have children shut their eyes and outstretch both hands so they are ready to receive some mystery objects. Explain that they are to keep their eyes shut until you say to open them. Indicate that the mystery objects should be kept in their closed hands until you say to open them. Distribute the mystery objects so that each child gets one pebble and one kernel. Go to the board and record children's observations of the objects, classifying them as right- or left-hand objects. Have the children open their hands to reveal their objects.

2. *Inquiry and Acquisition.* Discuss the differences between living and nonliving things. Ask the children to describe what their kernel will need in order to grow into a popcorn plant. Read *The Popcorn Book* to the class.

3. *Discovery and Application.* Form cooperative learning groups, three children per group. Distribute a few soaked kernels to each group. Explain the need to soak the kernels for a day or two before planting. Distribute the cups and the plastic bag with potting soil, and indicate that you will be asking them to record the growth of their plants on a large bulletin board chart for each of the following 8 weeks.

ASSESSMENT   Keep anecdotal records that show which groups are observing and attending to the needs of their planted kernels each day.

ASSIGNMENT   Ask the children to think about two or three good ideas they learned that they can use in writing stories about what a seed in a cornfield needs in order to grow into a corn plant. Have them write their stories the next day.

FIGURE 4.5   A sample discovery-based lesson for the middle grades

Lesson
Plan

What Is a Healthy and Tasty Meal?

OBJECTIVES   Classify foods on the hot lunch menu and those from a typical fast-food lunch into the categories of the food pyramid.
State examples of foods from each food category.
Construct a menu for a balanced lunch.

PROCESS SKILLS EMPHASIZED   Classifying, interpreting data, formulating hypotheses

MATERIALS   Today's hot lunch menu
Bag from fast-food restaurant containing wrappings or containers for the following: burger, salad, fries, cookies, soda, milk
Information pamphlet available from the major fast-food chain that details calorie and nutrient information for each product
Copy of food pyramid chart and chart paper for each group.
Transparency listing food items that would make a complete meal from a menu of a local fancy restaurant

LEARNING CYCLE PROCEDURES   1. *Exploration.* Show the closed bag from the fast-food restaurant to the class. Have children guess what's in it. Begin a discussion of why eating a well-balanced diet is important. Distribute copies of the food pyramid chart, and have children discuss where each part of their most recent fast-food meal would be placed within the pyramid.

2. *Inquiry and Acquisition.* Describe to the class how the digestive system processes foods from each portion of the pyramid. Encourage the children to take notes. Mention that sample foods from each group contribute to the functioning of other body systems—for instance, minerals from dairy products and vegetables are used in bone formation. Place the children in groups, and distribute chart paper to each group. Have them prepare a food pyramid chart with space for sample foods under each category. Reveal the contents of the bag, and have children classify the foods that the wrappings represent. Distribute copies of the nutrition pamphlet, and have students locate the information related to each item they put on their chart.

3. *Discovery and Application.* Write today's hot lunch menu on the board. Have the groups classify the foods from the hot lunch menu and record them on a pyramid chart. Have each group write a hypothesis that explains why the school lunch menu includes an assortment of foods that do or do not meet the requirements of the food pyramid.

ASSESSMENT   Project a copy of the menu for a complete meal from a local fancy restaurant. Ask children to classify each food item into its proper location on the pyramid. Also ask if they think they will be improving their food choices as a result of this lesson.

ASSIGNMENT   Ask children to design and bring in a hot lunch menu each day of the week that includes foods from each group on the pyramid.

The most important element of a science work space is a flat surface. If you have the opportunity to select furniture for your classroom, choose tables and chairs rather than conventional desks. The typical classroom desk for children is designed for *writing,* not for doing science activities. If your classroom has desks with slanted tops, you will need to acquire tables, build your own tables, or use the floor as the place for science activities. Some teachers find that the inflexibility presented by traditional desks can be overcome by placing tables along the periphery of the room. Students can then carry out their science activities on the tables and use their desks during other instructional activities.

MAKE THE CASE   *An Individual or Group Challenge*

■ **The Problem** Chaos can result if a teacher has not carefully thought out classroom management issues before children engage in hands-on, discovery-based science experiences.

■ **Assess Your Prior Knowledge and Beliefs** Based on your classroom observations or teaching/tutoring experiences, consider the probable classroom management consequences of including each of the following in your classroom or curriculum:

An aquarium _____

Small mammals in cages _____

Reptiles in cages _____

Insects in cages _____

Rock, mineral, or shell collections on science tables or in learning centers _____

Taking a nature walk along a stream or pond in a city park _____

Taking a field trip to a hands-on science museum _____

■ **The Challenge** Create a poster of "do's and don'ts" that identifies appropriate classroom behavior and could be used at the beginning of the year to prepare children for a curriculum that includes experiences with all of the above. Be sure to give special attention to taking the class on field trips.

Providing Clear Directions

*"I didn't know what I was supposed to do with the ice cubes,
so I put them down her back."*

Children (and adults) seem to get into trouble when they don't understand what they are supposed to be doing. So, it should come as no surprise that problems arise in the classroom when children don't understand what your expectations are. If you learn to announce these expectations clearly and simply, you will find that misbehaviors decrease.

If the science activity the children are going to do requires procedures or materials they are unfamiliar with, you will need to model the use of these materials or procedures (except, of course, when the objective of the activity is the discovery of how to use them). *Children who do not know how to read a meterstick will use it as a baseball bat or sword rather than as a device for making linear measurements.* By taking a few minutes to teach children how to use materials and equipment properly, you can make the process of discovery more pleasant—for you and for them.

Summary

The success of an inquiry-based, discovery-focused classroom depends on your abilities to both plan and manage. The science curriculum for children typically consists of a number of learning units. Unit plans are long-term plans for science experiences that focus on particular topics. Daily lesson plans are single components of unit plans. This chapter offers three sample lesson plans.

A classroom in which students carry out science activities as part of group work undoubtedly will face some classroom management challenges. Teachers can use various techniques to ensure that science time is rich in appropriate learning opportunities yet manageable, as well.

**GOING
FURTHER**

On Your Own

1. How you plan for teaching will probably depend to a great extent upon your general outlook on the nature of teaching and how children learn. To bring these perceptions into focus, respond to each of the following statements:
   a. Careful planning is consistent with how I carry out the activities in my life.
   b. Planning can restrict flexibility.
   c. I never had a teacher who planned.
   d. Children will learn regardless of how much teachers plan.

2. Review the sample lesson plans in this chapter. Then select a science topic appropriate for the grade level you are interested in and develop a lesson plan. If possible, teach the lesson to a group of children or peers who role-play children. Assess the extent to which your lesson relates to the three-stage learning cycle.

3. Sketch your vision of the ideal classroom in which to teach science. Label the special areas in your classroom. Note, in particular, the location

and arrangement of classroom seating and work space. What advantage does your ideal classroom have over a conventional elementary

school classroom? How could you use your ideas for classroom organization in a conventional classroom?

4. Brainstorm a science activity for each of the following science units. Then try to place the activities in the most appropriate order in which they should be taught. Which activity do you think will cause the most management problems? Why?
   a. Indoor Gardening
   b. Animals with Pouches
   c. The Changes in the Seasons
   d. Earthquakes
   e. Friction

5. Role-play a job interview between a school principal and a teaching candidate for either a self-contained classroom or a departmentalized school. During the interview, the "principal" should ask about the following:

   a. The teacher's awareness of the NSE Standards
   b. The science content and experiences appropriate for children at that grade
   c. The planning style the prospective teacher would use
   d. The management strategies the teacher would use
   e. Ideas the teacher has for giving children opportunities to explore
   f. Alternate techniques the teacher could use to introduce a concept
   g. Ideas that the teacher has for helping children apply concepts to new situations

RESOURCES FOR DISCOVERY LEARNING

Internet Resources
Websites for Planning and Managing

The National Science Education (NSE) Standards

www.nap.edu/html/nses/html

Every person who teaches children science should visit this site, the official site for the NSE Standards. It presents the standards, the rationale behind them, and suggestions for using them to plan and teach standards-based units and lessons. So, if you are planning activities that relate to the NSE Standards, this site is a must.

Eisenhower National Clearing House

www.enc.org/weblinks/lessonplans/science

This site will be of great help to you as you begin thinking about science unit and lesson plan possibilities. It has an extraordinary collection of links to

science education resources, many of which will take you to sites that contain specific science lessons appropriate to particular grade levels.

Whales and Oceans

whale.wheelock.edu/whalenet-stuff/curriculum.html.

If you are designing a unit on whales, in particular, or oceanography, in general, this site will be of great interest to you. First of all, it provides many suggestions for lessons and activities, with whales as the principal topic. Perhaps more important, it shows how to use the Internet as a resource for the very latest information about whales—how they are tracked and, in some cases, real-time tracking data. With this information, your students could carry out a variety of activities about the behavior of real-live whales from the dry comfort of your classroom.

Detailed Science Curriculum Units

www.cis.yale.edu/ynhti/curriculum/units.

This extensive collection of teacher-developed units covers every subject in the curriculum. When you reach this site, search for those units that are science related. Then, after you have followed the links to the units, assess whether the content and suggested grade level are appropriate for your classroom. These are very thoroughly prepared units and, as such, should prove very helpful to you.

Columbia Education Center

www.col-ed.org/lessons_page.html

This site is an extremely helpful collection of over 600 teacher-developed lesson plans in a variety of subject areas, plus web guides and other web-based teaching resources. Select "Teacher Developed Lesson Plans" when you reach the starting page, and you'll go to a page that will lead you to lessons in every elementary subject area, including science. The science lessons are grouped as elementary (K–5), intermediate (6–8), and high school (9–12). One aspect of this collection that is particularly helpful is that the lesson plans all follow a consistent format.

Science-Based Teaching Theme Units

teachers.teach-nology.com/themes/science/

I find this commercial site very interesting because the science portion provides a far-ranging group of resources that would be helpful to teachers in planning science units. Here, in one place, you can find bulletin board materials, WebQuest ideas, science content background, lesson plans, hands-on activities, and even interactive sites that support the listed units. This site provides many of the basic components you will need as you create teaching units.

Print Resources
Suggested Readings

Cummings, Carol. *Winning Strategies for Classroom Management.* Alexandria, VA: Association for Supervision and Curriculum Development, 2000.

Fetters, Marcia, et al. "Making Science Accessible: Strategies to Meet the Needs of a Diverse Population." *Science Scope* 26, no. 5 (February 2003): 26–29.

Giacalone, Valerie. "How to Plan, Survive, and Even Enjoy an Overnight Field Trip with 200 Students." *Science Scope* 26, no. 4 (January 2003): 22–26.

Gooden, Kelly. "Parents Come to Class." *Science and Children* 40, no. 4 (January 2003): 22–25.

Melber, Leah M. "Tap Into Informal Science Learning." *Science Scope* 23, no. 6 (March 2000): 28–31.

Molledo, Magdalena. "The Resourceful Teacher." *Science Scope* 24, no. 6 (March 2001): 46–48.

Redmond, Alan. "Science in the Summer." *Science Scope*, 24 no. 4 (January 2000): 28–33.

Roy, Ken. "Safety Is for Everyone." *Science Scope* 26, no. 5 (February 2003): 16–17.

Sussman, Beverly. "Making Your Science Program Work." *Science Scope* 23, no. 6 (March 2000): 26–27.

Sutton, Kimberly Kode. "Curriculum Compacting." *Science Scope* 24, no. 4 (January 2000): 22–27.

NOTES

1. Kenneth Grahame, *The Wind in the Willows* (New York: Macmillan, 1991).

2. Robert F. Mager, *Preparing Instructional Objectives,* 2nd ed. (Belmont, CA: Pitman Learning, 1975), pp. v, vi. Reprinted by permission of the publisher.

3. National Research Council, *National Science Education Standards* (Washington, DC: National Academy Press, 1996), p. 6. Reprinted with permission of National Academy Press.

4. Ibid., 104.

5. Ibid., 103.

5

Strategies and QuickChecks

How can I effectively use cooperative learning, questioning and wait-time strategies, active listening, demonstrations, and textbooks in my classroom?

Talk, Talk, and More Talk!

My greatest challenge as a teacher is to refrain from telling my students everything—far more than they want to know. This problem seems to be a highly contagious ailment that can be transmitted from professor to student. I have reached this conclusion because I find that teachers in grades K–8 tell their students too much—usually more than the children really want to be told. A favorite story of mine concerns a first-grade child who asks a teacher to explain nuclear fusion. The teacher replies, "Why don't you ask your mother? She is a nuclear physicist." The child replies, "I don't want to know *that* much about it."

Perhaps it is just human nature to tell people more than they really want to know. In my case, it happens when I get excited about the content I am sharing; I want everyone to get the information quickly. When I work in science classrooms, I try to restrain myself from talking so much because I know that I will enjoy watching children discover something special on their own, and I know that will happen only if I talk less. That smile or screech of excitement from a child who makes a discovery is powerful medicine that stops my wagging tongue.

How can we do more real science with children? Perhaps the first step is to talk less and to use more creative strategies that help children learn on their own—with our guidance, to be sure, but not with so much guidance that the smiles and screeches are lost.

Cooperative Learning Strategies

Each stage of the learning cycle can be enriched by the use of well-planned group work. One promising approach to improving the quality of group work is the use of *cooperative learning groups,* which consist of children who are, in fact, working *together* on a project. That is to say, they are supportive of one another and accountable for both their individual learning as well as the learning of every other person in their group.

The success of a cooperative learning group depends on the success of each of its members.

Creating and Using Cooperative Learning Groups

Cooperative learning groups have very special characteristics that distinguish them from traditional classroom learning groups. Figure 5.1 makes a point-by-point comparison of nine of those characteristics, clearly contrasting these two approaches to group work.

In fact, these characteristics of cooperative learning groups emerge from three more fundamental elements, or strategies, of cooperative learning. If you can incorporate these strategies into your work with children before, during, and even after group work, you will increase the chances for successful group work. Here is a brief discussion of each:

1. *Teach for positive interdependence.* Help all members of each group understand that their success depends on the extent to which they agree on goals, objectives, and the roles each member is expected to carry out. They also need to agree in advance on an acceptable way to share available resources and information.

2. *Teach for individual accountability.* Help all members of each group understand that they are not only accountable for their own learning and behavior but also for helping other group members learn and work productively.

3. *Teach interpersonal and small-group skills.* If you expect children to work together and display appropriate group process skills, you will have to take the time to teach them those skills. Before group work, discuss group process skills such as sharing leadership, praising good work done by others, and active listening. Also teach children how to analyze how well the group process itself is going and how to modify the process to improve it.

To make these three elements easier to observe or implement in an actual science classroom, use the Cooperative Learning QuickCheck described in the next section.

FIGURE 5.1
What are the differences between a cooperative learning group and a traditional learning group?

Cooperative Learning Group	Traditional Learning Group
■ Positive interdependence	■ No interdependence
■ Individual accountability	■ No individual accountability
■ Heterogeneous	■ Homogeneous
■ Shared leadership	■ One appointed leader
■ Shared responsibility for each other	■ Responsibility only for self
■ Task and maintenance emphasized	■ Only task emphasized
■ Social skills directly taught	■ Social skills assumed and ignored
■ Teacher observes and intervenes	■ Teacher ignores group functioning
■ Groups process their effectiveness	■ No group processing

■ *Do It! Use the Cooperative Learning QuickCheck*

Figure 5.2 is a tool that you can use as you guide group work in your own classroom or as you observe another teacher's groups at work. Simply observe a group or a number of groups at work for a period of time, and use the points in the QuickCheck to help you determine the true nature of the group work that's occurring. You should check off (✓) each cooperative learning behavior that you observe. Think about whether you are observing a cooperative or a traditional learning group. Then use the results of your observation for guidance when you create and oversee future cooperative group work during science time.

REAL TEACHERS TALKING   *A Starting Point for Thinking, Talking, and Writing*

Barbara: One of the problems I notice with cooperative learning is that sometimes one member of the group gets left out. So, it's really important for the teacher to create a science learning experience that really is going to involve everyone on the team.

Pat: I think part of the answer is trying to choose a task that has many subtasks. This way, there will be enough work to go around. Of course, one problem with this approach is that it makes it tempting for children to just work on their subtask, which flies in the face of the big ideas about cooperative learning.

Barbara: Well, you have to keep in mind that during an entire school year, you might use a number of different models of cooperative learning, although the emphasis is always on the team product. For example, there is a strategy called "think, pair, share" in which the students pair up, study, and discuss the topic or complete their projects. Then they share what they learn with the class. This type of cooperative project really fits science nicely.

Pat: What about the use of roles? Does the idea work for you? What roles and responsibilities make most sense to you as a science teacher?

Barbara: Each member of the team has a name that tells the type of task he or she must perform. The "materials manager" picks up and returns materials and leads the cleanup work. The "tracker" helps record and maintain information for the team. The "communicator" helps resolve problems and is the only member who can leave the team to seek help. The "checker" acts like the team captain, keeping everyone on task.

Pat: So, I guess the challenge is to have a task or project that is sufficiently challenging and, where appropriate, to give children roles that will keep them involved. Of course, even if we are able to do both, we still have to keep a sharp eye out for children who are left out. I think some teachers call these children "hitchhikers"—meaning that they are just along for the ride. I guess that's a role we don't have to create in advance!

▶ **POINT TO PONDER:** *In this conversation, Barbara discussed four possible roles for children in science groups. Teachers of young children might find the names for these roles are a bit complicated for their students. Suppose you are a teacher of young children. What names would you suggest for these roles?*

FIGURE 5.2   Use this checklist to determine the level of cooperative learning in science group work.

Cooperative Learning QuickCheck

1. Does the group display *positive interdependence?*
   _____ Group members agree on general goals.
   _____ Group members agree on specific objectives.
   _____ Group members agree on roles for each group member.
   _____ Group members are sharing resources.

2. Does the group display *individual accountability?*
   _____ Group members try to keep the group on task.
   _____ Group members help one another complete tasks.
   _____ Group members try to keep their resource materials organized.

3. Does the group demonstrate *interpersonal and group process skills?*
   _____ Leadership is being shared among group members.
   _____ Group members praise each other.
   _____ Group members actively listen to one another.
   _____ Group members say and do things that keep the group moving ahead.

Questioning Strategies

Every now and then, I visit a classroom that makes me feel like I've entered a time machine and been transported back to the days of the Spanish Inquisition. At those times, I feel like I'm an observer in an interrogation room—not a classroom. Questions, questions, and more questions!

Asking children a reasonable number of purposeful questions can be a helpful strategy. But too often, what I hear are rapid-fire questions that simply require recall and not much actual thought. In fact, sometimes children don't even have a chance to think about the possible answers before the next question is put forth.

Improving the Questions You Ask

Educational researchers have long been concerned about the quantity and quality of teacher questions. As a teacher, you have found or will soon find that it takes self-discipline to ask questions that actually stimulate thought and move children along the road to inquiry-based, discovery-focused learning.

Fortunately, you can take some practical steps to ensure that the time you spend probing what children actually know will be well spent. To begin, gather data about what you presently do in terms of question asking. You can do this by videotaping or audiotaping lessons or parts of lessons you teach to children or to peers. Then classify the types of questions you ask. One system for classifying questions has as its foundation the six cognitive levels—knowledge, comprehension, application, analysis, synthesis, and evaluation—which you learned about in Chapter 1.

After carefully studying these six cognitive levels, Orlich and others proposed a more simplified three-category system for classifying questions.[1] The three categories of questions are as follow:

1. *Convergent questions* get children to think in ways that focus on basic knowledge or comprehension.

   Examples

   How did the yeast help our dough rise?

   What did the three-horned dinosaur eat?

   How was the plant cell different from the animal cell?

   How many planets orbit the sun?

2. *Divergent questions* get children to think about a number of alternative answers.

   Examples

   What are some ideas about what caused the dinosaurs to become extinct?

   If you were a prey animal in the jungle, what could you do to keep safe from predators?

   What are some ways we could reduce the amount of water and electricity wasted in our school?

3. *Evaluative questions* get students to offer a judgment based on some criteria.

   Examples

   If a power plant was going to be built next to your house, which one source of energy would you want it to be?

   If you could pick only three foods to take on a week-long camping trip, what would they be?

   Where would be the safest place to be during an earthquake?

■ *Do It! Use the Questioning QuickCheck*

I have used these three categories in creating a Questioning QuickCheck (see Figure 5.3). By counting the number of each type of question asked, you can analyze the tapes that you make of your own teaching or as you observe others teach. Clearly, to create an inquiry-based, discovery-focused classroom, a balance must be reached among the types of questions you ask. Using the Questioning QuickCheck will help you start that process.

FIGURE 5.3   Use this form to count questions by type during a live or recorded teaching episode.

Questioning QuickCheck

Date of episode _____   Start time _____   End time._____

OBSERVE

1. *Convergent questions* get children to think in ways that focus on basic knowledge or comprehension.
   Tally of questions asked:

2. *Divergent questions* get children to think about a number of alternative answers.
   Tally of questions asked:

3. *Evaluative questions* get students to offer a judgment based on some criteria.
   Tally of questions asked:

EVALUATE

1. How long did you observe, listen to, or watch the teaching episode? _____

2. How many of each type of question was asked?
   Convergent _____
   Divergent   _____
   Evaluative _____

3. What was the total number of questions asked? _____

Wait-Time/Think-Time Strategies

Have you ever heard of *wait-time* or *think-time?* Unfortunately, teachers' questioning behavior tends to follow a certain pattern: We ask a question, receive a response from a child, and then *immediately* react to the response and ask another question. The generally too-short gap between our question and the child's answer is known as wait-time or think-time. Experts tell us that that time is usually just two or three seconds long, if that. Regardless, it is too brief for the children to actually think deeply about one question before hearing its answer or yet another question.

Allowing More Time

Allowing a very short wait-time/think-time turns your classroom into a game show of sorts, in which you are trying to catch the children and indirectly embarrass them. By increasing wait-time or think-time, you can produce some very positive results. In particular, by allowing more time between questions, you can change a traditional classroom into a richer environment for inquiry-based, discovery-focused learning.

Researchers Tobin and Capie, in building on the previous work of Mary Bud Rowe, describe the following benefits of increasing wait-time beyond three seconds:

1. The length of student responses increased.
2. The number of unsolicited but appropriate responses increased.
3. Failure to respond decreased.
4. Confidence, as reflected by a decrease in the number of inflected responses, increased.
5. The incidence of speculative responses increased.
6. The incidence of child-child comparisons of data increased.
7. The incidence of evidence-inference statements increased.
8. The incidence of questions asked by students increased.
9. There was an increase in the incidence of responses emanating from students rated by the teacher as relatively slow learners.
10. The variety in the type of verbal behavior of students increased.[2]

The pause provided by a sufficient wait-time seems to refresh and improve the learning process. Make a real attempt to slow down the pace of questioning in your classroom.

■ *Do It! Use the Wait-Time/Think-Time QuickCheck*

The QuickCheck in Figure 5.4 lists a variety of strategies you can use in the classroom to improve your own wait-time/think-time.[3] Check off (✓) the strategies as you try them, and make note of which ones seem especially effective using an asterisk (*).

Active Listening Strategies

"For the third time, you draw the food chain arrows so the arrow heads point to the living things that receive the energy. Why do I keep seeing people draw the arrows from the killer whale to the seal? Was anyone listening when we talked about the food chain?"

It's very frustrating when you suddenly realize that your students are not listening to you, their classmates, or even visiting speakers as intently as you might wish. To help them improve on this skill during science time, focus on the idea of *active listening,* which is the conscious effort to focus one's attention on what people are saying as they are saying it. This is an important life skill that children need to master—and *you* may need a little work on it yourself! (I am relatively easily distracted, since I find everything around me quite interesting, so I need to work on active listening, also!)

FIGURE 5.4   Use the strategies in this checklist to
slow down the pace of questioning.

Wait-Time/Think-Time QuickCheck

1. *To improve wait-time/think-time:*
   _____ Prompt the children to think about the answer before answering.
   _____ Mentally count off five seconds after you ask a question.
   _____ As you wait, look around the room to observe any signs of confusion about the question.
   _____ If the child's answer is appropriate, praise him or her and then count off another
   five seconds mentally before asking another question.

2. *If the children don't respond:*
   _____ Ask the childen if they would like you to ask the question in a different way.
   _____ Repeat the question with some modifications.
   _____ If possible, represent the question graphically on a chalkboard, whiteboard, or
   transparency.
   _____ Try to ask a simpler form of the question.
   _____ Ask if anyone in the class can rephrase the question for you.
   _____ Ask if part of the question is too difficult, and modify it accordingly.

3. *If the children do respond appropriately:*
   _____ Liberally praise the responding child or children.
   _____ Ask the child to elaborate on his or her answer.

4. *If the children offer a partial response:*
   _____ Focus on the adequacy of the answer and capitalize on it (for instance, by asking
   "Can anyone help Jamie's answer?")
   _____ Praise the act of responding, perhaps by saying "That was a very good try, Jamie."

Increasing Active Listening

You can take some practical steps to increase active listening in your classroom:

1. *Restructure the physical setting to minimize distractions.* A classroom in which children are involved in hands-on activities will not be as quiet as a library. As you speak, there will be the bubbling sounds of the fish tank, the background noise of shifting chairs and desks, and so on. The first step in providing an environment in which active listening can occur is to compensate for background noise. Do this by having the children asking or answering questions speak louder, by moving classroom furniture so that everyone can see the speaker, and by having the children look directly at and speak directly to the group or person they are addressing.

2. *Have children listen for key science words.* One way to keep their attention on the speaker is to listen for words such as *up, down, under,* and *above* that signal what is to follow. You will need to teach the children to use such terms as *observe, classify, graph, measure,* and *predict* and then to reinforce the use of these words through your praise. On a regular basis after a child has spoken or you have spoken, ask a question such as "Did you hear any key words when Emilio told us about last night's storm?" By teaching the children to listen for key words and what follows them, you and they will hear more of what is actually being said.

3. *Have children create questions for the speaker.* Challenge them to become such good listeners that you and they will be able to ask the speaker a question that uses some of his or her own words and ideas. For example, if Nadine is reporting the results of her group's work on rock classifying to the full class, ask the class at the end of the report if they have any questions for Nadine or her group. By doing this, you will help the children realize that they should be so attentive to the speaker that they can later ask good questions about what was said.

4. *Practice summarizing what the speaker has said.* When children speak or ask questions, listen so attentively that you can restate in summary form what they said. To do this, you have to use the natural gaps in a speaker's speech patterns to mentally summarize the key ideas as they emerge. Model this by occasionally restating or rephrasing a child's question in a shorter form and then checking with him or her to see if you have captured the point or question.

FIGURE 5.5   Use this checklist to apply specific strategies for improving the quality of listening in the science classroom.

Active Listening QuickCheck

_____ 1. Move the classroom furniture as needed so everyone can see the speaker.

_____ 2. Remind the children to look directly at and speak directly to the speaker.

_____ 3. Encourage children who are asking or answering questions to speak loudly enough for everyone to hear.

_____ 4. Remind the children to listen for signal words that the speaker uses, such as *up, down, under,* and *above.*

_____ 5. Remind the children to listen for key science words that the speaker uses, such as *observe, classify, measure,* and *predict.*

_____ 6. Challenge the children to come up with questions for the speaker that use some of his or her own words and ideas.

_____ 7. Model how to summarize what a speaker has said by restating or rephrasing what the children say.

_____ 8. Have the children practice summarizing or restating what the speaker has said.

■ *Do It! Use the Active Listening QuickCheck*

You can apply these four guidelines to a real classroom setting by using Figure 5.5, the Active Listening QuickCheck. It provides some very specific things you can do to increase active listening. Check off (✓) each strategy as you try it.

Demonstrations

> *"Do it again!"*

This exclamation should bring joy to your heart after you do a science demonstration for children. These three little words send a clear message that you have made contact with a child's mind.

Presenting a Good Science Demonstration

In recent years, I have observed fewer and fewer demonstrations in elementary science classrooms. It seems that a long-overdue emphasis on having *children* do activities has taken an important job away from the *teacher:* showing children phenomena they cannot efficiently, effectively, or *safely* discover for themselves. Because it has enormous potential for focusing attention on a given phenomenon, the science demonstration can be an important tool for promoting inquiry in children. A demonstration can raise many questions for children, which can then be addressed in greater detail by individual science activities.

Science demonstrations have enormous potential for focusing children's attention on specific phenomena.

Of course, demonstrations can be misused in the classroom. They should never replace children's involvement in science activities, and they should not be used solely to reproduce phenomena that children have already read about. Instead, demonstrations should be used to intensify children's curiosity about a unit to be studied; to clarify the confusion that may result from attaining contrary results by children who have carried out identical science activities; and to tie together various types of learning at the end of a unit.

■ *Do It! Use the Demonstration QuickCheck*

A number of sources of science demonstrations are provided in the resources at the end of this book. Bear in mind that by using larger equipment or materials, you can transform virtually any science activity into a demonstration you feel the children should experience as a class.

A number of considerations must be made in order to present effective demonstration. Use Figure 5.6, the Demonstration QuickCheck, to assess the effectiveness of the science demonstrations that you or others do. Check off (✓) each item that applies.

FIGURE 5.6   Use this checklist to evaluate a science demonstration for children that you observe or perform.

Demonstration QuickCheck

_____ 1. The teacher began the demonstration promptly; the children didn't have to wait an excessive amount of time while the teacher got prepared.

_____ 2. The demonstration was essentially simple and straightforward, not elaborate and complex.

_____ 3. All the children in the class could observe the demonstration.

_____ 4. It seemed as if the teacher had pretested the demonstration; there was no evidence that this was the first time it had been tried—for example, missing equipment, confusion in the sequence of steps.

_____ 5. The teacher was able to create a bit of drama by presenting purposely puzzling situations or outcomes that were unexpected to the children.

_____ 6. The demonstration did not endanger the health or safety of the children.

_____ 7. The demonstration seemed to fit the topic under study.

_____ 8. The demonstration was appropriately introduced, carried out, and concluded.

_____ 9. The children had an opportunity to ask questions, make statements, and give reactions.

_____ 10. The demonstration provided a significant learning experience for the children.

MAKE THE CASE *An Individual or Group Challenge*

■ **The Problem** A large class may make so many demands on a teacher's time and attention that some children who have a special aptitude for science may go unnoticed.

■ **Assess Your Prior Knowledge and Beliefs** Based on your personal experiences, comment on how much each of the following may increase the likelihood of a teacher recognizing children with a special aptitude for science:

1. The group leader shares the results of a science activity with the class as a whole.

   _____

2. The teacher leads a discussion about a field trip the class has recently taken.

   _____

3. The teacher asks questions that will reveal the children's knowledge of a topic.

   _____

4. The teacher discusses the results of a demonstration.

   _____

5. The teacher helps a cooperative learning group summarize its findings.

   _____

6. The teacher praises a group that has completed its science activity before other groups.

   _____

7. The teacher asks groups to select their own leaders.

   _____

■ **The Challenge** It has become clear that you must find some way to reach those children who are not working to their full potential in science. You have decided to teach a few students in higher grades some basic questioning and cooperative group skills and then use these students as assistants. You have already decided to call the project "Science Buddies." What factors should you consider in the early stages of planning for this project?

Science Textbooks

The year was 1489. The city was Florence, Italy. A young man, just 14 years old, was walking through the work yard next to a cathedral that was being built. He came upon an enormous old block of poorly shaped marble resting in the weeds, which was called "The Giant" by marble workers and sculptors. Many had tried to make some use of it and failed. "It had lain for 35 years in the cathedral's work yard, an awesome ghostly reminder to all young sculptors of the challenge of their craft."[4]

Twelve years later, the same man rediscovered and very carefully studied the sleeping, malformed Giant. Now, at 26, he saw something in the marble that only he could release. That something would become known as *David,* and the man who stripped away the excess marble to reveal perhaps the most extraordinary sculpture known to humankind was Michelangelo. Within the imperfect, he saw what few others could see: potential.

Using Textbooks as Resources

Your science classroom will be filled with imperfect resources: computers with Internet access that may lock up just as your children reach the best part of your research assignment, stacks of videotapes of nature adventures that really don't fit your curriculum, and bookshelves of textbooks that seem far too dull for your active children. You can spend a great deal of time wishing that you had better resources, but doing so will make no difference at all.

Science textbooks, bought with taxpayer money and intended as useful resources, will probably be flawed in one way or another. Their limitations will be obvious to all, but their potential will be unseen by many. Jones tells us that "U.S. textbooks are about twice the size of textbooks in other countries, and this is one situation where bigger is definitely not better."[5] She goes on to cite another expert who comments on the fact that textbooks seem unfocused, repetitive, and lacking coherence.

Although modern textbooks have definite weaknesses, they also contain some resources that you, a discovery-oriented teacher, can make good use of—*if* you are creative. They contain science content written at particular grade levels and provide many hands-on science activities. In addition, they usually come with teachers' guides that include enrichment ideas.

The activities in a textbook series, of course, reflect a particular scope and sequence of science content. If you have the freedom and the desire to create your own science curriculum, the textbook can still be quite useful. By omitting some of the structure present in the textbook's directions to the children, you can modify the activities so that they place more emphasis on discovery learning.

Textbooks are typically divided into a number of *units,* or groups of chapters. If you look over the units and the teacher's guide that accompanies the book, you will find many helpful teaching ideas. You will also find that many of the suggestions can be applied to learning units that you devise on your own. Many teachers' guides for textbooks provide bulletin board ideas, suggestions for field trips, lists of audiovisual materials, lists of children's books, and other helpful information that you can use to enrich your learning units.

FIGURE 5.7   Use this checklist to assess the quality of science textbooks available for children at your grade level.

QuickCheck

Textbook Quality QuickCheck

1. *Content*
   - _____ Does the content easily correlate with NSE Standards, state standards, and local standards?
   - _____ Are the inquiry process skills emphasized?
   - _____ Are there unit, chapter, section, and lesson objectives, and are they clearly written?
   - _____ Is the content accurate and up to date?
   - _____ Are the units, chapters, sections, and lessons logically organized?
   - _____ Are distinctions made between *fact* and *theory?*
   - _____ Are connections made between science and technology and personal/social perspectives?
   - _____ Are the accomplishments of women, individuals from diverse cultural backgrounds, and individuals with special challenges included?
   - _____ Do the end-of-unit, -chapter, or -section questions go beyond simple recall?
   - _____ Is the content relevant to students' daily lives?

2. *Reading Level*
   - _____ Is the reading level appropriate for the intended grade level?
   - _____ Will the material engage student interest?
   - _____ Is new vocabulary clearly introduced and defined?
   - _____ Is there a glossary?

3. *Approach to Instruction*
   - _____ Does the book appropriately relate the reading of science content to inquiry-based, discovery-focused activities?
   - _____ Can the science activities be done with readily available, inexpensive materials and equipment?
   - _____ Are there suggestions for follow-up activities that students could carry out on the Internet, at home, or as special long-term projects?

4. *Physical Characteristics*
   - _____ Does the book look interesting from the view of students at your grade level?
   - _____ Is the size and font of the print appropriate for students at your grade level?
   - _____ Are the photographs and artwork clear, purposeful, and engaging?
   - _____ Are the charts and graphs labeled well, and do they clarify the text?
   - _____ Is there an appropriate mix of photos and art representing females, males, students with challenges, and students from diverse cultural backgrounds?

5. *Availability of Supplemental Materials*
   - _____ Does the teacher's guide (teacher's edition) seem useful in terms of providing help in planning lessons and units?
   - _____ Are any of the following available?
     - _____ Transparencies
     - _____ Lab books, workbooks, or other student materials
     - _____ Assessment materials
     - _____ Videos/CD-ROMS
     - _____ Related software
     - _____ Correlated science materials and equipment kits

In sum, you should consider these criteria in determining the usefulness of a certain textbook:

1. Content
2. Reading level
3. Approach to instruction
4. Physical characteristics
5. Availability of supplemental materials

Textbooks can provide you and your children a general structure for science content and experiences, ensuring continuity both during a single school year and from year to year within a school. Keep in mind, however, that the extent to which textbooks lead to discovery learning will, in the final analysis, depend on you.

■ *Do It! Use the Textbook Quality QuickCheck*

If you have access to a collection of modern textbooks that are used in an elementary or middle school, you will likely find it very useful to systematically analyze a few of them, using the five criteria just listed. Doing so will reveal a great deal to you about the content that is commonly taught at particular grade levels as well as the quality of textbook resources that teachers might use. Use Figure 5.7, the Textbook Quality QuickCheck (page 95), to guide your efforts, checking off (✓) each criterion that applies. You may wish to add additional criteria to the checklist as you put it to use.

Summary

Classroom teachers can use a variety of strategies to teach children science in an effective yet creative way. Cooperative learning groups can be used as an important part of any learning environment that encourages discovery learning. Teachers' use of questioning and wait-time strategies, ability to teach children to become active listeners, inclusion of science demonstrations along with hands-on activities, and creative use of textbooks can all serve to enhance and enrich the learning environment.

GOING FURTHER

On Your Own

1. Reflect upon the science activities you experienced in elementary school:
   a. Specifically, what activities do you remember? Why do you think you remember them?
   b. If you do remember activities, were they carried out by individual children or by groups? What do you think motivated the teacher's decision in this respect?
   c. While the activities were underway, were there any specific problems with work space, classroom behavior, or the availability of science materials? If so, what?

d. Would you say that your teacher or teachers encouraged discovery learning?

2. Select a chapter from a conventional elementary school science textbook that contains some science activities. Develop a strategy for using the activities and text materials as the basis for a group of discovery-based lessons. How does your strategy compare with the more conventional use of chapters in science textbooks? Would your approach offer any cooperative learning possibilities?

3. How could you use some of the ideas in this chapter to create an ideal curriculum for children at the grade level you are most interested in? Be specific and focus upon the following:

   a. The content you would stress
   b. The concepts you would stress
   c. How the curriculum would reflect the teaching style you would use
   d. The use of cooperative learning groups
   e. The use of teacher demonstrations and hands-on student activities
   f. The use of effective questioning and wait-time strategies
   g. The use of textbooks as resources

On Your Own or in a Cooperative Learning Group

4. With others, role-play the best and worst science demonstrations you have ever observed. What factors contributed to the quality (or lack thereof) of each? If you are doing this activity by yourself, respond in writing.

5. Select a topic commonly covered in elementary school science, and create five questions the teacher could use to help children make discoveries in this field of study. Also try to think of a demonstration that the teacher could use to raise questions among the children that might lead to discoveries.

6. Formulate a position on each of the following statements. You may wish to have a minidebate in which various members of the group adopt extreme positions.

   a. Discovery learning uses up valuable classroom time.
   b. Textbooks cannot be used with inquiry-based techniques.
   c. By asking questions, you can slow down a child's thought processes.

RESOURCES FOR DISCOVERY LEARNING

Internet Resources
Websites for Discovery-Learning Strategies

Problem Solving

www.indiana.edu/~eric_rec/

One of the goals in creating a classroom environment that emphasizes inquiry-based, discovery-focused learning is to have children learn problem-solving skills. When you reach this site, type "Problem Solving" into the search engine to find ERIC resources.

Institute for Inquiry Activities

www.exploratorium.edu/IFI/activities/

This page is part of a site prepared and maintained by the Exploratorium and dedicated to helping teachers develop inquiry-oriented classrooms. Although other parts of the site discuss in-service training opportunities, this part shares specific activities that foster the best elements of discovery-focused teaching.

Center for Problem-Based Learning

www.imsa.edu/team/cpbl/

This site provides an in-depth presentation of the strategies and techniques that have been proven effective in having children learn as a result of inquiry that leads to discoveries. A good deal of background information is provided on the topic of *problem-based learning* along with examples of how children might engage in such activities.

Questioning Skills

www.petech.ac.za/robert/question.htm

This site may be the most comprehensive presentation of alternative questioning skills found on the Internet.

Select the "Questioning Skills" link to access a wide variety of practical resources about questioning, active listening, wait-time, and framing good questions.

Young Inventors Educational Resource

inventors.miningco.com/msub11 er.htm

This site is an excellent source of lesson ideas that bring children face to face with the challenge of creating inventions and learning from the discoveries they make as they engage in inventing. The lesson plans provided should give many opportunities to utilize cooperative group work as children create their inventions.

 **Print Resources**
Suggested Readings

Brune, Jeff. "Take It Outside!" *Science and Children* 39 no. 7 (April 2002): 29–33.

Corder, Greg, and Darren Reed. "It's Raining Micrometeorites." *Science Scope* 26, no. 5 (February 2003): 23–25.

Fones, Shelly White. "Engaging Science." *Science Scope* 23, no. 6 (March 2000): 32–36.

Freedman, Michael. "Using Effective Demonstrations in the Classroom." *Science and Children* 38, no. 1 (September 2000): 52–55.

Galus, Pamela. "Reactions to Atomic Structure." *Science Scope* 26, no. 4 (January 2003): 38–41.

Irwin, Leslie, et al. "Science Centers for All." *Science and Children* 40, no. 5 (February 2003): 35–37.

Kelly, Janet, et al. "Science Adventures at the Local Museum." *Science and Children* 39, no. 7 (April 2002): 46–48.

Krutchinsky, Rick, and William Harris. "Super Science Saturday." *Science and Children* 40, no. 4 (January 2003): 26–28.

MacKenzie, Ann Haley. "Brain Busters, Mind Games & Science Chats." *Science Scope* 24, no. 6 (March 2001): 54–58.

Reeve, Stephen L. "Beyond the Textbook." *Science Scope* 25, no. 6 (March 2002): 4–6.

Stivers, Louise. "Discovering Trees: Not Just a Walk in the Park!" *Science and Children* 39, no. 7 (April 2002): 38–41.

NOTES

1. Donald Orlich et al., *Teaching Strategies: A Guide to Better Instruction* (Lexington, MA: D. C. Heath, 1994), pp. 186–193.

2. Kenneth G. Tobin and William Capie, *Wait-Time and Learning in Science* (Burlington, NC: Carolina Biological Supply, n.d.), p. 2.

3. I drew ideas for the Wait-Time/ Think-Time QuickCheck from a variety of sources that you may find of interest, including Robert J. Stahl (1995), "Using 'Think-Time' and 'Wait-Time' in the Classroom" (ERIC Digest no. ED370885); it can be found on the Internet at <www.ed.gov/databases/ ERIC_Digests/ed370885.html>. Another useful source, which focused on college teaching assistants, is "Teaching Tips for TAs: WAIT-TIME" (June 14, 2000), published by the Office of Instructional Consultation, University of California, Santa Barbara, and located on the Internet at <www.id.ucsb. edu/IC/TA/ta.html>.

4. Robert Coughlan, *The World of Michelangelo* (New York: Time, 1966), p. 85.

5. Rebecca Jones, "Solving Problems in Math and Science Education," *The American School Board Journal* 185, no. 7 (July 1998): 18.

6

Assessment of Understanding and Inquiry

How can I put the NSE Standards approach, along with traditional and authentic assessment techniques, to work in my classroom?

"What D'ja Git?"

> *"What d'ja git?"*
> *"She gave me a C!"*

Would overhearing this exchange between two students—after you've taught a unit that took three weeks to plan and far too many afternoons shopping at discount stores for inexpensive activity materials—get your attention? And would it sting just a bit?

It would and should for two reasons. First of all, it would tell you that the end-of-unit test probably didn't assess whether your children actually learned some science. Second, it would tell you that your children have the extraordinary idea that the teacher *gives* a grade. Notice the phrasing *She gave.* Does that imply, even slightly, that the student's grade was *earned?*

In this chapter, you will learn about a range of assessment techniques that will help you discover whether your children are actually learning science. Carefully studying these materials will help you create a classroom in which the children are more concerned about what they *learned* and less concerned about the gifts they think you give!

Three Approaches to Assessment

Let me give you a quick overview of the three types of assessment we'll cover in this chapter. We will start with the newest approach to assessment: the recommendations included as part of the National Science Education (NSE) Standards. Their focus is on student's understanding of science ideas and their ability to do activities involving *inquiry.*

Next, we will consider the uses of *traditional assessment techniques,* such as chapter homework, quizzes, reports, and the like. For each technique, we'll look at its strengths and weaknesses—what it will and won't accomplish in terms of assessment.

Third, we will look at *authentic assessment,* an approach that focuses on whether children are actually learning the science they are intended to learn. Typically, authentic assessment is more closely related to children's real lives and includes techniques such as the use of portfolios, science conferences, concept mapping, and journals.

The last section of this chapter will give you strong guidance about how to synthesize the most helpful parts of all three approaches. You will create your own personal assessment checklist, which you can use to assess the units you plan or observe.

The NSE Standards Approach to Assessment

The NSE Standards recommend assessing children in two broad areas: understanding and inquiry. *Understanding* means what you would expect it to mean—whether children comprehend the science ideas you are teaching. *Inquiry* focuses on whether children have the ability to actually carry out their own science experiments.

The NSE Standards assessment suggestions are summarized in Figures 6.1 and 6.2 (pages 101 and 103). The following sections will further clarify the intent of the standards as well as provide some practical examples.

Assessing Students' Understanding

Definitions

Basic to the NSE Standards approach to assessment is the use of rubrics and prompts. A *prompt* is a question or group of questions that includes a statement about a task to be done along with directions on how to do it. A *scoring rubric* (pronounced "roo-brick") is used to describe the standard that should be used when assessing a child's performance.[1]

Let's look at examples of the use of prompts and scoring rubrics in the classroom.

FIGURE 6.1   Implementing the NSE Standards guidelines for assessing understanding

NSE Standards

Does the Child Understand?

Assessment

To assess whether a child understands a concept, law, principle, theory, or other "big idea," identify what you want him or her to assess and then take these steps:

1. Invent a *prompt* for the child to respond to.

   EXAMPLES   Puzzling demonstration, thought problem, natural phenomenon (such as a plant that has insect holes in leaves)

2A. Tell the child what *performance* you expect him or her to carry out.

   EXAMPLES   Oral report, class discussion, discovery activity, demonstration for classmates

2B. Tell the child what *product* you expect him or her to prepare.

   EXAMPLES   Model, labeled drawing, collection, photograph

Measurement

To measure success:

For most children:

1. Compare the performance or product to what the child could do earlier in the year.*

2. Compare the child's performance or product to what you would expect of most children at this grade/age.

For very able children:

   Compare the child's performance or product to what you would expect of a scientifically literate adult.**

*This is this author's suggestion. It does not appear in the NSE Standards.

**This does not mean you should assign a grade on this basis. The comparison is made to get a sense of how good the performance or product actually is.

Examples

- *Sound* (for young learners)

   The big idea children are to grasp: Sound and vibration are associated with one another.

   Prompt: "This little drum is made by stretching plastic wrap over a jar. I'd like you to tap the drum with the eraser, look at the plastic, and tell me what you see and what you hear. Then sprinkle some rice grains on the plastic and look at it as you tap it again."

   Scoring rubric: The teacher will listen to the child's responses and then ask him or her to guess at what might be causing the sound. If the child refers to the up and down movement of the plastic wrap (as evidenced by the bouncing of the rice grains) as being related to the sound, he or she will be considered to have made a correct response.

- *Density*

   The big idea children are to grasp: The densities of objects can be determined using simple equipment.

   Prompt: "Here are all the things you need to find the densities of these mystery objects on the tray. I would like you to find the density of each of the three objects."

   Scoring rubric: A chart is used that lists the mystery objects and the densities the teacher discovered when he or she calculated them. If the child gets answers within 10% of the teacher's results, they will be considered correct.

Assessing Students' Ability to Conduct Inquiry

Wouldn't you be delighted if your children learned so much and acquired so many skills that they could actually invent and carry out their own experiments? It's happened to me on occasion, and it's a wonderful feeling!

Steps in Assessing Inquiry

The NSE Standards encourage teachers to have children design and carry out their own experiments (which the standards refer to as *inquiry*) and then assess how well the children have done. The standards recommend that teachers assess achievement with a focus on whether children can actually function as young scientists. The following steps in the process *and* the final product should be evaluated:

1. Identifying a worthwhile and researchable question
2. Planning the investigation
3. Executing the research plan
4. Drafting the research report[2]

Again, let's consider some examples of how to develop your own techniques for assessing inquiry in the classroom.

Examples

■ *Light and plants* (for young learners)

Identifying an inquiry question: Does the plant on Ms. Riley's desk really need sunlight to live?

Planning the inquiry: The children make a set of four drawings that show what they intend do. They depict how the plant looks today, including the colors they see; how it will look in the closet; how they will water the plant in the closet; and how they will draw the plant once a week for four weeks (at the end of each week).

Executing the plan: The children carry out the steps listed under "Planning the inquiry."

Drafting the report: The children show all their drawings and share their conclusions.

Assessing the inquiry: The teacher makes an anecdotal record of the children's progress, noting whether all of the steps were followed and whether the actual color changes were captured in the drawings.

FIGURE 6.2   Implementing the NSE Standards guidelines for assessing inquiry

Can the Child Carry Out an Inquiry?

Assessment
To assess whether a child can carry out an *inquiry:*

1. Ask the child to identify a *researchable question.*
   EXAMPLE   What color of clothing is coolest on a hot, sunny day?

2. Ask the child to prepare a *research plan.*
   EXAMPLE   The child designs a plan to collect samples of cloth of different colors, invent an apparatus to hold cloth samples over thermometers, and measure temperature changes on a sunny day.

3. Have the child *carry out the plan.*
   EXAMPLE   The child follows through on item 2 above.

4. Ask the child to prepare a *report* on the inquiry.
   EXAMPLE   The child prepares a written and illustrated report.

Measurement
To measure success:

1. Assess the quality of the *research question.*
2. Assess the quality of the *research plan.*
3. Assess the quality of the *research.*
4. Assess the quality of the *report.*

■ *Melting a solid*

Identifying an inquiry question: What besides heat can make ice cubes melt faster?

Planning the inquiry: The children develop a plan that includes observing ice cubes (before and after their experiments), using a paper fan, crushing ice cubes, and adding salt to the cubes. The plan also calls for them to use a chart to record their observations and diagrams to show what changes they observed.

Executing the plan: The children carry out the steps in "Planning the inquiry."

Drafting the report: The children record their data on their charts and also write paragraphs that answer the inquiry question.

Assessing the inquiry: The teacher uses a three-point scale to assess children's work. A 3 means "extremely well planned and carried out," a 2 means "readable and complete," and a 1 means "incomplete or hard to follow."

As your teaching career unfolds, you will develop your own approaches to assessing how well children understand science and can propose and carry out inquiry. I hope that the examples just given will help you develop those strategies.

Traditional Assessment Techniques

End-of-Chapter Homework

> *". . . and then do numbers 1 through 5 on the last page."*

Does this bring back a few classroom memories? Giving children an end-of-chapter homework assignment is a common way for teachers to discover whether the children remember what they have read. When you make such an assignment, you believe that children will read the chapter first and then answer the questions. Perhaps in elementary and middle school, you read your science chapters before you did your homework. If so, I congratulate you! If you didn't, this is a good opportunity to consider what traditional end-of-chapter homework does and doesn't accomplish.

■ *What Does It Accomplish?*

An end-of-chapter assignment tells the children that you are serious about the content you are teaching. It forces them to look at and, if you are fortunate, read text material, if only to find answers to the questions they have been assigned. This type of assignment provides you with one small indicator of how serious a child is about his or her schooling. The actual appearance of a textbook in the home also tells parents that the child is doing something in science class. Finally, homework assignments that are *not* done provide you with a reason for talking with a child and the child's parents about his or her effort.

■ *What Doesn't It Accomplish?*

End-of-chapter homework does not tell you much about what children know, and it doesn't tell you if they like science. Completed homework seldom reveals any understanding of information beyond the recall level of the cognitive domain. End-of-chapter homework will probably not pique children's interest to the point that they will want to learn more about the topic.

Using End-of-Chapter Homework Effectively

Before making the assignment, talk with children about the purpose of the homework and the reading they have done. Use statements such as "You know this first chapter on living things told us about the differences between living and nonliving things. The questions at the end will help you find out if you remember and understand some of the big ideas." After this introduction, give children a few minutes of class time to begin the assignment. Doing so will increase the probability that children will do the homework and possibly make the experience somewhat more meaningful to them.

Quizzes

Do you still live in fear of the "pop" quiz? Does your heart flutter a bit just hearing the term *quiz?* Quizzes are a part of the classroom assessment process from elementary school through graduate school, and their effect on students seems to remain rather constant. A quiz takes little time and is usually used as a quick assessment of whether students remember or understand factual information or concepts.

■ *What Do They Accomplish?*

Quizzes tell teachers whether children can think fast and have a sufficient command of writing to get their responses on paper before time is up. They are easy to grade and provide a snapshot of the student's recall of information. They also serve to keep children "on their toes," but they should not divert teachers from the science experiences that should be taking place in the classroom.

■ *What Don't They Accomplish?*

Quizzes do not tell teachers much about in-depth understanding. Children's lack of success on quizzes may not reveal a deficit in knowledge or understanding but rather a deficit in being able to express themselves quickly.

Using Quizzes More Effectively

Quizzes should be used in moderation. If you wish to find out whether children are learning, giving a quiz now and then that is focused on the important ideas of a science unit can provide some information about student progress. Doing so can also help you discover that you need to modify your teaching or help a particular child before a unit is completed.

Tests

Given the large numbers of children in most classrooms, most teacher-developed tests are composed of short-answer questions and some multiple-choice items. At the end of the test, there may be a few so-called essay questions. In inquiry-based classrooms, teachers who use tests are likely to include some questions dealing with how science activities were conducted and what was learned from them.

Traditional assessment may not reflect all of the learning that occurs in a discovery-based science classroom.

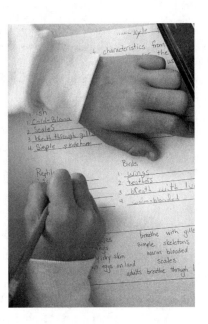

■ *What Do They Accomplish?*

Test results tell children, parents, and you how well the children answered the questions that were asked. Test results give children a way to assess their own progress and a way to compare themselves to others. They give you a neat and tidy way to get information to use for grading. They also tell you which children in the class are good test takers. That information is important if you want to teach children skills that will be useful in later life.

If you create a test with questions that discover more than children's recall abilities, you may get more useful information. The test results may reveal whether children understood concepts, were able to apply what was learned, and were able to analyze the science phenomena studied. If, however, the test consists of recall questions, only the children's memory will be assessed.

■ *What Don't They Accomplish?*

Tests only tell you what children know and understand about the particular questions you asked. Very few tests assess how well children can express their thoughts. Questions that elicit this information are challenging to create, require many minutes for children to complete, and demand that the teacher spend a considerable amount of time outside class carefully reading each response, reflecting on the work, offering written feedback, and assigning grades.

Tests probably do little to motivate children to think about science as an interesting subject area or to increase their career awareness. Nor does success on science tests indicate that children like science, are interested in science, will engage in free reading about science topics, will watch televised science programs, or even will become interested observers of the natural world.

Using Tests More Effectively

As you prepare a test, try to cross-reference each item to one of the cognitive, affective, or psychomotor objectives of the teaching unit. By doing this, you can measure student progress over all of the unit's objectives. To help you assess student achievement on the objectives of the unit and the quality of the questions you have asked, after the test, prepare a chart on which you will record the number of children who answer each question correctly.

Library Reports

Can you recall going to the school library or media center to do research on a topic for a science report? Perhaps you remember poring through encyclopedias and other reference books to find information on such topics as whales, volcanoes, tornadoes, and rockets. A great deal can be learned through library work that is related to the science experiences that occur in the classroom.

■ *What Do They Accomplish?*

Science reports are common assignments in elementary and middle school and provide students with information and ideas that can round out what they have learned through hands-on activities, demonstrations, and class discussions. Library reports can lead children to think about topics and questions that were not considered during class. They can also help improve a child's grade for a marking period by making up for low quiz or test grades.

■ *What Don't They Accomplish?*

When used in the traditional manner, library reports do little to extend and enrich the basic knowledge, skills, and attitudes emphasized in a discovery-focused classroom. They do not present children with an opportunity to touch science materials or to move through the full learning cycle. In the best circumstances, library reports tell you whether children can look up information in reference books and summarize what they have learned.

Using Library Reports More Effectively

In order for library reports to be meaningful, they should engage children in a quest that resolves some issue or problem. Therefore, if the children are engaged in inquiry-based science experiences related to the life cycle of insects, you might say, "I would like you to do work in the learning center that will help you answer the question 'Why don't we ever see baby butterflies?'" This type of assignment captures the same curiosity that you are hoping to capitalize on with hands-on discovery science. Children should be going to the library or learning center to learn how to use books and media as *tools* that are as essential to the pursuit of science as microscopes and metersticks.

Activity Write-Ups

How will you know that children are learning, fitting new learnings into previous knowledge, and constructing new meanings? You can discover this by observing them, by listening to them, and by reading what they have written in their activity write-ups.

■ *What Do They Accomplish?*

Having children synthesize and share what they have learned in activity write-ups tells them that you believe thinking, talking, and writing about what they have experienced is important. Listening to a child's observations of water droplets forming on an ice-filled glass or reading a list of written observations gives you valuable information about the learning that is occurring in your classroom.

■ *What Don't They Accomplish?*

A variety of problems can arise when you use activity write-ups. The most obvious one is that a child may have completed an activity successfully but not be a good writer. Under these circumstances, a poor report may tell you more about his or her language arts abilities than science abilities. Children with language difficulties will be unable to express what they have learned if you rely only on activity write-ups.

By necessity, the activity write-up is a very brief sketch of the work the child has done. While it will tell you a good deal about the results of a child's experimentation, it will tell you little about all the experiences he or she may have had as the activity was carried out.

Using Activity Write-Ups Effectively

When you look at or listen to a child's activity write-up, you need to be able to assess whether the efforts reflect the child's or the group's work on the activity. To help you do this, take some time to explain to the children the importance of clearly identifying all the group members involved in preparing the report.

Another component of assessing the quality of a write-up is determining whether an incomplete report shows a lack of effort on the child's part or a limitation in his or her ability to use language. The only way to make this distinction is to ask the child clarifying questions.

Standardized Tests

If you walk down a school hallway and notice that it is strangely quiet, that the children are seated quietly at their desks, and that the public address system is not blaring messages, chances are the children are taking a standardized test. For some reason, standardized tests create a time of palpable quiet and anxiety.

In addition to the usual battery of IQ tests and personality inventories, some school districts have children take achievement tests in a variety of subjects. If you teach in a school that requires a standardized science achievement test, you may find that *you* are more concerned about the results than the children are.

■ *What Do They Accomplish?*

A standardized achievement test in science compares how much the children in your class know compared to children nationwide, as reflected in norms. If the children in your class do well, it may make you feel very successful. If they do poorly, you may feel obliged to rethink what and how you are teaching. The results provide teachers, administrators, and members of the community with an opportunity to compare the success of their children to that of children around the country.

■ *What Don't They Accomplish?*

If you have been teaching science using a hands-on, discovery-focused approach, you may have good reason to be anxious when the children in your class are expected to display a command of the basic subject matter on a standardized test. After all, teaching science in a hands-on fashion may not provide the background in science knowledge that children from more traditional textbook-oriented classrooms have. On the other hand, the children in your class will probably have acquired many inquiry process skills and have developed a favorable attitude toward science. Standardized achievement tests will not reveal your success in helping children grasp central science concepts through hands-on experimentation.

Using Standardized Achievement Tests More Effectively

First, help children understand that the results of a standardized test will not measure all that they have learned. If, for example, your class has carried out a hands-on unit on the use and waste of water in your school, explain to the children that they should not expect to see questions about it on the test. Point out that some of the science units they have studied have given them a lot of information that will not be measured. Emphasize that they should not feel badly if many of the things they have learned are not on the test.

Also, take some class time before the test to teach basic standardized test-taking strategies. The children likely will take many standardized tests while they are students and when they pursue employment. Investing time and energy to improve test-taking skills may annoy you because of your own feelings about testing, but it may help children become more successful test takers.

Authentic Assessment Techniques

When modern teachers speak of *authentic assessment,* they are speaking of assessment that measures what students have actually *learned.* This is far more than what is measured by a test, quiz, or end-of-chapter list of questions. However, the strategies and techniques of authentic assessment are much more challenging to implement than the traditional techniques described earlier.

Authentic assessment is a goal for teachers. I have chosen the term *goal* purposefully. The defining quality of authentic assessment is the completion or demonstration of the desired behavior in a real-life context. Exceptional teachers are able to create classrooms in which children's experiences feel like real life! These rooms overflow with experiences that draw children in and involve them so fully that they forget they are children in a classroom and begin to act like scientists. In such an environment, we can move very close to authentic assessment.

Let me describe some commonly used methods of authentic assessment.

Portfolios

A *portfolio* is an organized collection of a person's work that shows the very best that he or she can do. While each piece placed in a portfolio can be assessed with respect to the degree to which the student achieved specific unit objectives, the portfolio as a whole will illustrate the child's progress.

Jodie: It's been quite a year! It was hard work, but the students were really challenged—especially with those inquiry-based discovery units.

Rick: Definitely! Those units took a lot of effort, but the children responded to them *so well.* Can you believe it? We've got to start planning for next year or we'll never get any budget money for new units and materials. Which ones should we hang on to, and which ones should we change?

Jodie: I really liked the ecosystem unit. We were able to tie it to the real world and even different areas right outside the school. The children even started to volunteer the observations they made about changes they noticed near the paths and around the bushes in front of the school. I think the one big weakness in this unit was that we didn't keep track of things real well. The children did some self-assessments and I gave them a few quizzes, but it all seemed trivial. I don't think they even realized all they had learned.

Rick: Actually, I even felt a little flatfooted at the end of the ecosystems unit. We had done so *many* wonderful things, but I wasn't sure where to go with it. So much of what we did got lost in the shuffle. I guess what I'm saying is that we did good work, but we did so much of it and moved so fast that what we really accomplished was lost on the kids.

Jodie: That's the feeling I got, too. I think we need to formalize what we do with the products. The kids work really work hard on these things, and then the stuff just seems to get jammed into folders and notebooks. Some of it winds up a crumpled mess!

Rick: Maybe if we had a big picture at the beginning of the unit about what to do with everything that is going to be produced. I wonder if a science portfolio would work?

Jodie: Well, traditionally, teachers do a KWL at the end of a unit—you know, "What did we *know?*" "What did we *want* to learn?" and "What did we *learn?*" But we could do a lot better. A portfolio would really make a huge difference as far as showing what the students really learned. We would be looking at actual products.

Rick: You know, it wouldn't be that hard to do. We are already doing science journals, and the children are supposed to be keeping data logs, observation logs, and logs of labeled diagrams. All of these could be portfolio samples.

Jodie: But it's a little disorganized now. What if the children do science portfolios that were organized around the inquiry process skills? In other words, they could put their best work samples that showed mastery of observation skills in one section, classifying skills in another section, and so on.

Rick: My only problem is going to be with my "hoarder." He'll never be able to sort through everything! I'm not sure he's even going to be able to *read* the science stuff he's got on those crumpled-up papers that are jammed into his desk.

Jodie: I've got the answer for you: You already have children ironing leaves to wax paper for that leaf collection you do. So when everyone else is ironing leaves, he can be ironing his science logs!

Rick: Can I borrow your iron for that one?

▶ **POINT TO PONDER:** *If you were teaching, what student work products would you select to assess a child's progress over a full academic year? Why?*

You may be wondering what specific examples of a child's science work should go in a science portfolio. Here are some products that could be included:

- Written observations and science reports
- Drawings, charts, and graphs that are the products of hands-on, discovery-focused activities
- Thank-you letters to resource people who have visited the classroom (e.g., bee-keepers, veterinarians, health care providers)
- Reaction pieces, such as prepared written responses to science software, videos, discovery experiences, field trips, and websites
- Media products, such as student-produced science work in audio, video, or digital form

Anecdotal Records

Name: Jimmy Green   *Age: 8*
Grade: 2   *Date: May 5*

This week Jimmy's group, the Science Stars, which was responsible for taking care of the aquarium, found a dead guppy. Jimmy volunteered to bury it in the school lawn. He told the group, "Even though it's dead, it'll help the grass grow."

A teacher's brief notes about a child's behavior can reveal a great deal about what the child has or has not learned. The notes, called *anecdotal records,* can help you assess how well individual children are doing. They can be particularly helpful when you wish to reflect upon and assess how well individual children are mastering inquiry process skills or developing desirable attitudes and values.

You can learn a great deal by observing a child at work.

Affective Development Checklists

"Boy, do I hate science!"

If you heard one of your students say this, what would you conclude about his or her affective development? Your only basis for assessing changes in *affect* is your observation of the affect-laden behaviors students exhibit. Their comments, smiles, frowns, in-class behavior, and out-of-class behavior reveal a great deal about how much they are developing favorable attitudes toward science and your teaching.

Figure 6.3 presents a list of behaviors that you may wish to draw on to create your own affective development checklist. Add your personal observations of student behaviors to create a more comprehensive list.

FIGURE 6.3
Draw from these behaviors to create an affective development checklist.

- Makes drawings and diagrams of science-related objects and events
- Is curious about new objects, organisms, and materials added to the classroom
- Talks about surprising things he or she notices in the environment
- Spends free time at the in-class science learning center
- Questions but is tolerant of the ideas of others
- Enters science fairs and school science expositions
- Brings science-related magazine pictures to class
- Checks science-related books out of the class or school library
- Reads science fiction
- Collects natural objects as a hobby
- Comments on science-related programs seen on TV
- Comments on science-related films
- Asks for class field trips to museums, planetariums, and so on
- Invents things
- Builds models
- Asks questions about science-related news stories
- Asks to do more science activities
- Asks to make or fix science equipment
- Volunteers to carry out demonstrations
- Asks to work on science-related bulletin boards
- Asks to distribute materials and equipment for activities
- Questions superstitions
- Asks to take care of classroom animals or plants

Science Conferences with Children

The words we speak tell a great deal about what we know and how we feel. The quickest and possibly most reliable way to find out if children in a discovery-oriented classroom are learning is to give them an opportunity to talk to you. If you learn to listen carefully and gently probe around the edges of a child's talk, you will discover whether he or she has grasped the real meaning of a food web, has had anything to do with creating the group's drawings showing the movement of the continents, or is becoming increasingly curious about the natural world.

Science Journals

Have you ever watched a child fish around in his or her desk to locate a bologna-stained sheet of paper that contains yesterday's science notes? Some teachers have found that a journal or notebook devoted only to science can be a great asset for children as well as a useful tool for assessing how well individual students are doing. Here are some suggestions for implementing the use of science journals:

1. At the start of the year, ask each child to get a notebook he or she will devote exclusively to science. You may wish to have the children construct their own science journals.

2. Encourage the children to design covers for their science journals. One way to do this is to have a general discussion about the major themes or units they will do during the year.

3. Encourage children to write in their journals each day, and provide time for them to do so. Offer some guiding questions, such as "What did you do? What did you learn? How do you feel about what you have learned?"

4. Schedule time at the end of each teaching unit for children to discuss some of the things they have written.

5. Consider using the science journals during parent-teacher conferences. Also consider putting the journals on display for Parents' Night or Back-to-School Night.

Children's Self-Assessment

As teachers, we may forget that children naturally reflect on how well they do in each activity that is a part of their science experience. And so it should seem logical to capitalize on self-reflection when you incorporate authentic assessment into your classroom.

There are many ways to stimulate children's self-assessment. For example, before the children begin to write in their science journals, you might say, "So far this month, you have worked on two projects. One was building a flashlight, and the other was using a flashlight and mirrors to study how light behaves. What did you learn in each project?" The children's responses will represent their efforts to assess what they have done. This is important information to you as a teacher.

Concept Mapping

A family is seated around the dinner table. The dad passes a bowl of reconstituted instant mashed potatoes to his son and asks, "So, what did you learn in science today?" The child responds, "Nuthin."

How can this be? That child spent the entire day in a lovely, pastel-walled classroom overflowing with books and science materials, was taught by knowledgeable and motivated teachers, had access to a variety of resources (including four or five computers with Internet access), took an around-the-school-yard nature field trip with his class, and also attended a special all-school assembly with Dr. Science, who performed demonstrations that flashed, popped, and banged. Yet the child answered his dad's question with "Nuthin." What went wrong?

The answer is simple: The child doesn't really know what he learned. By that, I mean that the child has had no opportunity to make what he learned *explicit*. He probably learned many things today, but he has not brought them to the forefront of his consciousness and tied them all together. Consequently, both the child and his dad finish their meal thinking that the day was as bland as those mashed potatoes.

One way to help a child assess self-learning is to have him or her make a concept map after an inquiry-based experience. You can even use a concept map as a personal unit-planning device. Even so, I am presenting it here as an authentic assessment tool, so you can see what children have learned in a concrete way. They will literally draw you a picture!

A *concept map* is a diagram that represents knowledge by identifying basic concepts and topics and showing how these items are related. Such a map is created using these two symbols:

1. *Node*—A shape (typically a circle or oval) that contains a word or phrase to represent the item of content knowledge.

2. *Link*—A line with an arrowhead at one or both ends that's used to connect the nodes and to show the relationship between them. A single arrowhead indicates that one node leads to or is part of another. A double arrowhead indicates that nodes are reciprocal or mutually supportive of each other.

Figure 6.4 shows the concept map a child drew after going on a school yard field trip to observe types of living things in the environment. Starting with "Animals" in the center of the page, the child branched out to classes of animals, such as "Mammals" and "Birds," and then became even more specific by noting types of animals within each class, such as "Dogs" and "Squirrels" under "Mammals." Note that all of the arrows point the same way: back to "Animals."

By studying a child's concept map, you can assess what he or she has really learned during an experience and how he or she has tied specific pieces of knowledge together. The child will benefit from creating the map because he or she will make what might have been abstract or general more concrete and specific. As a result, the child will have a much fuller knowledge of what was learned—and it won't seem like "Nuthin"!

FIGURE 6.4

This concept map represents what one child learned in a school yard field trip to observe types of living things.

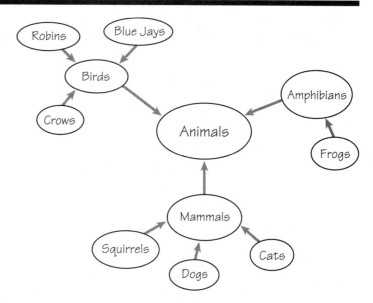

Putting It All Together

Now comes the real challenge: How do you create a meaningful assessment system that will tell whether your students understand the science content and can conduct inquiry?

Use as your foundation the three major approaches to assessment discussed in this chapter: The NSE Standards recommendations and both traditional and authentic assessment techniques. Then consider your curriculum—specific units you teach or observe being taught. With that material in mind, try to answer the question, What is the ideal way to assess whether children are understanding and inquiring successfully? Certainly, the answer must lie in your clever integration of parts of all three assessment strategies plus your familiarity with what you teach.

To put all this together, you need a straightforward and sensible approach. I recommend that you create your very own assessment checklist, which you can use for the units you teach or for units you observe being taught. A sample is shown in Figure 6.5. Look along the horizontal scale, and you'll see the major assessment areas of understanding and inquiry. Look along the vertical scale, and you'll see the general approaches discussed in this chapter.

Consider a specific science unit you are planning or one that you have recently observed. Use the checklist to gauge the range of assessment techniques used. After you have finished using the checklist, ask yourself questions such as these:

1. Is there too much traditional assessment?
2. Should more prompts and rubrics be used so the children's thinking can be more fully challenged?
3. Are any authentic assessment experiences built into the unit?

FIGURE 6.5   Use this personal assessment checklist to evaluate units
you plan or observe being taught.

	Assessment Focus	
Assessment Device	UNDERSTANDING	INQUIRY
NSE Standards Approach		
Prompts		
Rubrics		
Traditional Devices		
End-of-chapter homework		
Quizzes		
Tests		
Library reports		
Activity write-ups		
Standardized tests		
Authentic Assessment Devices		
Portfolios		
Anecdotal records		
Affective development checklists		
Science conferences with children		
Science journals		
Children's self-assessment		
Concept mapping		

Many other questions will also likely come to mind as you reflect on the results you acquired by using the checklist.

The "bottom line" for assessment is that you need to use a variety of measures because you will have a variety of students in terms of achievement levels, aptitudes, and attitudes. If you are able to assess them well and then use that information gathered sensibly, your students will become better students and you, of course, will become an even better teacher.

MAKE THE CASE   *An Individual or Group Challenge*

■ **The Problem**

Teachers may devote so much classroom time and personal energy to providing hands-on, discovery-based science experiences that the children do not have opportunities to display what they have learned.

■ **Assess Your Prior Knowledge and Beliefs**

Think for a moment about an inquiry process skill or a topic in science that you feel you understand well. For that topic or skill, respond to the following:

1. State the topic or skill.

_____

2. Where did you first learn about it?

_____

3. When did you learn about it?

_____

4. Did you learn it on your own, or did someone else help you?

_____

5. How did you know that you had learned it?

_____

6. How could you show that you have learned it?

_____

■ **The Challenge**

To have the children demonstrate that they are learning, you have decided to ask each child to create an invention that uses what he or she has learned. You would like to stage a Convention of Inventions for parents on Back-to-School Night. What five key points about the importance of children demonstrating their knowledge in this manner could you use to convince your school principal to provide financial support for the materials children will need?

Summary

There are three basic approaches you can take to assess children's progress in science. One is rooted in the recommendations from the NSE Standards regarding the assessment of understanding and inquiry using prompts and rubrics. The second approach, traditional assessment techniques, includes end-of-chapter homework, quizzes, and so on. Authentic assessment, the third approach, uses techniques such as anecdotal records, student portfolios, concept maps, and the like. Clearly, as a teacher, you must develop a sound understanding of what children are, in fact, learning. More than likely, you will integrate techniques from the three major strategies presented in this chapter. To help you identify assessment techniques for the science units you teach or observe, you should use a personal assessment checklist, like the one included in this chapter.

GOING FURTHER

On Your Own

1. Imagine that you are an elementary- or middle-grade science teacher who has just received a $1,000 grant to improve the strategies and techniques used to assess children in science. What would you spend the money on? Explain your rationale.

2. Consider the traditional student-teacher book conference. Then describe how a 10-minute *science* conference with a child might be similar and different from a book conference in terms of its purpose and the types of questions asked by the teacher.

3. Select a science topic you might teach to children at a grade level of your choice. For that topic, suggest a specific subject for an age-appropriate, inquiry-based project. Then briefly describe how you would apply the four steps suggested by the NSE Standards to determine whether the children were successful in completing the project.

On Your Own or in a Cooperative Learning Group

4. Create a poster listing five techniques children should use to prepare for a traditional science unit test. Highlight techniques that you or members of your group learned through direct experience as students.

5. Imagine that you and some other teachers have decided to give a Back-to-School Night presentation that will provide the rationale for using science portfolios in place of traditional assessment techniques. Prepare three overhead transparencies that you could use as part of the presentation.

6. On a sheet of newsprint, have your group identify one science topic at a grade level of interest. Under that topic, list three or four "big ideas" that children should understand by the time the unit has been completed. Show that you can implement the techniques suggested by the NSE Standards for gauging how well children understand the big ideas. Identify a prompt and a scoring rubric that a teacher could implement to assess understanding.

RESOURCES FOR DISCOVERY LEARNING

Internet Resources
Websites for Assessment of Understanding and Inquiry

Assessment Ideas for the Elementary Science Classroom

www.sasked.gov.sk.ca/docs/elemsci/ideass.html

This is one of few sites on the Internet that deals specifically with the needs of elementary-/middle-level science teachers. In addition to discussing conferences, interviews, contracts, and portfolios, this site provides *templates,* or guide sheets for creating and using various assessment techniques. This site has a very practical focus and should be of great use to you.

Alternative Assessment Techniques

www.indiana.edu/fleric_rec/ieo/bibs/altasses.html

This site provides a bibliography of ERIC documents dealing with alternative ways of assessing students as well as a procedure to help you acquire full-text copies of those documents. The available documents are organized both alphabetically and by category. The "Category" choice is particularly helpful.

ERIC Clearinghouse on Assessment and Evaluation

ericae.net/

This site provides access to a wide range of ERIC documents dealing with assessment and testing. It also provides an extremely well-organized list of Internet sites that deal with topics of interest to teachers and others. The links range from specific resources for

elementary teachers, such as ways of improving test construction, to general resources on how people in other countries deal with issues related to assessment and testing.

Project Zero

pzweb.harvard.edu

This portion of the Project Zero site includes a section called "Research Projects." Within it, you will find discussions of a variety of projects, including alternative and imaginative ways of assessing student progress in several disciplines, such as science. Most of the projects have an interdisciplinary focus, which makes issues of assessment rather interesting.

The National Assessment of Educational Progress

nces.ed.gov/NAEP/

You may have heard of the *The Nation's Report Card,* a continuing assessment of what American students know and can do in a variety of subjects, including science. The testing program itself is called the *National Assessment of Educational Progress,* or *NAEP.* It samples student achievement at grades 4, 8, and 12. A very interesting feature of this site is that it allows you to see science achievement levels in every state as well as how those results change from year to year. You can also look over sample test questions to judge whether they reveal important indicators of science achievement.

Print Resources
Suggested Readings

Barton, James, and Angelo Collins. *Portfolio Assessment.* White Plains, NY: Dale Seymour, 1997.

Brown, Janet Harley, and Richard Shavelson. *Assessing Hands-On Science.* Thousand Oaks, CA: Corwin Press, 1996.

Coray, Gail. "Rubrics Made Simple." *Science Scope* 23, no. 6 (March 2000): 38–49.

Craven, John A., and Tracy Hogan. *Science Scope* 25, no. 1 (September 2001): 36–40.

Davis, Elizabeth A., and Doug Kirkpatrick. "It's All the News: Critiquing Evidence and Claims. *Science Scope* 25, no. 5 (February 2002): 32–37.

Demers, Chris. "Beyond Paper-and-Pencil Assessments." *Science and Children* 38, no. 2 (October 2000): 24–29, 60.

Enger, Sandra, and Robert Yager. *Assessing Student Understanding in Science.* Thousand Oaks, CA: Corwin Press, 2001.

Franklin, John. "Assessing Assessment." *Curriculum Update* (Spring 2002): 1–8.

Gandal, Matthew, and Laura McGiffert. "The Power of Testing." *Educational Leadership* 60, no. 5 (February 2003): 39–42.

Goodnough, Karen, and Robin Long. "Mind Mapping: A Graphic Organizer for the Pedagogical Toolbox." *Science Scope* 25, no. 8 (May 2002): 20–24.

Guskey, Thomas R. "How Classroom Assessments Improve Learning." *Educational Leadership* 60, no. 5 (February 2003): 6–11.

Neill, Monty. "The Dangers of Testing." *Educational Leadership* 60, no. 5 (February 2003): 43–45.

Olson, Joanne K., and Anne M. Cox-Peterson. "An Authentic Science Conference." *Science and Children* 38, no. 6 (March 2001): 40–45.

Pelligrino, James W. "Knowing What Students Know." *Issues in Science and Technology* 19, no. 2 (Winter 2002–2003): 48–52.

Sclafani, Susan. "No Child Left Behind." *Issues in Science and Technology* 19, no. 2 (Winter 2002–2003): 43–47.

Shepardson, Daniel P., and Susan J. Britsch. "Analyzing Children's Science Journals." *Science and Children* 38, no. 3 (November/December 2000): 29–33.

Smith, Deborah C., and Ann Wesley. "Teaching for Understanding." *Science and Children* 38, no. 1 (September 2000): 36–41.

Stavy, Ruth, and Dina Tirosh. *How Students (Mis-) Understand Science and Mathematics.* New York: Teachers College Press, 2000.

Stearns, Carole, and Rosalea Courtney. "Designing Assessments with the Standards." *Science and Children* 37, no. 4 (January 2000): 51–55.

Sunda, Ruth. "Thinking about Thinking—What Makes a Good Question?" *Learning & Leading with Technology* 30, no. 5 (February 2003): 10–15.

Varelas, Maria, et al. "Examining Language to Capture Scientific Understandings." *Science and Children* 38, no. 7 (April 2001): 26–29.

Ward, Robin E., and James Wandersee. "Roundhouse Diagrams." *Science Scope* 24, no. 4 (January 2000): 17–27.

NOTES

1. For a detailed discussion of the use of prompts and scoring rubrics, see National Research Council, *National Science Education Standards* (Washington, DC: National Academy Press, 1996), pp. 91–98.

2. From National Research Council, *National Science Education Standards* (Washington, DC: National Academy Press, 1996), pp. 98–100.

7

Integrating Science

How can I integrate inquiry-based science with other subjects in a child's school day?

Inquiry as the "Superglue" of Knowledge

"You can't take off for spelling. This is science!"

If you haven't heard these words yet, be patient. You will! And you will feel very, very discouraged when you do. Even if you are normally a pleasant, calm, thoughtful, easy-going teacher, hearing a student utter these words could easily provoke you to delivering an arm-waving, too-loud exposition on the subject of "taking pride in your science work." In fact, if you hear this comment near the end of a feet-hurting, head-throbbing, "I've given all I have to give and the well is dry day," you might even be tempted to say,

"Yes, I can and I will! So get used to it!"

I hope you can resist the temptation to respond viscerally and instead put your focus on patiently and intelligently teaching children that human knowledge is *interconnected*. What's more, the people who *do* science and technology share some of the very same thoughts and do some of the very same things that great writers, artists, mathematicians, and athletes do. They explore, they inquire, and they inevitably discover and apply new knowledge and skills.

As you plan science units, remember that science experiences can draw together a variety of subjects, acting as a kind of "superglue" that connects the learning in a range

Project 2061: Implications for Integrating Science across the Subject Areas

Project 2061 provides strong guidance for integrating science with mathematics and technology using particular themes. And you can use these themes to find ways of integrating science with other subjects in the curriculum (something that Project 2061 does not do directly).

Here are the themes that Project 2061 provides for tying together science, mathematics, and technology:

- Systems
- Models
- Constancy and change
- Scale

Using "Systems" as a theme, for example, you would teach children that a whole object, event, or interaction is made of parts, that those parts relate to each other, and that those parts affect the whole. Using the theme of "Models," you would teach that models are either real things or ideas that are used as tools to understand the world. The theme of "Constancy and change" addresses those ideas and discoveries that have withstood the test of time along with the nature of change and how small changes can have large effects. Finally, in teaching the theme of "Scale," you would help children see that things that differ from one another in terms of size, weight, or any other variable may also behave differently.

Specific recommendations for implementing these four themes are available at the Project 2061 website: <www.project2061.org/>.

of areas and shows how human knowledge and experience fit together to form a larger, more meaningful whole. This is much easier said than done, however, so let's consider some practical things you can do to integrate science with other subjects.

Science and the Language Arts

"That cloud looks like a pregnant polar bear."

Children have a natural inclination to react to the world around them, and they absorb information from what they see, hear, taste, and touch as well as what they read. They can also respond in many ways, talking, writing, and drawing about what they absorb. Like scientists, children develop a repertoire of specific reading and writing process skills that enable them to carefully observe and react to what they experience through their senses. The next few sections will describe techniques you can use to help children expand both their science and their language arts abilities.

Selecting Trade Books That Stimulate Inquiry and Discovery

Do you love books? I certainly hope so! One feature of your classroom should be an extensive collection of books that motivate children to think and engage in inquiry-based, discovery-focused science.

Trade books are volumes distributed by commercial publishers that do just that. They are not textbooks. Instead, they tell about scientific adventures, the lives of scientists, science careers, and factual material about stars, planets, dolphins, the rain forest, and much more.

How can you select the best possible trade books for your children? Try using the following criteria, which were suggested by a distinguished panel of teachers and other science educators:

- The book has a substantial amount of science content.
- The information presented is clear, accurate, and up to date.
- Theories and facts are clearly distinguished.
- Facts are not oversimplified so as to make the information misleading.
- Generalizations are supported by facts, and significant facts are not left out.
- The book does not contain gender, ethnic, or socioeconomic bias.[1]

I won't provide you with a list of recommended science trade books, since so many new ones appear each month. Instead, I'll direct you to two excellent and easily accessible sources that *will* provide you lists of the very best modern trade books for children and youths:

1. An annual article in *Science and Children* whose title is always "Outstanding Science Trade Books for Students K–12"
2. The Internet site <www.nsta.org>, where you may select the feature "NSTA Recommends"

Three Integrating Techniques

As the children entered the classroom on Monday morning, their exclamations could be heard the length of the hallway. "Wow!" "What happened here?" "It's beautiful!"

Over the weekend, their fourth-grade teacher had transformed the classroom into a tropical rain forest. The children knew that this was going to be no ordinary day. But their teacher was no ordinary teacher.[2]

Indeed, any teacher who finds creative ways to cross subject matter barriers using language arts as the bridge is special. You can be such a teacher if you focus on actively finding techniques to tie science and language arts together. Rakow and Vasquez, who described the fourth-grade teacher in the preceding excerpt, suggest three ways to do this:

1. *Literature-based integration* is simply the use of modern nonfiction science books, such as the trade books just discussed, to help children acquire science-related information. Additionally, for those children who might benefit from getting science information through a story line, many fictional books by authors such as Eric Carle and Tomie dePaola have science information and concepts threaded through them.

2. *Theme-based integration* is instruction in which a major theme or concept becomes the foundation for a learning unit that cuts across subject lines. Think in creative ways as you identify a theme such as "The Rain Forest," "Space Neighbors" for astronomy, or "Animals with Pouches" for the life sciences.

Science-related projects provide excellent opportunities for integrating the language arts.

3. *Project-based integration* involves children in actually carrying out a long-term activity in which they investigate a real-world problem. Here are a few examples of science-related projects that provide excellent opportunities to tie language arts development to science content:

- Discovering the amount of paper wasted each day in a classroom or school and communicating ideas to others that will help solve the problem
- Discovering how much water is wasted at school water fountains each day or week and communicating ideas to others that will help stop the waste
- Discovering how well school hot lunch offerings and student choices match proper nutrition guidelines and communicating ideas to others that will help children choose better lunches[3]

Weaving It All Together with Whole-Language Instruction

The term *whole language* should mean something to you. The foundation for the popular whole-language approach to teaching the language arts rests on the belief that we become good readers and good language users as a result of our personal experiences with language.

Teachers who emphasize the whole-language approach draw on the real-life experiences of children and use children's speaking vocabulary as an important starting point for developing language arts skills. Class time overflows with children dictating stories, chanting, singing, speaking, writing, constructing "big books," and the like. These experiences help children develop and improve their language arts skills.

The teaching strategies of the whole-language approach can be easily adapted to enrich and extend children's science experiences. Writing stories about butterflies and rockets, making "big books" about insects, and writing and singing songs about saving the earth's natural resources are activities that involve children in a variety of science topics and help develop their language arts skills.

Whether you use the whole-language approach or another approach, I hope that you will create appropriate ways to develop each component of the language arts through science. In the sections that follow, you will find some very specific ways to achieve a science/language arts synergy.

Extending the Basics: Vocabulary, Comprehension, and Writing

Vocabulary

Someday, somewhere, some child will come up to you, look you straight in the eye, and ask with a giggle, "What part of a fish weighs the most?" or "What grows down while growing up?" And you will enjoy not only the joke but also what telling it has to say about that child's ability to use language.

Unfortunately, for many children, words and their meanings are *not* sources of jokes and riddles. For these children, words are mysterious combinations of ink marks that make little sense and create little pleasure. If you are not alert to the need to teach and reinforce reading skill development, the printed page of a science book can serve as a source of frustration for a child with limited vocabulary skills.

Here are some specific strategies you can use to help children learn new vocabulary words during science time:

1. Look through science trade books and elementary science textbooks before the children work with them to *identify terms that may be too difficult* to learn from the context, and then preteach those words.

2. *Pronounce science vocabulary words with children* before they reach them in their science materials.

3. *Have each child develop a personal word card file* that lists and defines each new science word. Each card should include the word, the sentence in which the word was found, a phonetic respelling of the word, and, if appropriate, a drawing or diagram showing the object or concept that the word defines.

Comprehension

You can help children build their comprehension skills in science by focusing their attention on prereading experiences. Before the children begin reading a specific text, trade book, or Internet article, focus your discussion of the material around three magic words:

1. *What?* When you distribute trade books, text material, or resource material on a science topic, take the time to discuss exactly what you expect the children to do with it. Describe how much time they will have and what they are expected to produce as a result of the reading.

2. *Why?* Take the time to explain to children why they are going to do the assignment. Do your best to describe how it will relate to work they have done before and work that will follow.

3. *How?* Describe how you expect children to learn from the material they are reading. You might say something like this: "Here are some topics you can use to organize the information you get about the planets from your reading: What is the planet's size compared to Earth? What is the surface like? How long is a day on the planet? Why don't you list them in your science notebook before you start reading. That way, you will have a specific place to put the information that you find in the book."

Writing

Writing is like talking to your best friend. —Eric, a first-grader

Writing is a dance in the sun. —Christi Ann, a second-grader

Writing is meeting the person in me I never knew. —Mike, a seventh-grader[4]

This excerpt from *Reading and Learning to Read* tells a lot about the power you give children when you help them learn how to move their thoughts to a page. Science classrooms that provide children with opportunities to explore the natural world are places that provoke thought and thus create an unending array of possibilities for communication through the powerful medium of the written word. When you are teaching science, you are offering the possibility of many "dances in the sun."

You are quite fortunate when you teach children science because the breadth of content, processes, and affect that you teach is well matched by the range of writing forms that elementary school children need to practice. In *Language Arts: Learning Processes and Teaching Practices,* Temple and Gillet suggest that there are six basic writing forms:

Description	Expression	Persuasion
Exposition	Narration	Poetry[5]

REAL TEACHERS TALKING   *A Starting Point for Thinking, Talking, and Writing*

Lynn: So you've been doing a lot of curriculum integration in your classroom. Has it been worth the time and energy?

Toni: Oh, definitely! One of the hurdles teachers face is the amount of material that needs to be covered in the school year. With a more integrated curriculum, I can combine lots of things. This saves a lot of time that used to be spent teaching the same type of content within the separate subjects (I like making charts and graphs), and I get more depth of coverage than I had before.

Lynn: That sounds really practical, but I think there is something bigger going on when you integrate. You know, in Eastern cultures, the focus of learning is more on the whole and less on the parts. Western education is more focused on the parts—the segmented disciplines. I think the Eastern idea of how we think and learn makes a great deal of sense, since the mind seems to retain information when it's placed in a larger context. For your classroom, the larger context is the *theme.*

Toni: I agree completely. It seems that the more I integrate my curriculum, the easier it is to tie it to real-life experiences. The learning seems to take on more meaning for the student. After all, life isn't departmentalized!

Lynn: I totally agree. I teach thematically, and I accept the student's evaluations through multiple assessment. They have multiple intelligences that need to be addressed in different ways.

Toni: I'm glad the curriculum is getting more "seamless." The topics we cover now have a purpose and focus. We don't do them just because I say we have to.

Lynn: Another plus that I have found is that sometimes my students get so involved with integrated science projects that they forget they are learning. I work with students who are at risk, so integrating has been a great bonus for the children and for me.

▶ **POINT TO PONDER:** *Based on your personal experiences in classrooms, do you see the integration possibilities as being as rich and promising as these two teachers see them? Are these teachers the exception to the rule, or do you sense a movement toward a more integrated approach to teaching children science?*

Here are some examples of how you can help children develop their abilities with each writing form. I am sure that you can suggest many others.[6]

- *Description.* Have the children describe in detail an animal they observe on a class trip to a zoo.
- *Exposition.* Have the children explain how to make a flashlight lamp light using just one battery, one wire, and one bulb.
- *Expression.* Have the children write thank-you letters to a park ranger who visited the class to talk about protecting the natural environment.
- *Narration.* Have the children write stories about an incident in the life of a young girl who decides to be the first astronaut to set foot on the planet Mars.
- *Persuasion.* Have the children write scripts for a children's television commercial that will convince others to eat more green, leafy vegetables.
- *Poetry.* Have the children observe and draw a seashell and then write poems that use at least three of the observations they made about the shell.

Science and Mathematics

"Whose mine is it?" asked Milo, stepping around two of the loaded wagons.

"BY THE FOUR MILLION EIGHT HUNDRED AND TWENTY-SEVEN THOUSAND SIX HUNDRED AND FIFTY-NINE HAIRS ON MY HEAD, IT'S MINE, OF COURSE," bellowed a voice from across the cavern. And striding toward them came a figure who could only have been the Mathemagician.

He was dressed in a long flowing robe covered entirely with complex mathematical equations and a tall pointed cap that made him look very wise. In his left hand he carried a long staff with a pencil point at one end and a large rubber eraser at the other.[7]

This excerpt from *The Phantom Tollbooth* comes from the part of the book in which Milo, the watchdog Tock, and the Dodecahedron are about to find out where numbers come from.

"So that's where they come from," said Milo, looking in awe at the glittering collection of numbers. He returned them to the Dodecahedron as carefully as possible but, as he did, one dropped to the floor with a smash and broke in two. The Humbug winced and Milo looked terribly concerned.

"Oh, don't worry about that," said the Mathemagician as he scooped up the pieces. "We use the broken ones for fractions."[8]

The journey of Milo and his friends to the numbers mine has always struck me as an excellent frame of reference for both understanding the difficulties children may have with mathematics and helping them overcome those difficulties. Some children view numbers as squiggly lines on paper that have no basis in reality. For all they know, numbers come from number mines! Although there are many aspects of elementary school mathematics that can be reinforced, extended, and enriched as children do science, three are particularly important: computational skills; data collection and expression; and logical reasoning.[9]

Computational Skills

Figure 7.1 provides examples of various ways in which computational skills can be practiced and put to real work during science. As you look over the figure, see if you can think of other ways to have children work on computation as they carry out science activities and projects.

Data Collection and Expression

> Zing! Another rubber band flies across the science classroom. Is this a sign of unmotivated students in an undisciplined classroom? Not this time. This otherwise unruly behavior is actually part of a hands-on activity that teaches students the basics of graphing and experimental design.[10]

Although I definitely don't suggest this particular activity for either brand-new or veteran teachers with limited classroom management skills, I share it with you to focus attention on what a creative science teacher can do to build a child's science/math skills. Even though shooting rubber bands will not be your first choice as an activity to use when your school principal is observing your magnificent teaching talents, it does

FIGURE 7.1
A variety of science activities can be done to improve math computational skills.

Computational Skill	Science-Teaching Example
■ Counting	Determine the number of pieces of litter on the school lawn.
■ Addition	Keep track of the number of birds that visit a feeder.
■ Subtraction	Measure children's heights at the beginning and end of the year and calculate growth.
■ Multiplication	Estimate the number of birds in a flock on the school lawn by first counting a small group and then multiplying by the number of groups.
■ Division	Do a school survey of animals in classrooms, and find the average number in each.
■ Working with fractions	Place half a collection of seeds in moist soil and half in dry soil and compare their relative growth.
■ Working with decimals and percentages	Study the list of ingredients and the nutrition chart on a box of sweetened cereal, and figure out what part of the weight of the cereal is sugar.

provide a good data-collection and data-expression experience. Notice the true sophistication of the activity:

> In this experiment the independent (or manipulated) variable is the width of the rubber bands and the dependent (or responding) variable is the distance they fly. Does the width of a rubber band affect the distance it travels? Ask students to write a hypothesis using an if-then sentence format that states how the independent variable will affect the dependent variable. Once they have constructed a hypothesis, let the rubber bands fly![11]

Even if you are not quite ready (or will never be ready) to extend science through rubber band shooting, you can do equally interesting, if not equally exciting, activities

MAKE THE CASE   *An Individual or Group Challenge*

■ **The Problem**

As a result of their school and real-world experiences, children may conclude that science is an isolated and complex branch of human knowledge.

■ **Assess Your Prior Knowledge and Beliefs**

Check your beliefs and knowledge about the following:

1. Children in the elementary grades learn that science is separate and different from other subjects.

   strongly disagree   disagree   agree   strongly agree

2. Children in the elementary grades learn that science is difficult.

   strongly disagree   disagree   agree   strongly agree

3. In the middle grades, children experience science as a separate subject.

   strongly disagree   disagree   agree   strongly agree

4. In the middle grades, children learn that science is a difficult subject.

   strongly disagree   disagree   agree   strongly agree

5. Science activities in most elementary- and middle-grade textbooks and resource books connect science to other school subjects.

   strongly disagree   disagree   agree   strongly agree

■ **The Challenge**

Before being interviewed for a teaching position, you review the science curriculum and notice that it includes sample science activities. At the end of each activity is the side heading Connections, which suggests how to relate the activity to other subjects. During the interview, the interviewer tells you, "We are so excited about our new curriculum. It is really interdisciplinary. I think you've had a chance to look it over. What do you think of it?" How would you respond?

that lead to data collection and expression. For example, you can have the children observe changes in the level of water in an open container. Begin by having a child place a mark on the container to show the present water level. The children can then mark the level each day for several days. At the end of the time, the children can measure the distance from the first mark to the new marks and make graphs to show the changes.

Can very young children express data through graphs and charts? They certainly can! By cutting paper strips that represent the distance from the water level to the original mark in the preceding example, the measurement for each day can be recorded. The paper strips can then be placed in sequence to produce a rudimentary graph of changes in water level.

Following the data-gathering process, the children can be led through a discussion of the lengths of their paper strips. Their understanding of math concepts can be probed and developed with questions such as these:

1. Can you explain why the strips are different lengths?
2. How much longer is the longest strip than the shortest?
3. How do the changes shown by your strips compare with those shown by other children's strips?

Logical Reasoning

An important goal of mathematics education for children is to develop an understanding of the logical structure of mathematics. In practice, this means a child is able to look at collections of items and make statements about them and the outcomes of grouping and regrouping them. This is the mathematics of sets and subsets, open sentences, and the commutative, associative, and distributive properties. Science experiences can provide children with opportunities to put their understanding of mathematical concepts to work. You could, for example, have the children in your class do these activities:

1. Group collections of plants into sets and subsets.
2. Devise a system for classifying organisms into the set of all plants and the set of all animals.
3. Identify the similarities and differences of various elements of the set of all birds and fish.
4. Use a list of characteristics to determine whether an organism is part of such subsets as fish, birds, and reptiles.

Science and the Social Studies

"After analyzing what kind of garbage was in and around the creek (like grocery carts, litter, and car tires), the students agreed that the source of the trash was from various people and places. When the students had decided who was responsible, it was more difficult for them to decide who should help with their cleanup. How could they ask people in the apartments to come clean up the creek safely and without offending them?"[12]

Social studies and science can easily be integrated, since societal problems, in many cases, lend themselves to real-life inquiry-based experiences for children. The outdoor experience just described shows how challenging children with meaningful projects can tie together science and social studies. And in doing so, it can raise important issues about individual and societal attitudes and values.

Attitude and value development is an important dimension of social studies that can easily be integrated with science. Children who learn that questions of values cut across content areas are more apt to appreciate the significance of such topics. Here is a sampling of the types of questions you can use to stimulate attitude- and value-based science discussions and to generate ideas for activities and projects that relate science and social studies:

1. Should animals be kept in zoos?
2. Should cities and towns have animal control officers?
3. Should a factory that provides many jobs for people but also pollutes the town's air and water be closed down?
4. Should people be required to wear seat belts?
5. Should commercials for sugar-sweetened cereals be shown during Saturday morning children's shows?

Also see Figure 7.2, which shows how a number of social studies topics can be extended through related science content. Integrating these two content areas will help children realize the science/social studies connection.

FIGURE 7.2
Many social studies topics can be extended through science activities.

Social Studies Topic	Related Science Concept
■ The natural resources of a country	The sun as the original energy source in the solar system
	The protection of air and water resources
	The use of alternative energy sources
■ The history and development of a country or part of the world	Contributions made by specific scientists and inventors
■ The employment of North Americans in diverse occupations	Career awareness for occupations in science and technology
■ The structure of the family and other social groups; the interaction of group members	The effect of improved technology on providing increased leisure time
■ The production, transportation, and consumption of goods and services	The improvement of the quality and quantity of agricultural products through selective breeding and food preservation technology

Science and Art

Recently, I began to plan a unit on the human body. In an art unit that I had done a few years ago, the class used fabric crayons to make a wall mural for display in the hall. So I decided to use these crayons to make ourselves walking, anatomically correct models of the digestive and respiratory systems.[13]

Jackie Moore, the teacher who came up with this clever idea, goes on to explain that first she had each child bring in a white, cotton-blend T-shirt. The fabric crayons were used to draw the systems and organ labels on paper, and the drawings were then ironed on the shirts. She describes the culminating activity this way:

To show off our beautiful bodies all my 125 students wore their shirts on the same day. Quite a sight to behold! Interestingly enough, the students do better on questions dealing with these two systems than on any of the other systems that we study.[14]

This activity shows how you can easily encourage children to use art with science and thereby help them see the relationship between art and science. There are many other activities that you can use to accomplish this. Use those described in Figure 7.3 to get you started on developing your own strategies for relating science and art.

FIGURE 7.3
These sample activities integrate art and science.

- *Tree Stump Rubbings:* Place paper on a smooth, recently cut tree stump, and rub the paper with a pencil. Follow-up activities may include discussions about climatic changes, as reflected in changes in the annual ring pattern, and how to find the age of the tree.

- *Leaf Rubbings:* Place paper over a variety of leaves, and rub the paper with the side of a crayon. Follow-up activities can include observation of leaf veins in the print and discussion of the variety of leaves found or defects in leaf surfaces as a result of insect activity.

- *Native Crafts:* Use natural objects to make sculptures, including mobiles or stabiles, and pictures. Examples include stone people, acorn people, apple-head dolls, fruit and vegetable prints, dried flowers, and shell sculptures.

- *Sand Painting:* After studying the origin and characteristics of sand, dye the sand to use in sand paintings. This can be integrated with social studies, since it is an activity that comes from the heritage of native North Americans.

- *Moving Sculpture:* Build simple circuits to operate sculptures that have moving parts as well as blinking lights.

Science and Music

Music has become so much a part of our daily lives that we are sometimes oblivious to it, but the children that you teach are not. Even very young children are able to hum, dance, whistle, and sing a multitude of breakfast cereal commercials and know some of the words and phrases of the most popular songs on MTV. Music has had a profound impact upon our culture, and we should be able to take advantage of its ability to attract and hold a child's attention when we teach science.

Hapai and Burton have prepared a helpful resource book called *BugPlay* that offers many strategies for integrating one common science topic—insects—with the rest of the school curriculum. One of my favorite songs from this book, and a favorite of children for obvious reasons, is "Cock-a-Roaches." I have included the words and music in Figure 7.4 as an example of a creative way to integrate science and music.[15]

Another strategy for relating music and science is to locate music that was composed to express feelings about topics that you are covering in science. For example, if you teach the four seasons, you can fill your classroom with selections from Vivaldi's Concerto in F Minor, op. 8, no. 4, "Winter," from *The Four Seasons.*

FIGURE 7.4

Music and science can make an irresistible combination for a child.

Science and Health
and Physical Education

The sun is shining. Feel its warm glow on your seed bodies. Now it's raining . . . a gentle rain. You are beginning to grow ever so slowly. Feel your sides enlarge. What are you growing into? A dandelion? A flower? A blade of grass? A young sapling? Feel your arms and fingers stretch into leaves, petals, or branches. S-T-R-E-T-C-H. Reach for the sky. Reach for the sun. Now there's a wind, a gentle breeze. Now there's a rainstorm. Move as a flower, plant, or tree would move in a rainstorm. Now the sun is peeking out from behind a cloud. Fill your body with its wonderful warmth. Breathe in the air . . . in and out . . . in and out.[16]

Wouldn't doing this activity be a nice way to review some of the concepts taught in a unit on green plants while helping a child develop his or her motor skills? The concepts that underlie physical education activities for children are clearly related to many of the topics of elementary school science.

The physical education component of a child's day focuses on such matters as engaging in recreational activities that may be carried out over a lifetime, improving general health, and developing strength and coordination through a variety of movement activities. Thus, much of what is done during a modern physical education class actually is related to common science vocabulary terms, such as *time, space,* and *force.* Whether children become aware of this relationship is certainly a debatable question.

To build your own bridge between physical education and science, you need to establish a working relationship with your school's physical education teacher. If you teach in a self-contained classroom, strive to develop each curriculum—science and physical education—in a way that emphasizes and extends the concepts common to both.

Summary

Inquiry and discovery are at the heart of science experiences for children and can also serve as the "glue" that ties together various subjects during the school day. Science experiences offer many opportunities to build and extend language skills, whether taught through the whole-language approach or through other methods. Math experiences for children—including computation, data collection and expression, and logical reasoning—can be easily tied to science work, as can activities in subjects such as social studies, art, music, and health and physical education. There is great potential for the teacher who is willing to invest the energy in helping children become aware of the connections between human knowledge and skills and engage in work that makes the integration of these two things real.

GOING FURTHER

On Your Own

1. Identify a reading or language arts activity that you could have children do when they are learning about each of these topics:
   a. The seasons
   b. Sound energy
   c. Endangered animal species
   d. Rocks and minerals
   e. The role of technology in their lives

   For each activity, suggest whether you would do it at the beginning, middle, or end of a unit of study.

2. What special techniques might you use to help poor readers read science materials successfully? How could you help children with writing problems improve their written communication skills while they learn science? Be specific in your responses, citing techniques that could be used with a wide variety of science content.

3. Can you recall a science experience that you had as an elementary school child that integrated at least one other content field? If you can't recall such an experience, try to recall a science activity that could have been related to another content field with minimal teacher effort. What benefits could result from such an integrated activity?

4. The study of current events can provide many opportunities to relate science and social studies. Identify a recent news story that had a significant scientific or technologic dimension. For this current event, describe a series of classroom activities that would provide children with experiences that highlight the relationship of science and social studies.

On Your Own or in a Cooperative Learning Group

5. Select a topic in science that could be used as a theme in a variety of subject areas. If you are working with a group, have each person play the role of the teacher of a specific subject in a departmentalized elementary or middle school. Discuss how a group of teachers at the same grade level might plan a teaching unit that integrates the subject areas. (If you are doing this on your own, prepare a written statement that highlights possible comments each teacher might make.)

6. Interview a teacher who works in a self-contained classroom. During the interview, determine the following:
   a. The major science topics emphasized during the year

   b. The science processes that are emphasized
   c. The extent to which the topics are enriched as a result of his or her efforts to relate other subjects to science

7. Interview a teacher in a departmentalized elementary or middle school. During your discussion, determine the following:
   a. The major topics and processes emphasized during the year
   b. The approximate length of a science class
   c. Whether other teachers at the grade level are aware of the topics dealt with in the science curriculum
   d. Whether all the teachers at the grade level ever work together to plan and teach units with interdisciplinary themes

RESOURCES FOR DISCOVERY LEARNING

Internet Resources
Websites for Integrating Science with Other Subjects

Writing in the Science Classroom

www.indiana.edu/fleric_rec

This site by the ERIC Clearinghouse on Reading, English, and Communication at Indiana University provides links to resources related to science and writing. It has links to sites within the ERIC system as well as to other Internet resources.

Links

www.ssec.org/

Select "Education Links" to access many units and lesson plans that have a cross-disciplinary focus. As you scan the links, locate those that have terms such as *interdisciplinary* and *thematic.* They will take you to sites that will prove helpful in your own planning for integrated science teaching.

Interdisciplinary Lesson and Unit Plans

www.stark.k12.oh.us/Docs/units/

The lessons and units at this site were developed by a group of teachers for middle-grade and upper-grade students. All emphasize technology, and many have a clear science focus, such as "Ecology," "Cycles," and "Wetlands." All units also follow a consistent format, which makes it easy to use them as resources.

Additionally, the connections made between the science or technology content and other subjects, such as language arts or fine arts, are very clearly shown.

CRPC GirlTECH Lesson Plans

teachertech.rice.edu

The excellent units and lessons at this site are focused on integrating mathematics with science and technology. An additional feature is the strong emphasis on ensuring gender equity by providing examples that have appeal for girls as well as boys. The units and lessons range across grade levels, so you will have to identify those most appropriate for your grade level of interest.

Science, Technology, and Society

serp.la.asu.edu/sts_dir/sts_idx.html

This page is a compilation of lessons prepared by elementary and middle school teachers that are intended to integrate science, technology, and society-related concepts. The units are clearly marked with respect to grade level and, in fact, cut across more subject areas than the three that are their principal focus. Among the interdisciplinary units at this site are those dealing with weather, planetary survival, the environment, and energy conservation.

Print Resources
Suggested Readings

Akerson, Valerie. "Teaching Science When Your Principal Says 'Teach Language Arts.'" *Science and Children* 38, no. 7 (April 2001): 42–47.

Barman, Charles, et al. "Assessing Students' Ideas about Plants." *Science and Children* 40, no. 1 (September 2002): 25–29.

Burns, John E., and Jack Price. "Diving into Literature, Mathematics, and Science." *Science Scope* 26, no. 1 (September 2002): 15–17.

Butzow, John, and Carol Butzow. *Science through Children's Literature.* Engelwood, CO: Libraries Unlimited, 2000.

Fioranelli, Debra. "Recycling into Art." *Science and Children* 38, no. 2 (October 2000): 30–33.

Freedman, Robin Lee Harris. *Science and Writing Connections.* White Plains, NY: Dale Seymour, 1999.

Keena, Kelly, and Carole G. Basile. "An Environmental Journey." *Science and Children* 39, no. 8 (May 2002): 30–35.

Kupfer, Joseph H. "Engaging Nature Aesthetically." *Journal of Aesthetic Education* 37, no. 1 (Spring 2003): 77–89.

Lee, Michele, Maria Lostoski, and Kathy Williams. "Diving into a Schoolwide Science Theme." *Science and Children* 38, no. 1 (September 2000): 31–35.

Minton, Sandra. "Using Movement to Teach Academics: An Outline for Success." *Journal of Physical Education, Recreation and Dance* 74, no. 2 (February 2003): 36–40.

National Science Teachers Association (NSTA), Children's Book Council Joint Book Review Panel. "Outstanding Science Trade Books for Students K–12." *Science and Children* 39, no. 6 (March 2002): 31–38.

Nikitina, Svetlana. "Movement Class as an Integrative Experience: Academic, Cognitive, and Social Effects." *Journal of Aesthetic Education* 37, no. 1 (Spring 2003): 54–63.

Terrell, Arlene G. "Leaders, Readers, and Science." *Science and Children* 39, no. 1 (September 2001): 28–33.

Young, Rich, Jyotika Virmani, and Kristen M. Kusek. "Creative Writing and the Water Cycle." *Science Scope* 25, no. 1 (September 2001): 30–35.

NOTES

1. National Science Teachers Association (NSTA), Children's Book Council Joint Book Review Panel, "Outstanding Science Trade Books for Students K–12," *Science and Children* 39, no. 6 (March 2002): 33.

2. Steven J. Rakow and Jo Anne Vasquez, "Integrated Instruction: A Trio of Strategies," *Science and Children* 35, no. 6 (March 1998): 18.

3. Ibid., 19.

4. Jo Anne L. Vacca, Richard T. Vacca, and Mary K. Gove, *Reading and Learning to Read* (Boston: Little Brown, rpt. 1991), p. 127.

5. Charles Temple and Jean Wallace Gillet, *Language Arts: Learning Processes and Teaching Practices* (Glenview, IL: Scott, Foresman, 1989), p. 231.

6. You may wish to refer to the presentation of a sample unit on space exploration, which shows a detailed integration of the language arts with a science topic, in Susan I. Barcher, *Teaching Language Arts: An Integrated Approach* (New York: West, 1994), pp. 351–367.

7. From *The Phantom Tollbooth* by Norman Juster, copyright © 1961 and renewed 1989 by Norton Juster. Used by permission of Random House Children's Books, a division of Random House, Inc.

8. Ibid., 180.

9. AIMS Activities that Integrate Math and Science and GEMS (Great Explorations in Math and Science) are two interesting curriculum development projects involved in the preparation of teaching materials that cut across the traditional boundaries of mathematics and science. To receive overviews of available integrated activities from these projects, write to AIMS Education Foundation, P.O. Box 8120, Fresno, CA 93747, and GEMS, Lawrence Hall of Science, University of California, Berkeley, CA 94720.

10. Richard J. Rezba, Ronald N. Glese, and Julia H. Cothron, "Graphing Is a Snap," *Science Scope* 21, no. 4 (Januay 1998: 20.

11. Ibid.

12. Kelly Keena and Carole G. Basile, "An Environmental Journey," *Science and Children* 39, no. 8 (May 2002): 32.

13. Jackie Moore, "Iron-On Respiratory System," *Science and Children* 28, no. 1 (September 1990): 36.

14. Ibid.

15. From *BugPlay*, © 1990 Addison-Wesley Publishing Co., Menlo Park, CA. Used with permission. Words and music © 1990 Leon H. Burton and Marlene Nachbar Hapai.

16. Milton E. Polsky, "Straight from the Arts," *Instructor* 99, no. 7 (March 1990): 57.

8

Science WebQuests

How can I create inquiry-based, discovery-focused Internet projects for children?

A Strange Thing Happened on My Way to a School One Day

I was peacefully driving to an elementary school to visit with teachers who were about to receive some new computers when a very distracting question entered my mind: What about the computers that were being *replaced*—those dead or dying dinosaurs whose dust-covered corpses were quietly lying on the back counters of the classrooms? Did they die a natural death from exhaustion, or did they waste away after enduring a mind-numbing and sedentary lifestyle? More specifically, did they spend most of their time presenting arcade-type fact games, tired cross-country simulations, and diversions intended to teach the dates of obscure historical events?

As I drove along, pondering these questions, the real reasons for the computers' demise emerged: Perhaps they succumbed because most of the so-called educational software in use had little to do with the curriculum teachers were expected to teach. Perhaps the computers died of dust inhalation from being surrounded by software packages that were only rarely disturbed when the children or teacher sought educational diversions. Or perhaps the computers were bored to death!

Whatever the case, if teachers and students had real reasons to use computers, they would be used more often and much more appropriately. Then the computers would eventually die of exhaustion but happy in knowing they had led full and productive lives.

The Internet: An Important Resource for Inquiry and Discovery

The most purposeful and exciting reason I can think of for using computers in your classroom is to access the Internet. Now, I am not saying that children should use the Internet instead of doing hands-on, inquiry-based science. In fact, if you forced me to rate science experiences for children, the "gold medal" would go to *outdoor* hands-on experiences in the earth/space, life, or physical sciences; the "silver medal" would go to *indoor* hands-on science experiences; and the "bronze medal" would go to using the Internet.

Without a doubt, the Internet is an extraordinary resource that shapes our lives in countless ways. Access to the Internet provides you and your children an opportunity that no other generation has had: to tap the resources of almost every library, school, museum, and laboratory in the world!

Yet productive use of the Internet requires planning. I will share a planning technique that you may wish to use as it stands or to adapt to fit your professional needs. It is called a *Science WebQuest* and is based, in part, on ideas originally put forth by Bernie Dodge and Tom March at San Diego State University and other experts in the field of educational technology.[1] I suggest an approach that focuses on the discipline of

Most of us find it difficult to keep up with the rapidly changing technology in our lives and in our classrooms, as well. Even so, as you invest time and energy in creating and using WebQuests, try not to lose sight of the fact that in doing so, you are harnessing a very powerful technology: the Internet. And with that realization, also try to comprehend the enormous implications that come with the ability to access the Internet.

Project 2061 provides an in-depth look at technology and its specific effects on children and adults. It emphasizes three components of technology within the benchmark "The nature of technology":

- Technology and science
- Design and systems
- Issues and technology

You will find more information about these three components by visiting the Project 2061 website at <www.project2061.org/>.

science and is geared toward elementary- and middle-grade teachers. This WebQuest approach has three components whose names are understandable to children: *challenge, journey,* and *report.* Finally, this approach requires teachers to correlate children's Internet explorations with the inquiry process skills as well as the NSE Standards and/or local science curriculum guides.

What Is a Science WebQuest?

A *Science WebQuest* is a discovery project for children that requires the use of Internet resources. Specifically, it's a three-step guide for students that will bring them into direct, focused contact with the Internet as a way to acquire knowledge, concepts, and skills. The three steps are as follow:

1. The challenge
2. The journey
3. The report

Although I will describe the Science WebQuest as being teacher prepared, you may wish to consider whether some of your students could prepare WebQuests for themselves or to challenge peers. Additionally, the Science WebQuest can serve as an opportunity for cooperative learning when a team of children engage in a WebQuest together.

Computers with Internet access open unlimited learning possibilities for children. Science WebQuests can guide children to find and use appropriate resources as they respond to "challenges."

Figure 8.1 (pages 144–145) illustrates the three-part Science WebQuest form. Parts 1 and 2 should be completed by the teacher and given to the student or cooperative group. These parts structure and give direction to the quest. The student or cooperative group should complete Part 3 and prepare the WebQuest final report, which can take a variety of formats: a written summary, a set of answers to questions, a story, a skit, a piece of art, a poem, or a multimedia presentation in which the children use computers and related technology.

Relationship to the Inquiry Process Skills

Using Science WebQuests with students is a teaching strategy that can effectively give individuals and groups practice with some of the key inquiry process skills (discussed in Chapter 3). Using these skills also provides experiences that are consistent with and supportive of discovery learning. In order to grasp how Science WebQuests and the inquiry process skills are related, let's look at a few examples:

Basic Inquiry Process Skills	Possible Science WebQuest Experiences
Observing	Viewing recent Hubble telescope photos of stars and star clusters
Classifying	Compiling lists of rain forest animals and grouping them into categories
Predicting	Studying weather maps over a three- or four-day period and preparing weather forecasts

Integrated Inquiry Process Skills	Possible Science WebQuest Experiences
Interpreting data	Gathering earthquake location data, plotting them on a map, and observing the emergence of the "ring of fire" pattern
Formulating hypotheses	Studying information gathered about the characteristics and locations of asteroids and making a hypothesis to explain their origins
Experimenting	Gathering data from other schools who report their experiences with Oobleck and using that information in combination with locally obtained data to prepare experiments for further hands-on explorations

Relationship to the Discovery-Learning Cycle

You may recall that earlier in the book (Chapter 3), I presented a model for discovery learning known as the *learning cycle.* That cycle has three components that can easily be incorporated in lesson and unit plans:

1. Explore
2. Inquire and acquire
3. Discover and apply

By creating a well-crafted Science WebQuest and providing strong teacher guidance, you can support the learning cycle in at least two ways. You can prepare three small Science WebQuests that each focus on one stage, *or* you can prepare a larger Science WebQuest that moves a student through all three stages.

Relationship to the NSE Standards and Local Curriculum Guides

Why should you add Science WebQuests to your repertoire of teaching skills? What will doing so help you accomplish?

Consider how a child or cooperative group carrying out a Science WebQuest will achieve meaningful local or national curriculum goals as a result of the experience. Also consider the boundless variety of information, ideas, and opportunities for skill development that exist on the Internet and how learning or acquiring them will help students achieve curriculum goals.

FIGURE 8.1   A master science WebQuest form

Title: _____

Your Name or Cooperative Group's Name _____

Start Date _____   Completion Date _____

1. Your Challenge
A. Introduction

_____

_____

_____

_____

_____

_____

_____

_____

_____

_____

_____

B. The Challenge

_____

_____

_____

_____

2. Your Journey: Starting Your Search
A. To get more information, visit these sites:

Site   *URL*

_____   _____

_____   _____

_____   _____

_____   _____

B. To get even more information, use these key words with search engines:

_____ _____ _____

3. Your Report: Sharing Your Results

A The report <u>must</u> be your answer to the Science WebQuest challenge.

B. Which of these words best describes your report? (You may check more than one.)

___ Written summary of what I (we) learned

___ Story	___ Play	___ Poetry	___ Art
___ Music	___ Chart	___ Graph	___ Multimedia

___ Other: _____

C. In two or three sentences, describe your Science WebQuest report. In other words, tell what the reader or viewer will observe in your report.

_____

_____

_____

Please attach your report to this Science WebQuest form.

Teacher Space

- Intended Grade Level(s) _____   Is adult help/supervision needed? _____

- Inquiry Process Skill(s) Emphasized

___ Observing	___ Using space/time relationships	___ Using numbers
___ Classifying	___ Defining operationally	___ Communicating
___ Predicting	___ Controlling variables	___ Inferring
___ Interpreting data	___ Formulating hypotheses	___ Measuring
___ Experimenting		

- NSE Standards content area(s) to which this Science WebQuest is most closely related:

___ Physical science	___ Life science	___ Earth and space sciences
___ Science and technology	___ Personal and social	
___ History and nature of science	perspectives	

- Specific NSE Standard to which this Science WebQuest is most closely related:

_____

_____

- Local science curriculum guide topic to which this Science WebQuest is most closely related:

_____

_____

Let me be more explicit by listing a few goals from various curriculum sources and identifying some possible Science WebQuest challenges you could develop:

■ *From the NSE Standards*

Goal or objective: "As a result of activities in grades K–4, all students should develop understanding of personal health."(Content Standard F)[2]

Possible Science WebQuest challenge: Use the Internet to find and creatively present four examples of how smoking cigarettes and using alcohol can harm a person's health.

■ *From a Local Science Curriculum*

Goal or objective: Students should understand the advantages and disadvantages of using each of the following energy sources to make electricity: coal, oil, and nuclear energy.

Possible Science WebQuest challenge: Use the Internet to locate information about the advantages and disadvantages of using each of these energy sources to make electricity: coal, oil, and nuclear energy.

Alternative Strategies for Using Science WebQuests in Your Classroom

The Science WebQuest planning model will support many different teaching styles, many different curriculum approaches, and the needs of diverse groups of children. The following examples will help you see the range of possibilities for you and your classroom:

- Make multiple copies of the same Science WebQuest, and have all children or cooperative groups pursue the same challenge. When the individuals or groups have completed their work, all will benefit from observing the various reports. Bear in mind that the *forms* that the individual and group reports take will vary greatly, including writing pieces, graphs and charts, poetry, art, skits, and multimedia presentations.

- Prepare two or three Science WebQuests that all deal with one general topic. Assemble the WebQuests to create a packet, and have individuals or groups select the one of most interest to them. (*Note:* If you use cooperative groups as part of your overall instructional strategy, the within-group negotiations that go on as students select a WebQuest will reveal each group's social interaction skills.)

- Individually or in cooperative groups, have students do Internet research to prepare Science WebQuests for others. If you happen to teach science to more than one class (a typical pattern in middle-grade settings), have each class prepare Science WebQuests to challenge the other classes. You will, of course, need to be deeply involved to make sure the WebQuests are not so difficult as to be impossible for a given class to complete.

- Use Science WebQuests as long-term assignments that students do at home or in association with free time at computers connected in the classroom or school learning center.

How to Plan and Prepare a Science WebQuest

As you read this section, you may find it helpful to refer to the completed Science WebQuests shown in Figures 8.2, The Whale Deal—It's a Killer, and 8.3, The Space Warp Weather Network Gives You a Chance (pages 148 and 149).

REAL TEACHERS TALKING — *A Starting Point for Thinking, Talking, and Writing*

Marti: One of my favorite pieces of new technology is the digital camera. I was able to use one last year, and I really loved it.

Eileen: I've seen them, but I always thought they looked complicated. Was it easy to take and print the pictures you took? I know that no film is involved.

Marti: Oh, it's not hard at all. You just use the camera like an ordinary camera—point, click, and you've got the picture. Then you plug the camera into the computer, and the computer stores all the pictures on its hard disk. You just move the picture into a desktop-publishing program, so the pictures that you take of children doing science, pictures of objects and equipment you use, and pictures of children in costume doing science-related dramatics all become part of reports children write. Some teachers create science newsletters to send home. You can imagine the impact on parents of seeing pictures of their children in a newsletter that the class created. It really isn't very hard to do.

Eileen: It must make your newsletters really interesting. Besides the use for the science newsletter, are you using the camera with student science portfolios?

Marti: You know, I've been thinking about that. It would be wonderful to have the children keep their science journals, or parts of them, as computer files and include digitized pictures of their work. If a child did a project on plant growth, he or she could take digital pictures of the plants to include in a science portfolio.

Eileen: I'm still amazed that we can now have a camera in the classroom that uses no film. It almost sounds too good to be true! We don't have to send film out to be developed, since it's all recorded as digital information, and if the picture doesn't turn out well, we just take another one. We can take pictures, put them in a computer file, and then immediately print them on a laser printer, and it all happens right in our classroom. Who could ask for anything more?

Marti: Well, I could. I was thinking about how nice it would be to have a laser printer that prints in color. Now, that would really be something!

▶ **POINT TO PONDER:** *The digital camera is only one example of a technological innovation that is changing what we do in science time and how we do it. What new technology have you observed teachers using to carry out interesting science projects with children? Would your science experiences in the elementary and middle grades have been much different if your teachers had some of the technology that today's teachers have?*

FIGURE 8.2   A sample science WebQuest

The Whale Deal—It's a Killer

Your Name or Cooperative Group's Name _____

Start Date _____   Completion Date _____

1. Your Challenge

A. Introduction

You are paying some book fines when Mr. Bookman complains that not many of your friends take books home to read. "Hmmmmm," you think for a moment and then say that you would like to make a deal with him. If you can get more kids to check out books, then he will let you take home as many books as you want for as long as you want—with no fines. He agrees! Then you tell him you will cover the school walls with posters that advertise books. He likes it! You also tell him you'll start with the theme "Killer Whales," since he has a shelf of whale books that are covered with a thick layer of dust. Amazingly, Mr. Bookman agrees again, shakes your hand, reaches under the counter to get out his feather duster, and walks toward the whale books.

B. The Challenge

Do research on the Internet to find information about the size, shape, and life of killer whales. Try to discover what they eat, what tries to eat them, and where they live. Then make a poster for each topic that includes drawings, information, and questions that will get other children interested enough to check out killer whale books.

2. Your Journey: Starting Your Search

A. To get more information, visit these sites:

Site	URL
Sea World	www.seaworld.org/infobooks/KillerWhale/home.html
Whale Museum: Orca Adoption Program	www.whale-museum.org/
Killer Whales	www.abc-kid.com/killerwhales/
Whale Times: Kids Page	www.whaletimes.org/whakids.htm
Whales Page	www.geocities.com/heather_malone/whales.html

B. To get even more information, use these key words with search engines:

Marine Mammal	Orca	Shamu

Note: See Part 3, Your Report, on page 145.

FIGURE 8.3 A sample science WebQuest

The Space Warp Weather Network
Gives You a Chance

Your Name or Cooperative Group's Name _____

Start Date _____ Completion Date _____

1. Your Challenge
A. Introduction
You have just been selected by the SWWN (Space Warp Weather Network) as one of
three finalists for the job of SWWN's first Solar System Weather Person. If you get the
job, your forecasts will be used by space travelers to decide where they will take their
vacations. Unfortunately, there is a small problem. To get the job, you will have to prepare
and present a script that announces tomorrow's weather on each planet. If SWWN likes
the script, you might get the job. If they don't, you will keep your present job serving
french fry pills at Jason's Hyperfast Food Restaurant.

B. The Challenge
Locate information on the Internet about the weather and climate on each of the nine
planets. Use the information to write a sample script for the weather forecast. You may
audiotape or videotape yourself giving the actual forecast. You may also create weather
maps to use during your presentation. If you are doing this Science WebQuest as a
member of a group, each group member should be involved.

2. Your Journey: Starting Your Search
A. To get more information, visit these sites:

Site	URL
NASA	www.nasa.gov/
The Planets	www.dustbunny.com/afk/planets/planets.htm
Jet Propulsion Laboratory	www.jpl.nasa.gov/index.cfm
Astronomy for Kids	www.frontiernet.net/~kidpower/astronomy.html
Welcome to the Planets	pds.jpl.nasa.gov/planets/welcome.htm

B. To get even more information, use these key words with search engines:

Planets	Solar System	Astronomy

Note: See Part 3, Your Report, on page 145.

Planning Challenges That Fit Your Students

Your success in getting children to carry out an Internet-related learning experience will depend on how well *you* carry out the essential first step: *to motivate them.* To successfully motivate children, you must establish a context or frame of reference for the actions you want them to take. This may mean, for instance, spinning a science-related tale that engages children's minds and builds their interest in accomplishing the Internet research task.

Your opportunity to motivate children's pursuit of a Science WebQuest comes in Part 1, "Your Challenge." Notice in Figure 8.2 that you need to prepare an *introduction* to set the context and then state the *challenge*. The *context,* or introduction, as a comedy writer will tell you, is equivalent to the setup for the punchline. It draws the reader's or listener's attention away from whatever he or she is thinking about and to your topic. It serves to pique the reader's or listener's curiosity about the topic and builds some positive psychological tension that begs to be resolved. The *challenge,* on the other hand, is a clear statement of the process and product that will channel the child's motivation in a direction that will resolve the problem or issue raised in the introduction.

To help you understand these points more completely, here are a few examples of introductions and challenges for Part 1 of the Science WebQuest document.

Early-Grade Samples

■ *Animals in Danger*

Introduction: Tashia and Nathan's grandmother, Mrs. Nancy Nicelady, wants to take them on a trip to see animals that might soon disappear from the earth. She gives money every month to a group that tries to protect the animals and also takes people to see them in their natural environments. The trips are designed so they don't disturb the animals or their environments. If Mrs. Nicelady was willing to take you along on such a trip, which animals would you like to see?

The Challenge: Make a drawing of North and South America. Add the animals you want to see, drawing each where it actually lives. Also draw the plants and animals that each animal needs for food.

■ *Is There a Volcano Near Your House?*

Introduction: While running to catch your school bus, you almost trip over a morning newspaper someone left on the sidewalk. You look down before you, kick it out of the way, and notice this headline: "Volcano Explodes, Killing 50 People." On the school bus, you look out the windows and notice some nearby mountains. You begin to wonder if there are any volcanoes in those mountains.

The Challenge: Using the Internet, find the locations of at least 10 volcanoes on the earth's surface. Make a map that shows where each volcano is. Also write the date of the last time each erupted. Circle the five volcanoes that are closest to your state or province.

Middle-Grade Samples

■ *Atom Crushers*

Introduction: Most people think that the atom is the smallest piece of matter, but they are wrong! Scientists have been smashing atoms for many years and discovered that there are smaller parts. There are even some parts that are smaller than protons and neutrons. Would you like to surprise some adults by telling them about these tiny pieces of matter?

The Challenge: Go to the Internet to find out about five pieces of matter that are smaller than a proton or a neutron. Write down the name of each small piece of matter, and list two of its characteristics. Also tell the names of atom smashers used to break apart atoms and produce these tiny parts and where these atom smashers are located.

■ *Be a Dino Detective*

Introduction: Are any dinosaur fossils buried under your school playground? How do you know for sure? This may sound like a strange question, but the answer might surprise you. This Science WebQuest will help you discover whether dinosaur fossils might be buried under your playground.

The Challenge: Make a map of your country that includes your state or province. On the map, show five places where dinosaur fossils have been found. If no fossils have been found in your state or province, show the nearest locations of dinosaur fossils. Name the dinosaurs discovered at these places, describe their characteristics, and make a hypothesis about whether dinosaur fossils are under your playground.

Notice that some of the introductions are written in a more fanciful way than others. Keep in mind that the tone and content of the introduction and challenge should fit the sophistication of the children you teach and your own creativity, too!

Planning Journeys That Fit Your Students

None of us has enough time to discover everything we need to know completely on our own. If we expected students to discover everything for themselves, there would be no time left for them to use their newly gathered information and concepts. Therefore, even discovery-based experiences require teacher guidance to ensure that children will achieve success in a reasonable amount of time.

The same is true for Science WebQuests. Guiding discovery during these experiences occurs naturally, since individual children or cooperative groups carry out their explorations in response to teacher-created challenges. The "road map" for children's journeys is actually quite simple to prepare. In fact, it's just a list of websites on the Internet with their accompanying *universal resource locators,* or *URLs.*

Before sending children on the journey, plot the course. To do so, you must have access to the Internet and conduct your own searches to locate suitable websites. Keep in mind that you are compiling a short list of prime sites that will help your students meet the challenge you gave them in Part 1.

As you prepare the journey, keep track of key words that students might use to go beyond the specific sites you identify with search engines. By identifying these key words, you will provide additional guidance but in a manner that's true to the basic concept of guided discovery. Figure 8.4 will help you think through the key word identification process.

MAKE THE CASE   *An Individual or Group Challenge*

■ **The Problem**   It is difficult, if not impossible, for the busy science teacher to keep up with advances in instructional technology and to integrate them into day-to-day instruction.

■ **Assess Your Prior Knowledge and Beliefs**   As a person who will be or is now teaching children science, rate yourself on each of the following:

	Minimal knowledge and skill	Some knowledge and skill	Confident in knowledge and skill
1. General computer ability	_____	_____	_____
2. Ability to select hardware for classroom use	_____	_____	_____
3. Ability to select software for classroom use	_____	_____	_____
4. Knowledge of available software	_____	_____	_____
5. Ability to locate teaching/learning resources on the Internet	_____	_____	_____
6. Ability to edit videos made by children	_____	_____	_____
7. Ability to create a multimedia presentation	_____	_____	_____
8. Knowledge of available videotaped programs	_____	_____	_____

■ **The Challenge**   While thinking about how you teach children science, consider how your role will change as new technologies find their way into the classroom. Based on your present level of knowledge and skills, predict how teaching children a unit on volcanoes and earthquakes may be different 10 years from now.

FIGURE 8.4   One way to identify key words for Internet searches is first to prepare possible questions you might use in a challenge. The questions should lead you to appropriate key words.

WebQuest Topic	Questions about the Topic	Possible Key Words
Manatees	What is a manatee? Is a manatee a mammal? Where would you find a manatee? What do manatees look like? Are manatees a threat to people? Are people a threat to manatees? Are manatees an endangered species?	manatee manatee picture manatee drawing mammal endangered species
Elephants	Are all elephants endangered species? Are Indian elephants the same as African elephants? What problems do wild elephants cause people? Are people a threat to elephants? What is a poacher?	Elephants Indian elephants African elephants endangered species poacher
Planets in Other Solar Systems	How many planets have been found in orbit around stars besides our sun? Do all astronomers agree that other planets have been found? Are any of the objects in orbit around stars like any of our planets? How can astronomers know that there are other planets if they can't see them? What is a radio telescope?	planets astronomy new planets other solar systems telescopes nearby stars radio telescope planet hunters

Assessing the Report

Students summarize the work they do in pursuit of the challenge in Part 3 of the Science WebQuest: the report. The final product of the Science WebQuest is then either attached (if it is a written document) or presented (if it is produced in another medium).

You should assess the report through simple observation, comparison with the original challenge, conferences with students in which they self-assess their work, and other strategies and techniques. (See Chapter 6 on assessment techniques.)

Summary

The computer and its related technologies have become more important to teachers as the potential of the Internet has been recognized in classrooms and schools around the world. The Science WebQuest is one practical technique teachers can use to guide students' work on the Internet. The challenge, journey, and report components of the Science WebQuest channel students' attention to focus on local, state, and national science curriculum goals, including those of the NSE Standards.

GOING FURTHER

On Your Own

1. Using curriculum resources, identify five science-related topics commonly dealt with at a grade level of your choice. Select one topic for which a Science WebQuest might be an appropriate project for a child or cooperative group. Then actually prepare a Science WebQuest. Be sure to create a Part 1, Challenge, and Part 2, Journey, that are appropriate for the grade level you chose. If possible, field test part or all of your Science WebQuest with a child or group of children at that grade level. In a few paragraphs, reflect on the success of the WebQuest.

2. Based on your previous experience as a child in elementary or middle school, your observations of classrooms, and any personal teaching experience you might have, identify the major classroom management problems you feel might result from having computers in the classroom. Briefly describe what preventive steps a teacher might take to minimize one such problem.

On Your Own or in a Cooperative Learning Group

3. Try to achieve consensus among your group members as you prepare one response to each of the following questions:
   a. What are the long-term benefits of having a classroom in which children are able to link to the outside world through computer networking?
   b. Are there any negatives for children and teachers who use this networking capability? If so, what are they?

4. Imagine that you are teaching in a school in a community that is the corporate headquarters of a well-known global telecommunications company. As part of its effort to support local education, the company has agreed to provide five long-distance phone lines for Internet connection with no monthly charges to the school. The only requirement is that the teachers agree to use this service to support the networking of their classrooms with other classrooms around the country and around the world. You already have a computer and printer in your classroom, and the parents of one of the children are willing to donate a new high-speed modem to the class. On large sheets of newsprint, prepare a list of Science WebQuests you could use to convince the school principal to have one of the lines connected to your classroom.

5. Visit an elementary or middle school, and observe the extent to which individual classrooms use computers and related technology. If possible, interview the teachers to determine

how each computer is used by children. Try to learn whether any science software is used and whether computers are used to keep track of science observations or to prepare science journals. Without identifying individual classrooms or teachers, prepare a chart that summarizes your observations of the number of computers, their placement, the availability of related technology (e.g., printer, modem), the principal uses of the computer in support of the science curriculum, and the percentage of computers that are connected to the Internet.

6. Conduct an in-depth interview with an elementary- or middle-grade teacher or someone who has recently had a student-teaching internship in an elementary or middle school to discover what he or she feels is his or her present level of computer literacy (e.g., word processing, telecommunications), the extent to which he or she presently uses a computer and related technology in support of the science curriculum, and the extent to which children access the Internet in support of assignments.

RESOURCES FOR DISCOVERY LEARNING

Internet Resources
Websites for Integrating Technology

Creating Web-Based Lessons

www.esc20.net/etprojects/

This site offers ideas for integrating technology into the curriculum. It also provides sample WebQuests and a method to access to a WebQuest WebRing, which will lead you to many related sites on the Internet.

Shelby County, Tennessee, Schools Searchable WebQuest Data Base

www.scs.k12.tn.us/

This site includes WebQuests prepared by teachers at all grade levels, and they have been carefully organized and made accessible through the use of a search engine. To access this part of the site, select "Teacher Resources" and then "WebQuest Searchable Database."

WebQuests in Our Future

discoveryschool.com/schrockguide/webquest/webquest.html

At this website, you will find links to articles about WebQuests, a sample WebQuest, and links to collections of WebQuests. In one part of this site, you can even share your WebQuests with other educators.

WebQuests for Learning

www.ozline.com/webquests/

This site provides ideas for creating your own WebQuests, ideas for the basic design and layout of a WebQuest, and a method of evaluating the quality of your WebQuests. It also has links that will take you to some of the original thinking of Bernie Dodge and Tom March as they worked to develop the general concept of the WebQuest.

The WebQuest Page

edweb.sdse.edu/webquest/webquest.html

This site, created and maintained by the Educational Technology Department of San Diego State University, will give you a good overview of WebQuest development, including links to training sites and lists of teacher-developed WebQuests.

Matrix of Examples

edweb.sdsu.ed/webquest/matrix.html

This is part of the San Diego State University Educational Technology Department site mentioned above, but it's so important that I have provided a separate and direct link to it. Commonly referred to as "the matrix" by educators, this site has a constantly updated collection of WebQuests that are prepared by teachers and others and grouped by content area and grade level. It is an excellent resource!

WebQuests and Resources for Teachers

www.davison.k12.mi.us/academic/hewitt14.htm

A listing of WebQuests from different content areas and grade levels is provided at this site, along with other educational resources such as sources of lesson plans.

WebQuests in Middle School

www.siue.edu/~jandris/north/questn.html

This site contains a well-organized article about the history and nature of WebQuests, and the article has extensive links to specific WebQuests that will be of greatest interest to middle-grade teachers.

 ## Print Resources
Suggested Readings

Cradler, John. "Research on E-Learning." *Learning and Leading with Technology* 30, no. 5 (February 2003): 54–57.

Holzberg, Carol S. "Online Tutorials." *Technology & Learning* 23, no. 7 (February 2003): 32–33.

Kennedy, Kristen. "Writing with Web Logs." *Technology and Learning* 23, no. 7 (February 2003): 11–14.

Laposta, Michael, et al. "Current Events and Technology: Video and Audio on the Internet." *Science Scope* 25, no. 6 (March 2002): 82–85.

Mackay, Pete. "Building and Using WebQuests." *Technology and Learning* 23, no. 6 (January 2003): 32–33.

Marcum-Dietrich, Nanette I., and Danielle Ford. "The Tools of Science." *Science Teacher* 70, no. 2 (February 2003): 48–51.

McMahon, Maureen. "Picture This!" *Science and Children* 39, no. 7 (April 2002): 42–45.

Perry, Laurie. "MultiMedia Rocks." *Science and Children* 37, no. 8 (May 2000): 24–27.

Schachter, Ronald. "Visiting the Virtual Library." *Technology and Learning* 23, no. 6 (January 2003): 12–17.

Smith, Stephen W. "Getting Connected to Science." *Science and Children* 37, no. 7 (April 2000): 22–25.

Sterling, Donna R. "Science on the Web: Exploring Hurricane Data." *Science Scope* 25, no. 6 (March 2002): 86–90.

Young, Lisa Rednadette, and Kristen M. Kusek. "Eye in the Sky: The Big Picture." *Science and Children* 24, no. 7 (April 2001): 22–27.

Zertouche, Albert A. "Travel without Leaving the Classroom." *Science Scope* 26, no. 3 (November/December 2002): 28–31.

NOTES

1. I greatly appreciate the work of Bernie Dodge and Tom March at San Diego State University, whose exploration of this general area has helped many educators develop strategies for helping students access the Internet for instructional purposes. As reported in "Some Thoughts about Web-Quests" (available at edweb.sdsu.edu/courses/EdTec596/About_WebQuests.html), Dodge's model suggests a six-component approach to WebQuests: introduction, the task, resources, the process, learning advice, and conclusion. My three-step model focuses specifically on the exploration of Internet science-related resources by elementary- and middle-level science students.

2. From the National Research Council, *National Science Education Standards* (Washington, DC: National Academy Press, 1996), p. 138.

9

Adapting the Science Curriculum

How can I adapt the science curriculum for children from diverse cultural backgrounds, children with special needs, and children with special gifts and talents?

Treasuring the Fleeting Moments

The time that you have with each child who steps through your classroom door into your care is fleeting—so brief that you are seldom able to respond fully to the numerous ways in which children differ from one another. This chapter will help you plan science experiences for children who have special needs. I hope that it will prepare you to say to every child who enters your classroom, "Hello, I'm glad you are going to be in my class. This is the place where *everyone* learns science."

The "Digital Divide": A Cautionary Tale

A classroom computer that's connected to the Internet is a special "window on the world." It can bring children the images of young hawks being fed and raised, cavorting rain forest animals, and a dolphin giving birth. Children who don't have this "window"—due to the fact that they attend underfunded schools or live in homes that lack the resources or inclination to own a computer—see none of these real-world wonders.

As you study this chapter, which focuses on the unique needs of special children, keep in mind that not all children have access to the technology that will bring these wonders and other advantages to their lives—now or in the years ahead. And when these children encounter one more thing that divides them from the larger society, they may become more removed, more distant, and even alienated from their schooling.

As you teach *all* children through the medium of science, try to bring to bear as much technology as your school has to offer. If you can help children cross the "digital divide," you will be doing much to broaden their self-confidence, their career aspirations, and ultimately their horizons.

Children from Diverse Cultural Backgrounds

Getting Science Reading Materials for Non-English Speakers

Las Cremalleras Tienen Dientes Y Otras Preguntas Sobre Inventos

If English is your only language, you must really be puzzled by the above quote! Even if you have studied the language used, my guess is that you only partially understand it.

I will give you the translation later in this section, but for now, I want you to think about what it's like for a non-English-speaking child, likely new to the United States, to see books and headings that look as foreboding as the quote above looks to *you*. Add to this language confusion the idea that the quote probably has something to do with science, a potentially difficult subject, and you should more fully appreciate the challenge that science time must be for non-English speakers as well as their teachers.

In a perfect world, all teachers would be fluent in at least one other language. But unless you were fortunate enough to be raised in a dual-language home, the odds of your being able to communicate effectively with a newly immigrated non-English-speaking child are slim, at best. Even if you are fluent in a second language, the odds are still not in your favor (or more importantly, the child's), since that language may not be Spanish, Cantonese or Mandarin Chinese, Bosnian, Laotian, Cambodian, or Vietnamese—the home languages of many new arrivals to the United States.

Your success in helping non-English-speaking children learn science and expand their abilities with English will depend on whether you can bring to your classroom resources in other languages. At present, it's easiest to find age-appropriate science materials in Spanish. Whether you can acquire science-related materials in other languages will depend on your own resourcefulness.

One way to find such materials is to contact community groups that represent speakers of various languages and find out what science resources might be borrowed from scientifically literate community members. Another strategy is to contact a local university to see if undergraduate or graduate students studying a given language would be available to make translations from English. Finally, if you are a world traveler, you might consider visiting one or more of the countries represented by your students. During your visit, you may be able to acquire resource materials that can be put to good use in your classroom.

Are you still curious about the quote presented at the start of this section? It's the title of a book for children that, roughly translated from Spanish, reads, *I Wonder Why Zippers Have Teeth and Other Questions about Inventions*. It is one of many Spanish language science books available from the Center for the Study of Books in Spanish for Children, which maintains a database of thousands of titles with brief descriptions. (See the Notes at the end of the chapter for the center's Internet address.)[1]

Isabel Schon, an expert in the use of books for children in Spanish, makes the following point about the availability of books in Spanish. But I think what she says can be applied to books in other languages, as well:

> Encouraging young Spanish speakers into the world of science is becoming easier every day. The ever-increasing number of high-quality, informative, and appealing books being published in Spanish make the observation, identification, description, experimental investigation, and/or theoretical explanation of phenomena much more rewarding.[2]

Reinforcing Reading and Language Arts Skills

Hands-on, discovery-based science experiences can be great confidence builders for children from diverse cultural backgrounds, even if their present reading and language arts skills in English are weak. Your challenge as a teacher is to remember that you can use a child's success in science as a starting point to build a positive attitude toward school. Let's take a unit on weather as an example. Here are some very specific ways to extend the unit to the areas of reading and language arts, which can be applied to any science unit:

1. Use daily weather observations by students to create a language experience chart. You may have learned this technique in reading and language arts methods courses or workshops. To make such a chart, transcribe the children's oral observations onto a large sheet of paper, and have them read and discuss the material.

2. Have cooperative learning groups make model weather instruments and maintain their own language experience charts. You or a child with advanced writing abilities can transcribe the observations to the chart.

3. Expect children to make labels for the parts of their model weather instruments.

4. Expect children to keep personal logs of their daily weather observations, and occasionally read to them from their logs.

5. Have children record their individual weather reports on audiocassette tape or videotape.

6. Read or have one of the children read weather-related passages from children's books.

7. Encourage children to cut out weather-related headlines from a daily newspaper, and read them to the class.

8. Using suggestions from the class, write short poems about weather on chartpaper.

9. Have the children create dictionaries of weather terms, including pronounciation hints and drawings.

10. Have the children create a school weather report and present it on the school public address system every morning.

These techniques will be most effective if they are rooted in your belief that children from diverse cultural backgrounds who have language difficulties need every possible opportunity to practice the skills of reading, speaking, and writing. Two other techniques are especially helpful for children who are not fluent in English in the classroom: peer tutoring and parent/classroom connections.

Organizing Peer Tutoring

The key to success in peer tutoring lies in the selection of the tutors. Ideally, tutors are good students who are fluent in both languages, who understand the content you are teaching, and who possess those special personal characteristics that permit them to function as positive, supportive tutors.

Peer tutors also need some help from teachers. If possible, you should provide them with materials that display and explain science concepts in the child's native language as well as in English. If you happen to be fluent in the native languages of the children in your classes, you may wish to prepare alternative materials similar to those shown in Figure 9.1.[3] Children who only speak English may enjoy the challenge of trying to explain what the foreign terms on such diagrams mean.

Fostering Parent/Classroom Science Connections

Science time can be a learning experience that fully and appropriately involves the parents of children from diverse cultural backgrounds. Reaching out to these parents is well worth the effort, even though time and energy are at a premium for modern

FIGURE 9.1
With a little effort, you should be able to find drawings that are labeled in children's native languages.

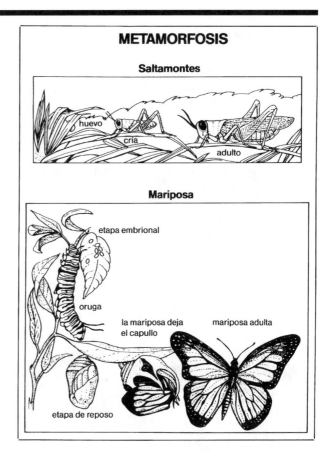

parents and teachers. You may need the assistance of someone who is fluent in the child's home language to use the following ideas:

1. Send a letter to parents at the beginning of the year explaining what science time for students will be like. Write the letters in English and in the children's home languages, and send both copies to parents.
2. Send home a monthly science newsletter in the children's home languages that includes examples of students' work.
3. Call five parents a week to make contact for future communication.
4. Invite parents to school for a Science Open House, and invite school professionals who speak the home languages to be present.
5. Prepare home study science activity sheets in children's home languages.
6. Send a letter to parents asking for volunteers to accompany the class on field trips or to come to class when science activities are done. If you are not fluent in children's home languages, having a helper who can communicate in more than one language can be a boon.

Creating Discovery-Based Lessons with Multicultural Dimensions

Figures 9.2 and 9.3 (pages 163 and 164) are sample lesson plans that reflect instructional techniques to interconnect science and multicultural education. Notice the implementation of the discovery-learning cycle—explore, inquire and acquire, and discover and apply—in each of the lessons.

For additional ideas on how to meet the special needs of minority and bilingual children in the classroom, contact one of the bilingual educational multifunctional support/resource centers listed in the For the Teacher's Desk section at the end of this book. As you review the listing, notice that the resource centers provide services for specific geographic regions.

Children with Special Needs

Perhaps we, as teachers, should take a vow with respect to children who have impairments—namely, that we will not give these children additional challenges while they are in our care. My language may seem a bit strong, but it is possible to put these children at even greater risk when we make *content* adjustments when we should be

MAKE THE CASE   *An Individual or Group Challenge*

■ **The Problem**

Because technological innovations occur so rapidly these days, it is difficult for teachers to select the best classroom technology for children with impairments.

■ **Assess Your Prior Knowledge and Beliefs**

Based on your personal experience in science classrooms, assess your present knowledge about the classroom devices that could help you achieve the fullest possible participation of children with these impairments:

1. Hearing _____

2. Visual _____

3. Orthopedic _____

■ **The Challenge**

Four engineers have formed a company to design and manufacture instructional equipment for children with impairments. They have asked you to suggest ideas for new devices or for improvements in existing devices that would assist these children in a hands-on, discovery-based classroom. What will you suggest?

FIGURE 9.2   This discovery lesson on nutrition has a multicultural
dimension that extends the topic into the subjects of social studies and health.

Lesson
Plan

Food and Nutrients

OBJECTIVES
1. The children will be able to list the nutrients found in rice, corn, and wheat.
2. The children will be able to identify countries in which these cereal grains are an important part of the typical diet.
3. The children will develop an appreciation of the roles that cereal grains play in the diets of different cultures.

MATERIALS
Three sandwich bags for each group, each containing rice, corn, or wheat (2–3 grains per bag)
Newsprint and watercolor markers
Food guide pyramid chart for each group
Photocopies of menus from ethnic restaurants

EXPLORE
1. Have the children join their cooperative learning groups. Distribute a sheet of newsprint and samples of rice, wheat, and corn to each group.
2. Have the groups spend 5 to 10 minutes discussing the following questions and recording their responses on the newsprint: What part of the plants did you receive? How does this part help the plants? What do you think these plants need to grow well? In what countries do people use these plants as a source of food?

INQUIRE AND ACQUIRE
1. Teach the term *nutrient* and write its definition on the board. Have children practice pronouncing and spelling *nutrient*. Then create a chart to show the amounts of starch, water, and protein in rice, corn, and wheat.
2. Have the groups display their newsprint and give their responses to the questions.
3. Ask the children about the type of climate they think that each plant needs. Then describe the climate characteristics needed for each plant.
4. Using wall maps, show the children where the cereal grains are typically grown and identify countries that rely on rice, corn, and wheat.
5. Review their previous work on the food groups shown on the food guide pyramid, and ask the children to classify rice, corn, and wheat into the proper group.

DISCOVER AND APPLY
Distribute photocopies of menus from ethnic restaurants. Have the children identify all of the foods that contain cereal grains and contribute to meeting the requirements of the "Rice, bread, cereal, and pasta" group.

ASSIGNMENT
Choosing foods from the photocopied menus, write a list of the items you would select for one day. Be sure to include foods from all six food groups, but watch out for the "Fats, oils, and sugars" group.

making *methodology* adjustments. Children with impairments need to learn the same things as other children, but they may need to learn these things in different ways or at different rates. Every child needs opportunities to explore, to inquire and acquire knowledge and skills, and to discover and apply what he or she has learned.

FIGURE 9.3   This discovery lesson on weather has a multicultural dimension that extends the topic into social studies work.

Lesson Plan

Weather and Climate

OBJECTIVES	1. The children will compare seasonal weather here with seasonal weather in their country of origin or their parents' or neighbors' countries of origin. 2. The children will make a chart comparing the climates of all the countries they have lived in or visited.
MATERIALS	A wall map showing the continents Index cards with weather and climate information for "mystery" countries A giant "mystery" card A globe
EXPLORE	Have the children join their cooperative learning groups. Give each group a climate information card for a "mystery" country. Have each group discuss the information on its card and then go to the wall map to make an educated guess about the location of their country.
INQUIRE AND ACQUIRE	1. At the board, distinguish between *climate* and *weather.* Write out a definition of each after receiving ideas from the class. 2. Discuss the seasonal differences between the Northern and Southern Hemispheres using the globe. 3. Have each group read the information from the index card and tell in what part of the world the country can be found. 4. After each group has had a turn, reveal the "mystery" countries and have the groups check their results.
DISCOVER AND APPLY	Have the students contribute ideas for a master chart that uses the climate information from their cards to show various climate types. Display the giant "mystery" card and encourage each group to prepare a hypothesis about the most likely part of the world for the location of the "mystery" country.
ASSIGNMENT	Interview relatives or neighbors about their recollections of the climates in their countries of origin, and bring the information to class tomorrow.

All children—including those with special needs—need opportunities to explore, acquire knowledge and skills, and apply what they have learned.

The Inclusion Illusion

In many schools, children with special needs have been moved from traditional special education or resource rooms to regular classrooms in a practice known as *inclusion* or *mainstreaming.* While educating these children in classrooms with their agemates may seem like a good idea, actually doing it can be a difficult, intense process. In too many cases, it's assumed that the physical placement alone is enough and that good things will automatically happen for everyone involved. It isn't quite that easy, however, especially in a science program designed to provide appropriate inquiry-based experiences for everyone. The strategies discussed in the next few sections will help you ensure that every child who is *physically* included in your classroom will be *educationally* included, as well.

Science Experiences for Children with Visual Impairments

Children with visual impairments don't need to be placed in special classrooms. A visual impairment affects only the *manner* through which knowledge enters a child's mind; it should not, in any way, affect the *nature* of the knowledge you select for the curriculum. (I am, of course, using *knowledge* in its broadest sense to include skills, attitudes, values, and so forth.)

But if you do not modify the curriculum, then what do you do? The answer is straightforward: You modify equipment, materials, and experiences that are visually based by incorporating the use of touch, taste, and smell.

Science Reading Materials

One convenient approach to delivering printed science information to children with visual problems is to have sighted students with good oral-reading skills audiotape books, chapter sections, newspaper stories, and other printed materials. This can be an ongoing class project, in which children take turns preparing instructional materials. Another strategy is to have the school purchase large-type books, talking books, and braille books (if your children have braille reading skills). (See the Notes at the end of the chapter for major sources of such materials.)[4]

Science Activities and Equipment

Some children with visual impairments have a degree of residual vision; that is, they may be able to distinguish light areas from dark areas and to differentiate shapes. To capitalize on these abilities, speak with the child, the child's parents, and perhaps the child's physician (with parental permission, of course) to get ideas about how to modify equipment for him or her.

A small audiocassette player can be an important addition to your classroom equipment. It can take the place of a notebook by permitting the child to record the results of science experiences. The audiotaping procedure will also help the child understand that you are holding him or her as accountable as the other students for taking and maintaining notes.

Here is a challenge for you: How would you have a child with a visual impairment observe a fish in an aquarium? Since aquarium fish usually are not noisy creatures and are tucked in water, which is itself encased in glass or plastic, this problem may seem insurmountable—but it isn't. If you place within the aquarium a slightly smaller plastic aquarium that has holes drilled in it, the child will be able to lift and tip the inner aquarium until most of the water drains into the larger aquarium. The fish will become trapped in the water that remains at the bottom of the inner aquarium and can be thoroughly studied through the child's sense of touch—a pleasant educational experience for the child, if not the fish.

As the aquarium question illustrates, the real challenge to a child's learning may be the difficulty the teacher has in finding a way around or through a seemingly insurmountable problem. You are not completely on your own, however, as you think through these problems. Through research in specialized catalogs and your personal contacts with special education personnel, you will discover that adapted equipment is available to help children and adults with visual impairments measure such variables as elapsed time, length, volume, mass, and weight.

There should be an "eleventh commandment" for teachers who work with children who have visual impairments: Do not be meek in your demeanor as you go forth to make requests for special adapted materials and equipment. Your efforts to accommodate the needs of children with visual impairments will be rewarded in many ways. The children will learn, and their peers will gain important knowledge and attitudes about people who may seem different but, in fact, are not.

Science Experiences for Children with Hearing Impairments

Mainstreamed children with hearing impairments range from those who do not require a hearing aid to those who have no hearing. Some of these children will be skilled lip readers, some will be adept at sign language, and some will have neither of these skills.

Children who have hearing impairments can benefit greatly from the multi-sensory, hands-on approach to science used in any discovery-oriented classroom. Your principal challenge will be helping these children participate fully in the experiences. Written or pictorial directions for activities and assignments, directions on task cards, and even acting out the steps of an activity will prove helpful. In the upper-elementary grades and in the middle grades, you may wish to have children take turns taking notes from your oral presentations and sharing them with students who have hearing impairments.

REAL TEACHERS TALKING
A Starting Point for Thinking, Talking, and Writing

Dale: Some teachers are really challenged when they have a child with a hearing impairment in class. I think this even happens when the child has a sign language interpreter. You've had a lot of experience with this, Karen. What are some practical things the rest of us should remember?

Karen: This sounds so obvious—but I think teachers can easily make a big mistake if there is an interpreter in the room, so I am going to say it: You must direct your conversation to the child and let the interpreter facilitate the communication. Don't speak to the interpreter! A child with residual hearing or with speech-reading ability will benefit from you speaking directly to him or her. So, face the child when you talk, teach children who are in the same cooperative group with the deaf child or the child with a hearing impairment to do the same thing, and always face the child when you talk and write on the board.

Dale: I learned that lesson a long time ago. I stopped "talking to the board" because even hearing children miss instructions and information when you fall into that pattern. I've got another question that might be debatable: Should I downplay lessons and projects dealing with sound and hearing? I hate to make anyone feel uncomfortable.

Karen: Oh, no. Any activity can be made more visual or tactile with a little extra preparation. Of course, you also have the benefit of having a child who, if both the child and the parents agree, can show and explain audiograms, hearing aids, and any devices that the child uses to make sound visual or tactile. These are all items that most children will be unaware of. The rest of the class will probably be motivated to ask the child many questions about how these devices work.

Dale: So, the advice is not to stay away from sound but to take advantage of the resources that the child brings by virtue of his or her presence in the classroom. I like to think of the presence of children who may have physical impairments as an opportunity to subtly teach the rest of the class some important lessons about life. *All* the children need to be better prepared to live in a world where people are a little different from one another. I think that is the most important advantage of having a classroom that welcomes everyone.

▶ **POINT TO PONDER:** *What steps would you take to change the physical setting in a traditional classroom to help children who are deaf or who have hearing impairments be successful with hands-on, discovery-oriented projects?*

Children with hearing impairments benefit greatly from participating in multisensory, hands-on science activities.

The child with a hearing impairment should have an unobstructed view of you and the location where you carry out demonstrations. This will allow the child to search for visual cues to supplement any information that you transmit orally. As you carry out demonstrations, explain content, and give directions, try to position your head so that the child can read your lip movements and facial expressions. You may want to remind the child's classmates to do the same.

When working with a child who has a hearing impairment, be careful not to form an opinion about his or her intellectual abilities based only upon listening to his or her speech. The inability to articulate properly results from not having a model for the spoken words and does not indicate intellectual ability. By encouraging the child's oral responses, you will provide him or her with an opportunity to build self-confidence and practice articulation.

Science Experiences for Children with Physical Impairments

Physical impairments may range from mild to severe and differ widely in origin. Some physical challenges may result from accidents and diseases, and some may be congenital. As a science teacher, your concern should focus on the specific problems that the child may have as the class does hands-on activities. Think about whether the child has problems grasping objects, moving, stopping, or remaining steady. Also keep in mind the space needed for the child to put crutches, the room required for a wheelchair to navigate, and the access available at some field trip sites.

As you consider these matters, you may find that you have to make a few minor modifications in the classroom to accommodate a child with a physical challenge or some adaptations in the science materials or equipment that he or she will use. For example, you may need to arrange seating so that a child in a wheelchair has ready access to all parts of the room. Or you may need to be sure that a child who has a problem moving quickly has a work space that is close to the distribution point for science materials. Of course, the modifications needed will vary with each child.

A child's physical challenge can provide a growth experience for the classroom if you capitalize on the opportunities it provides for building a sense of community among all the children. By helping children interact positively with *all* their peers, you not only help the child with a physical impairment but also the entire class.

Science Experiences for Children with Emotional Problems

Some children display emotional behaviors that interfere with their ability to function well academically or with their personal and social development in the classroom. These children may have little self-confidence, be frightened easily, be depressed, be disobedient or defiant, or simply spend their time daydreaming. The child with emotional problems acts the way he or she does for a reason. Unfortunately, the reason may have eluded even the most skilled school psychologist or psychiatrist.

The causes for the behavior you observe will probably lie outside your ability to remediate. However, the science activities you offer can serve an important therapeutic function. They can enable the child to manipulate and control variables and thus give him or her a unique opportunity to operate in responsible ways. If children can find success through such activities, they will gain self-confidence and pride in accomplishment. You may not be able to remedy children's basic emotional problems, but you can create an environment that can enhance feelings of self-worth.

As a teacher of science in a regular classroom, you should help your students welcome and encourage any child with emotional problems who joins the class for the day or a portion of the day. Remember, children with emotional problems need ever-increasing contact with children who display appropriate behaviors. Some teachers may be concerned that the rest of a class will learn inappropriate behaviors from a mainstreamed child with emotional problems. If this occurs, it may be that the teacher has been unable to create a total classroom environment that values and affirms productive and appropriate social behaviors.

Children with Special Gifts and Talents

Many of the children in our schools have extraordinary intellectual abilities, and many have other abilities that are far more advanced than those of their agemates. In fact, it is estimated that between 3% and 5% of the school-age population fits this definition. How can you tell which children have special abilities? The following definition may help:

> Children capable of high performance, including those with demonstrated achievements or ability in any one or more of these areas—general intellectual ability, specific academic aptitude, creative or productive thinking, leadership ability, visual and performing arts, or psychomotor ability.[5]

Also keep in mind that gifted and talented children may come from diverse cultural backgrounds or they may have impairments, as discussed in previous sections of this chapter. Think of your classroom as a garden in which each gifted and talented child can blossom. Science can provide these children with unique opportunities to design and carry out explorations of their environment. Because gifted and talented children may move very quickly through the planned learning experiences you provide for your class, the challenge is to keep them growing and blossoming. You will need to find ways to extend and enrich your science activities so that these children do not become bored.

Day-to-Day Enrichment Activities

Here are some activities you may wish to use even if your school has a standard science curriculum or a specific set of textbooks or other resource materials:

1. Get single copies of advanced levels of the materials for each child you think will benefit from such materials or activities.
2. Each time the class begins a new unit of work, have conferences with your gifted children to identify enrichment readings and activities for them to work on in the course of the unit and establish a schedule of follow-up conferences.
3. Develop some strategy that will enable these children to share their readings and related experiences with the rest of the class.
4. In general, expect these children to participate fully in all regular activities, but try to put their special gifts and talents to use as they go beyond the basic curriculum.

Challenge Projects

Gifted and talented children are a special joy to teach because many are able to function with considerable independence in the classroom. This capacity for independent, self-directed work is well suited to long-term science projects. I call such activities *challenge projects.* Here are a few examples:

Can You Make:

A sundial and use it as a clock?

A model wind-speed indicator?

A water filter using sand and pebbles that will clean up muddy water?

A compound machine from a group of simple machines?

A working model of a liquid-based fire extinguisher?

A simple battery-operated electric motor?

A balance that really works?

A clay contour map of the school grounds?

All challenge projects should begin with a teacher/student conference that focuses on the child's interest in and capacity to undertake various projects.

Responding to the special needs of gifted and talented children will provide you with many opportunities to stretch your own intellectual and imaginative abilities. You will find helping these children to reach their full potential is an extremely enjoyable part of teaching.

Summary

Teachers need to know how to use and provide access to the latest classroom technology so that special-needs children are not limited in their progress as a result of the "digital divide." Science time should be seen as an opportunity for all children to practice their reading and language development skills. Inquiry-based, discovery-focused activities, and the stimuli such activities provide, can help children from diverse cultural backgrounds increase their language skills as they learn science.

Children with special needs—whether visual or physical impairments, hearing problems, or emotional problems—must participate as fully as possible in the science activities that take place in the classroom. Your response to their special needs requires both an understanding of the unique challenges they offer and the ability to develop a variety of ways to make the curriculum accessible to them.

Gifted and talented children also have special needs. The science curriculum for these children should include various enrichment activities, challenge projects, and other opportunities to use their unique talents and abilities.

GOING FURTHER

On Your Own

1. If you are part of a racial or ethnic group that was a minority in your school, comment on any special challenges you had to overcome to be a successful student in science class. If you feel that there were no such challenges, note whether this was due to special circumstances, such as a particularly responsible and encouraging teacher, parental support, and so on. If you are not a member of a minority group, interview someone who is and record his or her responses to these questions.

2. How serious is the problem of science career awareness for children from diverse cultural backgrounds? Would broader media coverage of minority-group members in scientific fields

counterbalance the underrepresentation of such individuals in curricular materials? What do you see as the teacher's role in building scientific career awareness?

3. Identify a science activity you would do with children, and then describe how you would adapt it to the needs of a child with a visual or hearing impairment.

4. Write a sample letter that you could use to establish communication among yourself, a scientist living in the community, and a gifted child with a strong interest in science. In the letter, highlight the benefits that both the child and the scientist would enjoy.

On Your Own or in a Cooperative Learning Group

5. Develop an inquiry-based lesson or group of lessons that are organized around the three-step learning cycle, and capitalize on the presence of children from other parts of the world in your classroom. Focus the lesson or lessons on how musical instruments from other countries produce sound. Be sure that each lesson or group of lessons is organized around the three stages of the learning cycle: explore, inquire and acquire, and discover and apply.

6. Role-play the following situations with your group. When you are done, discuss each situation:
   a. A parent/teacher conference regarding a gifted child whose parent is dissatisfied with

your response to the child's special abilities. This parent is particularly concerned about accelerating the child's learning in both science and mathematics.
   b. Same as in "a," except the child has a hearing or visual impairment.
   c. A conference in which the teacher encourages the parents of a child with a physical impairment to allow the child to participate in a field trip to a water treatment plant.

If you are doing this activity by yourself, write a brief description of what might take place in each of these three conferences.

RESOURCES FOR DISCOVERY LEARNING

Internet Resources
Websites for Inclusive Classrooms

ERIC Clearinghouse on Disabilities and Gifted Education

www.cec.sped.org

This comprehensive site leads you to a variety of sources that will help you plan units and lessons for children with disabilities and children with special gifts and talents. It contains the results of the most recent research dealing with both groups as well as fact sheets and minibibliographies. Perhaps most important, it permits you to search the entire ERIC database to locate materials appropriate for your unique planning needs.

The National Information Center for Children and Youth with Disabilities

www.nichcy.org

This federally sponsored site provides information on disabilities and disability-related issues for educators, families, and others. You will find information about the nature of specific disabilities, the importance of

early intervention, and, most important for teachers, the preparation of IEPs (individualized education programs).

Top Language Groups for LEP (Limited-English-Proficiency) Students

www.ncbe.gwu.edu/links/langcult/toplangs.htm

This is an excellent site for anyone with a special interest in making curriculum adaptations for a child whose native language is not English. Links will take you to sites dealing with educating children representing 12 different languages, including Spanish, Vietnamese, Hmong, Tagalog, Russian, Haitian, and Arabic.

California Department of Education: Resources for English Learners

www.cde.ca.gov/el

This site will be a useful resource if you teach science to children who are not fluent in English. The part of the site that offers the most help to teachers is called "Resources," which has links to very specific information on unit and lesson planning.

Bilingual Books for Kids

www.bilingualbooks.com/

I have included this commercial site because of the rather unique materials available at it. The books are literally bilingual in that their text is written in both English and Spanish. Look at the book selections to find detailed descriptions of "Bilingual Nonfiction" choices for science. You may want to acquire some to support teaching science- and technology-related issues.

Center for Research on Education, Diversity, and Excellence (CREDE)

www.cal.org/crede/credeprj.htm

If you have a strong interest in educating children from culturally diverse backgrounds, this site will lead you to helpful resources. The center sponsors a variety of education-related projects that include attention to "Instruction in Context," which deals with teaching various subjects (including science) to these students, and "Assessment Programs," which suggest alternative ways of assessing their progress.

Print Resources
Suggested Readings

Allan, Alson. "The Minority Student Achievement Network." *Educational Leadership* 60, no. 5 (December 2002/January 2003): 76–78.

Bernstein, Leonard, et al. *African and African-American Women of Science.* Saddle Brook, NJ: Peoples Publishing Group, 1998.

Bernstein, Leonard, et al. *Latino Women of Science.* Saddle Brook, NJ: Peoples Publishing Group, 1998.

Bernstein, Leonard, et al. *Multicultural Women of Science.* Saddle Brook, NJ: Peoples Publishing Group, 1996.

Buck, Gayle A. "Teaching Science to English-as-Second-Language Learners." *Science and Children* 38, no. 3 (November/December 2000): 38–41.

Cassano, Paul, and Rayna A. Antol. "Integration and Integrity." *Science Scope* 24, no. 7 (April 2001): 18–21.

Farenga, Stephen J., et al. "Rocketing into Adaptive Inquiry." *Science Scope* 25, no. 4 (January 2002): 34–39.

Fetters, Marcia, Dawn M. Pickard, and Eric Pyle. "Making Science Accessible: Strategies to Meet the Needs of a Diverse Student Population." *Science Scope* 26, no. 5 (February 2003): 26–29.

Garrett, Michael Tlanusta, et al. "Open Hands, Open Hearts: Working with Native Youth in the Schools." *Intervention in School and Clinic* 38, no. 4 (March 2003): 225–235.

Gooden, Kelly. "Parents Come to Class." *Science and Children* 40, no. 4 (January 2003): 22–25.

Hrabowski, Freeman A., III. "Raising Minority Achievement in Science and Math." *Educational Leadership* 60, no. 5 (December 2002/January 2003): 44–48.

Krutchinsky, Rich, and William Harris. "Super Science Saturday." *Science and Children* 40, no. 4 (January 2003): 26–28.

Lord, Thomas R., and Tandi Clausen-May. "Giving Spatial Perception Our Full Attention." *Science and Children* 39, no. 5 (February 2002): 22–25.

Nitzberg, Joel, and Judith Sparrow. "Parent Outreach Success." *Science and Children* 39, no. 3 (November/December 2001): 36–40.

Pemberton, Jane B. "Integrated Processing: A Strategy for Working Out Unknown Words." *Intervention in School and Clinic* 38, no. 4 (March 2003): 247–250.

Rolon, Carmen A. "Educating Latino Students." *Educational Leadership* 60, no. 5 (December 2002/January 2003): 40–43.

Schon, Isabel. "Libros de Ciencias en Espanol." *Science and Children* 39, no. 6 (March 2002): 22–25.

Schon, Isabel. "Libros de Ciencias en Espanol." *Science and Children* 38, no. 6 (March 2001): 23–26.

Schon, Isabel. "Libros de Ciencias en Espanol."
Science and Children 37, no. 6 (March 2000):
26–29.

Talanquer, Vicente, and Grieselda Sarmiento. "One
Foot = One Cenxocoalli: Measuring in the
Pre-Hispanic World." *Science Scope* 25, no. 7
(April 2002): 12–15.

Williams, Gregory J., and Leon Reisberg. "Successful
Inclusion." *Intervention in School and Clinic* 38,
no. 4 (March 2003): 205–210.

NOTES

1. You may reach the Center for the Study of Books in Spanish for Children at <www.csusm.edu/campus.centers/csb>.

2. Isabel Schon, "Libros de Ciencias en Espanol," *Science and Children* 35, no. 6 (March 1998): 30.

3. Many major publishers of educational materials prepare direct translations of some or all of their elementary- and middle-grade science books. I extend my thanks to Holt, Rinehart and Winston for their permission to reproduce Figure 9.1, which first appeared in J. Abruscato et al., *Ciencia de Holt, Grade 5 Teacher's Guide* (New York: Holt, Rinehart and Winston, 1985), p. TM10.

4. Major sources of materials, such as large-type books, talking books, and braille books are the American Printing House for the Blind (Box 6085, 1839 Frankfort Avenue, Louisville, Kentucky 40206) and The Lighthouse for the Blind and Visually Impaired (1155 Mission Street, San Francisco, California 94103).

5. Dorothy Sisk, *What If Your Child Is Gifted?* (Washington, DC: Office of the Gifted and Talented, U.S. Office of Education, n.d.).

For the Teacher's Desk

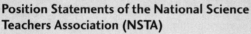

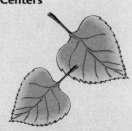

Position Statements of the National Science Teachers Association (NSTA)*

Women in Science Education

The continuing policy within NSTA is, and has been, to involve and encourage all teachers and members of the scientific community, regardless of sex, to participate in all organizational activities.

As teachers, however, our responsibility for contributing to the development of the science skills and interests of women lies principally in the classroom. Three elements within the educational system have subtle but significant roles in supporting or negating our efforts in this regard. They are (1) the development and use of criteria for the selection of student-used materials, e.g., textbooks, films, filmstrips, to insure the equitable portrayal of girls and boys, women and men involved in science; (2) the support of guidance departments that encourage students to develop to their full potential and to advise them of the course options available to them in school and the career options available to them after school; (3) the encouragement and guidance provided by the teacher regarding student achievement and careers in science; and (4) the inclusion of appropriate role models.

Because of the importance of these three elements, NSTA takes the following positions:

I. Any teacher whose charge includes the responsibility of evaluating or selecting instructional materials should demand that the materials (a) eliminate sex role stereotyping and (b) reflect a realistic female/male ratio in relation to the total number of people portrayed. Materials should be rejected by the teacher if they do not meet the above two criteria.

II. Science teachers must exert their influence to encourage guidance counselors to treat female students identically to male students relative to career opportunities and program planning. Science teachers can assist guidance counselors in this endeavor by providing them with detailed updated information and data on the interests and abilities of specific female students.

III. Science teachers must consciously strive to overcome the barriers created by society which discourage women from pursuing science for its career opportunities and for the enjoyment it brings to involved students.

—Adopted by the NSTA Board of Directors, July 1985

*The position statements on pages 176–178 are reprinted courtesy of the National Science Teachers Association, Arlington, VA <www.nsta.org/position>.

Multicultural Science Education

Science educators value the contributions and uniqueness of children from all backgrounds. Members of the National Science Teachers Association (NSTA) are aware that a country's welfare is ultimately dependent upon the productivity of all of its people. Many institutions and organizations in our global, multicultural society play major roles in establishing environments in which unity in diversity flourishes. Members of the NSTA believe science literacy must be a major goal of science education institutions and agencies. We believe that ALL children can learn and be successful in science and our nation must cultivate and harvest the minds of all children and provide the resources to do so.

Rationale

If our nation is to maintain a position of international leadership in science education, NSTA must work with other professional organizations, institutions, corporations, and agencies to seek the resources required to ensure science teaching for all learners.

Declarations

For this to be achieved, NSTA adheres to the following tenets:

- Schools are to provide science education programs that nurture all children academically, physically, and in development of a positive self-concept;
- Children from all cultures are to have equitable access to quality science education experiences that enhance success and provide the knowledge and opportunities required for them to become successful participants in our democratic society;
- Curricular content must incorporate the contributions of many cultures to our knowledge of science;
- Science teachers are knowledgeable about and use culturally-related ways of learning and instructional practices;
- Science teachers have the responsibility to involve culturally-diverse children in science, technology and engineering career opportunities; and
- Instructional strategies selected for use with all children must recognize and respect differences students bring based on their cultures.

—Adopted by the NSTA Board of Directors, July 2000

Substance Use and Abuse

Rationale

There is abundant evidence that the general public considers substance abuse a major problem. Students have revealed the same concern in surveys conducted nationwide. NSTA endorses the efforts of many school systems to conduct programs to help students understand the problem.

NSTA proposes the following guidelines for the development and implementation of such programs:

- The science education curriculum should include information about the effects of substance use and abuse.
- The thrust of such programs should be to promote healthful living.
- The programs should include information to help students make rational judgments regarding the consumption of commonly accepted over-the-counter drugs such as nicotine, alcohol, caffeine, and aspirin.
- The fact that the use of tobacco or tobacco products in any form is harmful to good health should be clearly documented.
- Student should be informed of the research which demonstrates clearly that marijuana, cocaine, and other illegal substances does cause physiological harm.
- Facts concerning the effects of the use of substances that may be abused should be presented, rather than counter-productive detailed discussion and explanation of the substances themselves.
- The programs should make available to students medical evidence that will help them to understand the inherent dangers of substance use and abuse.
- The ultimate goal of substance use/abuse awareness programs should be to eliminate substance abuse by giving students the up-to-date scientific knowledge they must have in order to make informed decisions.

—Adopted by the NSTA Board of Directors, January 2000

Science Competitions

The National Science Teachers Association recognizes that many kinds of learning experiences, including science competitions, can contribute significantly to the education of students of science. With respect to science competitions such as science fairs, science leagues, symposia, Olympiads, and talent searches, the Association takes the position that participation should be guided by the following principles:

I. Student and staff participation in science competition should be voluntary.
II. Emphasis should be placed on the learning experience rather than on the competition.
III. Science competitions should supplement and enhance other educational experiences.
IV. The emphasis should be on scientific process, content, and/or application.
V. Projects and presentations must be the work of the student with proper credit to others for their contributions.

—Adopted by the NSTA Board of Directors, July 1986

Keeping Living Things . . . Alive

Living Materials in the Classroom*

Animals

Before introducing animals into the classroom, check the policy of your local school district. When animals are in the classroom, care should be taken to ensure that neither the students nor the animals are harmed. Mammals protect themselves and their young by biting, scratching, and kicking. Pets such as cats, dogs, rabbits, and guinea pigs should be handled properly and should not be disturbed when eating. Consider the following guidelines for possible adoption in your science classroom.

1. Do not allow students to bring live or deceased wild animals, snapping turtles, snakes, insects, or arachnids (ticks, mites) into the classroom, as they are capable of carrying disease.
2. Provide proper living quarters. Animals are to be kept clean and free from contamination. They must remain in a securely closed cage. Provision for their care during weekends and holidays must be made.
3. Obtain all animals from a reputable supply house. Fish should be purchased from tanks in which all fish appear healthy.
4. Discourage students from bringing personal pets into school. If pets are brought into the classroom, they should be handled only by their owners. Provision should be made for their care during the day—give them plenty of fresh water and a place to rest.
5. When observing unfamiliar animals, students should avoid picking them up or touching them.
6. Caution students never to tease animals or insert fingers, pens, or pencils into wire mesh cages. Report animal bites and scratches to the school's medical authority immediately. Provide basic first aid.
7. Rats, rabbits, hamsters, and mice are best picked up by the scruff of the neck, with a hand placed under the body for support. If young are to be handled, the mother should be removed to another cage—by nature she will be fiercely protective.
8. Use heavy gloves for handling animals; have students wash their hands before and after they handle animals.
9. Personnel at the local humane society or zoo can help teachers create a wholesome animal environment in the classroom.

Plants

Create a classroom environment where there are plants for students to observe, compare, and possibly classify as a part of their understanding of the plant world. Plants that are used for such purposes should be well-known to you. Plants that produce harmful substances should not be used.

*From "Living Materials in the Classroom," *Science Scope* 13, no. 3 (November/December 1989), p. 517. Used with permission of the National Science Teachers Association.

Since many plants have not been thoroughly researched for their toxicity, it is important for students and teachers to keep in mind some common-sense rules:

1. Never place any part of a plant in your mouth. (*Note:* Emphasize the distinction between nonedible plants and edible plants, fruits, and vegetables.)
2. Never allow any sap or fruit juice to set into your skin.
3. Never inhale or expose your skin or eyes to the smoke of any burning plant.
4. Never pick any unfamiliar wildflowers, seeds, berries, or cultivated plants.
5. Never eat food after handling plants without first scrubbing your hands.

The reason for these precautions is that any part of a plant can be relatively toxic, even to the point of fatality. Following is a list of some specific examples of toxic plants. This list is only partial; include additional poisonous (toxic) plants for your specific geographical area.

A. Plants that are poisonous to the touch due to exuded oils are:

Poison ivy (often found on school grounds)	Poison oak
Poison sumac	(other)

B. Plants that are poisonous when eaten include:

Many fungi	Belladonna	Pokeweed	Indian tobacco
(mushrooms)	Wake robin	Tansy	Jimson weed
Aconite	Henbane	Foxglove	(other)

C. The saps of the following plants are toxic:

Oleander	Trumpet vine	Poinsettia	(other)

Note: Also be aware that many common houseplants are toxic.

The Plant Picker

Plants That Will Survive with Little Sunlight

African Violet	Corn Plant	Peperomia	Spider Plant
Asparagus Fern	English Ivy	Philodendron	Spiderwort
Begonia	Ficus	Piggyback (Tolmeia)	(Tradescantia)
Boston Fern	Hen and Chickens	Snake Plant	Staghorn Fern
Chinese Evergreen	Parlor Palm		

Plants That Need a Great Deal of Sunlight

Agave	Echeveria	Mimosa (Acacia)	Spirea
Aloe	Geranium	Oxalis	Swedish Ivy
Blood Leaf	Hibiscus	Sedum	(filtered sunlight)
Cactus	Jade Plant		Yucca
Coleus	(filtered sunlight)		

Safety Management Helper

Safety Checklist*

The following general safety practices should be followed in your science teaching situation:

_____ Obtain a copy of the federal, state, and local regulations which relate to school safety, as well as a copy of your school district's policies and procedures. Pay special attention to guidelines for overcrowding, goggle legislation and "right to know" legislation.

_____ Know your school's policy and procedure in case of accidents.

_____ Check your classroom on a regular basis to insure that all possible safety precautions are being taken. Equipment and materials should be properly stored; hazardous materials should not be left exposed in the classroom.

_____ Before handling equipment and materials, familiarize yourself with their possible hazards.

_____ Be extra cautious when dealing with fire, and instruct your students to take appropriate precautions. Be certain fire extinguishers and fire blankets are nearby.

_____ Be familiar with your school's fire regulations, evacuation procedures, and the location and use of fire-fighting equipment.

_____ At the start of each science activity, instruct students regarding potential hazards and the precautions to be taken.

_____ The group size of students working on an experiment should be limited to a number that can safely perform the experiment without confusion and accidents.

_____ Plan enough time for students to perform the experiments, then clean up and properly store the equipment and materials.

_____ Students should be instructed never to taste or touch substances in the science classroom without first obtaining specific instructions from the teacher.

_____ Instruct students that all accidents or injuries—no matter how small—should be reported to you immediately.

_____ Instruct students that it is unsafe to touch their faces, mouths, eyes, and other parts of their bodies while they are working with plants, animals, or chemical substances and afterwards, until they have washed their hands and cleaned their nails.

*Reprinted with permission from *Safety in the Elementary Science Classroom.* Copyright © 1978, 1993 by the National Science Teachers Association, 1840 Wilson Boulevard, Arlington, VA 22201-3000.

When working with chemicals:

_____ Teach students that chemicals must not be mixed just to see what happens.

_____ Students should be instructed never to taste chemicals and to wash their hands after using chemicals.

_____ Elementary school students should not be allowed to mix acid and water.

_____ Keep combustible materials in a metal cabinet equipped with a lock.

_____ Chemicals should be stored under separate lock in a cool, dry place, but not in a refrigerator.

_____ Only minimum amounts of chemicals should be stored in the classroom. Any materials not used in a given period should be carefully discarded, particularly if they could become unstable.

Glassware is dangerous. Whenever possible, plastic should be substituted. However, when glassware is used, follow these precautions:

_____ Hard glass test tubes should not be heated from the bottom. They should be tipped slightly, but not in the direction of another student.

_____ Sharp edges on mirrors or glassware should be reported to the teacher. A whisk broom and dustpan should be available for sweeping up pieces of broken glass.

_____ Warn students not to drink from glassware used for science experiments.

_____ Thermometers for use in the elementary classroom should be filled with alcohol, not mercury.

Teachers and students should be constantly alert to the following safety precautions while working with electricity:

_____ Students should be taught to use electricity safely in everyday situations.

_____ At the start of any unit on electricity, students should be told not to experiment with the electric current of home circuits.

_____ Check your school building code about temporary wiring for devices to be used continuously in one location.

_____ Electrical cords should be short, in good condition, and plugged in at the nearest outlet.

_____ Tap water is a conductor of electricity. Students' hands should be dry when touching electrical cords, switches, or appliances.

Materials to Keep in Your Science Closet

Primary Grades

Depending on the maturity of your students, you may wish to keep some
or most of these items in a secure location in the room:

aluminum foil
aluminum foil pie plates
aquarium
baking soda
balance and standard
    masses
basic rock and mineral
    collection
beans, lima
camera and supplies
cardboard tubes from
    paper towel rolls
clipboard
cooking oil
corks
dishes, paper

dishes, plastic
egg cartons
feathers
first aid kit
flashlight
food coloring
globe
hand lenses
hot plate
iron filings
latex gloves
lemon juice
lunch bags, paper
magnets, various sizes
    and shapes
masking tape

measuring cups
measuring spoons
meterstick
microscope
mirrors
modeling clay
peas, dried
plastic bucket
plastic jugs
plastic spoons
plastic wrap
potholder
potting soil
rain gauge
rubber balls of various
    sizes

salt
sandwich bags, plastic
scales and masses
seeds, assorted
shell collection
shoe boxes
small plastic animals
small plastic trays
sponges
string
sugar
tape measure
terrarium
vinegar
yeast, dry

Middle Grades

Depending on the maturity of your students, you may wish to keep some
or most of these items in a secure location in the room:

aluminum foil
assorted nuts and bolts
balance and standard
    masses
balloons
barometer
batteries
beakers
binoculars
cafeteria trays
calculator
candles
cans, clean, assorted,
    empty
cellophane, various
    colors
chart of regional birds
chart of regional rocks
    and minerals
clothespins, spring-
    variety

compass, directional
compass, drawing
desk lamp
extensive rock and
    mineral collection
eyedroppers
first aid kit
flashlight
flashlight bulbs
forceps or tweezers
glass jars
graduated cylinders
graph paper
hammer
hand lenses
hot glue gun*
hot plate*
hydrogen peroxide (3%)*
incubator
iron filings
isopropyl alcohol*

latex gloves
lenses
litmus paper
map of region, with
    contour lines
map of country, with
    climate regions
map of world
marbles
microscope slides and
    coverslips
mirrors
net for scooping material
    from streams and/or
    ponds
petroleum jelly
plastic bucket
plastic containers, wide-
    mouth, 1 and 2 L
plastic straws
plastic tubing

plastic wrap
pliers
prisms
pulleys
safety goggles
screwdriver
seeds, assorted vegetable
sponge, natural
steel wool
stop watch
sugar cubes
switches for circuits
tape, electrical
telescope
test tubes (Pyrex or
    equivalent)
thermometers
toothpicks
washers, assorted
wire for making circuits
wood scraps

*Keep these items in a locked closet.

183

The Metric Helper

Length

1 centimeter (cm) = 10 millimeters (mm)

1 decimeter (dm) = 10 centimeters

1 meter (m) = 10 decimeters

1 kilometer (km) = 1,000 meters

Liquid Volume

1,000 (mL) = 1 liter (L)

Dry Volume

1,000 cubic millimeters (mm3) = 1 cubic centimeter (cm3)

Mass

1,000 milligrams (mg) = 1 gram (g)

1,000 grams (g) = 1 kilogram (kg)

Some Important Metric Prefixes

kilo = one thousand

deci = one-tenth

centi = one-hundredth

milli = one-thousandth

micro = one-millionth

Temperature

Water freezes at 0° Celsius

Normal body temperature is 37° Celsius

Water boils at 100° Celsius

Approximate Sizes

millimeter = diameter of the wire in a paper clip

centimeter = slightly more than the width of a paper clip at its narrowest point

meter = slightly more than 1 yard

kilometer = slightly more than ½ mile

gram = slightly more than the mass of a paper clip

kilogram = slightly more than 2 pounds

milliliter = 5 milliters equal 1 teaspoon

liter = slightly more than 1 quart

Content Coverage Checklists

The following content checklists can be used to evaluate various elementary science textbooks, curriculum materials, audiovisual materials, software packages, and other resource materials for use in your classroom. Obviously, these lists do not include every concept, but they will provide a framework for analysis.

The Earth/Space Sciences and Technology

_____ The universe is 8 to 20 billion years old.

_____ The earth is about 5 billion years old.

_____ The earth is composed of rocks and minerals.

_____ Evidence of the many physical changes that have occurred over the earth's history is found in rocks and rock layers.

_____ The study of fossils can tell us a great deal about the life forms that have existed on the earth.

_____ Many species of animals and plants have become extinct.

_____ Our knowledge of earlier life forms comes from the study of fossils.

_____ Such forces as weathering, erosion, volcanic upheavals, and the shifting of crustal plates, as well as human activity, change the earth's surface.

_____ Natural phenomena and human activity also affect the earth's atmosphere and oceans.

_____ The climate of the earth has changed many times over its history.

_____ _Weather_ is a description of the conditions of our atmosphere at any given time.

_____ The energy we receive from the sun affects our weather.

_____ The water cycle, a continuous change in the form and location of water, affects the weather and life on our planet.

_____ Weather instruments are used to assess and predict the weather.

_____ The natural resources of our planet are limited.

_____ The quality of the earth's water, air, and soil is affected by human activity.

_____ Water, air, and soil must be conserved, or life as we know it will not be able to continue on the earth.

_____ The responsibility for preserving the environment rests with individuals, governments, and industries.

_____ Our solar system includes the sun, the moon, and nine planets.

_____ The sun is one of many billions of stars in the Milky Way galaxy.

_____ Rockets, artificial satellites, and space shuttles are devices that enable humans to explore the characteristics of planets in our solar system.

_____ Data gathered about the earth, oceans, atmosphere, solar system, and universe may be expressed in the form of words, numbers, charts, or graphs.

The Life Sciences
and Technology

_____ Living things are different from nonliving things.

_____ Plants and animals are living things.

_____ Living things can be classified according to their unique characteristics.

_____ The basic structural unit of all living things is the cell.

_____ All living things proceed through stages of development and maturation.

_____ Living things reproduce in a number of different ways.

_____ Animals and plants inherit and transmit the characteristics of their ancestors.

_____ Species of living things adapt and change over long periods of time or become extinct.

_____ Living things depend upon the earth, its atmosphere, and the sun for their existence.

_____ Living things affect their environment, and their environment affects living things.

_____ Different areas of the earth support different life forms, which are adapted to the unique characteristics of the area in which they live.

_____ Animals and plants affect one another.

_____ Plants are food producers.

_____ Animals are food consumers.

_____ Animals get their food by eating plants or other animals that eat plants.

_____ The human body consists of groups of organs (systems) that work together to perform a particular function.

_____ The human body can be affected by a variety of diseases, including sexually transmitted diseases.

_____ Human life processes are affected by food, exercise, drugs, air quality, and water quality.

_____ Medical technologies can be used to enhance the functioning of the human body and to diagnose, monitor, and treat diseases.

The Physical Sciences
and Technology

_____ _Matter_ is anything that takes up space and has weight.

_____ Matter is found in three forms: solid, liquid, and gas.

_____ All matter in the universe attracts all other matter in the universe with a force that depends on the mass of the objects and the distance between them.

_____ Matter can be classified on the basis of readily observable characteristics, such as color, odor, taste, and solubility. These characteristics are known as _physical properties of matter._

_____ Matter can undergo chemical change to form new substances.

_____ Substances consist of small particles known as *molecules.*

_____ Molecules are made of smaller particles known as *atoms.*

_____ Atoms are composed of three smaller particles called *protons, neutrons,* and *electrons.* (Protons and neutrons are composed of yet smaller particles known as *quarks.*)

_____ Atoms differ from one another in the number of protons, neutrons, and electrons they have.

_____ Some substances are composed of only one type of atom. These substances are known as *elements.*

_____ In chemical reactions between substances, matter is neither created nor destroyed but only changed in form. This is the law of conservation of matter.

_____ An object at rest or moving at a constant speed will remain in that state unless acted upon by an unbalanced external force.

_____ *Acceleration* is the rate at which an object's velocity changes.

_____ The amount of acceleration that an object displays varies with the force acting on the object and its mass.

_____ Whenever a force acts on an object, an equal and opposite reacting force occurs.

_____ The flight of an airplane results from the interaction of four forces: weight, lift, thrust, and drag.

_____ *Energy*—the capacity to do work—manifests itself in a variety of forms, including light, heat, sound, electricity, motion, and nuclear energy.

_____ Energy may be stored in matter by virtue of an object's position or condition. Such energy is known as *potential energy.*

_____ Under ordinary circumstances, energy can neither be created nor destroyed. This is the law of conservation of energy.

_____ The law of conservation of matter and the law of conservation of energy have been combined to form the law of conservation of matter plus energy, which states that under certain conditions, matter can be changed into energy and energy can be changed into matter.

_____ The basic concepts of matter, energy, force, and motion can be used to explain natural phenomena in the life, earth/space, and physical sciences.

_____ The diminishing supply of fossil fuels may be compensated for by the increased utilization of alternate energy sources, including wind, water, and synthetic fuels, and by energy conservation measures.

Your Science Survival Bookshelf

The Bookshelf

Abruscato, Joseph. *Whizbangers and Wonderments: Science Activities for Young People.* Boston: Allyn and Bacon, 2000.

Abruscato, Joseph, and Jack Hassard. *The Whole Cosmos Catalog of Science Activities.* Glenview, IL: Scott Foresman/Goodyear Publishers, 1991.

Blough, Glenn, and Julius Schwartz. *Elementary School Science and How to Teach It.* Fort Worth, TX: Holt Rinehart & Winston, 1990.

Carin, Arthur A. *Teaching Science through Discovery.* Columbus, OH: Merrill, 1996.

Esler, William K., and Mary K. Esler. *Teaching Elementary School Science.* Belmont, CA: Wadsworth, 1996.

Friedl, Alfred E. *Teaching Science to Children.* New York: Random House, 1991.

Hassard, Jack. *Science Experiences: Cooperative Learning and the Teaching of Science.* Menlo Park, CA: Addison-Wesley, 1990.

Jacobson, Willard J., and Abby B. Bergman. *Science for Children.* Englewood Cliffs, NJ: Prentice-Hall, 1991.

Lorbeer, George C., and Leslie W. Nelson. *Science Activities for Children.* Dubuque, IA: W. C. Brown, 1996.

Neuman, Donald B. *Experiencing Elementary Science.* Belmont, CA: Wadsworth, 1993.

Tolman, Marvin H., and Gary R. Hardy. *Discovering Elementary Science.* Boston: Allyn and Bacon, 1999.

Van Cleave, Janice Pratt. *Chemistry for Every Kid.* New York: Wiley, 1989.

Victor, Edward, and Richard E. Kellough. *Science for the Elementary School.* New York: Macmillan, 1997.

The Magazine Rack

For Teachers

Audubon Magazine
National Audubon Society
1130 Fifth Avenue
New York, NY 10028

Natural History
The American Museum of
   Natural History
Central Park West at Seventy-Ninth Street
New York, NY 10024

Science Activities
Heldref Publications
1319 Eighteenth Street, NW
Washington, DC 20036

Science and Children
National Science Teachers Association
1840 Wilson Boulevard
Arlington, VA 22201-3000

Science Scope
National Science Teachers Association
1840 Wilson Boulevard
Arlington, VA 22201-3000

Science Teacher
National Science Teachers Association
National Education Association
1742 Connecticut Avenue, NW
Washington, DC 20088-0154

For Children

Chickadee
Young Naturalist Foundation
P.O. Box 11314
Des Moines, IA 50340

The Curious Naturalist
Massachusetts Audubon Society
208 South Great Road
South Lincoln, MA 01773

Current Science
Xerox Education Publications
5555 Parkcenter Circle Suite 300
Dublin, OH 43017

Junior Astronomer
Benjamin Adelman
4211 Colie Drive
Silver Springs, MD 20906

Junior Natural History
American Museum of Natural History
Central Park West at Seventy-Ninth Street
New York, NY 10024

Ladybug
Cricket Country Lane
Box 50284
Boulder, CO 80321-0284

National Geographic World
National Geographic Society
Seventeenth and M Streets, NW
Washington, DC 20036

Odyssey
Kalmbach Publishing Company
1027 North Seventh Street
Milwaukee, WI 53233

Owl
Young Naturalist Foundation
P.O. Box 11314
Des Moines, IA 50304

Ranger Rick
National Wildlife Federation
1412 Sixteenth Street, NW
Washington, DC 20036-2266

Science Weekly
Subscription Department
P.O. Box 70154
Washington, DC 20088-0154

Science World
Scholastic Magazines, Inc.
50 West Forty-Fourth Street
New York, NY 10036

SuperScience
Scholastic Magazines, Inc.
50 West Forty-Fourth Street
New York, NY 10036

WonderScience
American Chemical Society
1155 Sixteenth Street, NW
Washington, DC 20036

Free and Inexpensive Materials

American Solar Energy Society
2400 Central Avenue, Suite G–1
Boulder, CO 80301

American Wind Energy Association
777 North Capitol Street, NE, Suite 805
Washington, DC 20002

Environmental Protection Agency Public
    Information Center and Library
401 M Street, SW
Washington, DC 20460

Environmental Sciences Services Administration
Office of Public Information
Washington Science Center, Building 5
Rockville, MD 20852

Fish and Wildlife Service
U.S. Department of the Interior
1849 C Street, NW
Mail Stop 304 Web Building
Washington, DC 20240

Jet Propulsion Laboratory (JPL)
Teacher Resource Center
4900 Oak Grove Drive
Mail Stop CS–530
Pasadena, CA 91109

National Aeronautics and Space
    Administration (NASA)
NASA Education Division
NASA Headquarters
300 E Street, SW
Washington, DC 20546

National Park Service
U.S. Department of the Interior
1849 C Street, NW
Washington, DC 20240

National Science Foundation
Division of Pre-College Education
1800 G Street, NW
Washington, DC 20550

National Wildlife Federation
8925 Leesburg Pike
Vienna, VA 22184-0001

Superintendent of Documents
U.S. Government Printing Office
732 North Capital Street, NW
Washington, D.C. 20401

U.S. Bureau of Mines
Office of Mineral Information
U.S. Department of the Interior
1849 C Street, NW
Washington, DC 20240

U.S. Department of Education
555 New Jersey Avenue, NW
Washington, DC 20208

U.S. Department of Energy
Conservation and Renewable Energy
    Inquiry and Referral Service
P.O. Box 8900
Silver Spring, MD 20907

U.S. Department of the Interior
Earth Science Information Center
1849 C Street, NW, Room 2650
Washington, DC 20240

U.S. Forest Service
Division of Information and Education
Fourteenth Street and Independence Avenue, SW
Washington, DC 20250

U.S. Geological Survey
Public Inquiries Office
U.S. Department of the Interior
Eighteenth and F Streets, NW
Washington, DC 20240

U.S. Public Health Service
Department of Health and Human Services
66 Canal Center Plaza, Suite 200
Alexandria, VA 22314

The "Wish Book" Companies

AIMS Education Foundation
P.O. Box 7766
Fresno, CA 93747

Carolina Biological Supply Co.
2700 York Road
Burlington, NC 27215

Central Scientific Company (CENCO)
3300 CENCO Parkway
Franklin, Park, IL 60131

Connecticut Valley Biological
 Supply Co., Inc.
82 Valley Road
Southhampton, MA 01073

Delta Education, Inc.
P.O. Box 915
Hudson, NH 03051-0915

Exploratorium Store
3601 Lyon Street
San Francisco, CA 94123

Flinn Scientific, Inc.
131 Flinn Street
P.O. Box 291
Batavia, IL 60510

Frey Scientific
905 Hickory Lane
Mansfield, OH 44905

Hubbard Scientific
3101 Iris Avenue, Suite 215
Boulder, CO 80301

Learning Things, Inc.
68A Broadway
P.O. Box 436
Arlington, MA 02174

LEGO Systems, Inc.
555 Taylor Road
Enfield, CT 06802

NASCO West, Inc.
P.O. Box 3837
Modesto, CA 95352

Ohaus Scale Corp.
29 Hanover Road
Florham Park, NJ 07932

Science Kit and Boreal Labs
777 East Park Drive
Tonawanda, NY 14150

Ward's Natural Science
 Establishment, Inc.
5100 West Henrietta Road
P.O. Box 92912
Rochester, NY 14692

Wind and Weather
P.O. Box 2320-ST
Mendocino, CA 95460

Young Naturalist Co.
614 East Fifth Street
Newton, KN 67114

Bilingual Child Resources

**Alabama, Florida, Georgia, Kentucky,
Mississippi, South Carolina, Tennessee**

Bilingual Education South Eastern Support
Center [BESES]
Florida International University
Tamiami Campus, TRM03
Miami, FL 33199

**Alaska, Idaho, Montana, Oregon,
Washington, Wyoming**

Interface Education Network
7080 SW Fir Loop, Suite 200
Portland, OR 97223

American Samoa, Hawaii

Hawaii/American Samoa Multifunctional
Support Center
1150 South King Street, #203
Honolulu, HI 97814

**Arizona, California (Imperial, Orange, Riverside,
San Bernardino, San Diego Counties)**

SDSU-Multifunctional Support Center
6363 Alvarado Court, Suite 200
San Diego, CA 92120

**Arkansas, Louisiana, Oklahoma,
Texas Education Service Regions V–XIX**

Bilingual Education Training and Technical
Assistance Network [BETTA]
University of Texas at El Paso
College of Education
El Paso, TX 79968

**California (all counties north of and including
San Luis Obispo, Kern, and Inyo), Nevada**

Bilingual Education Multifunctional Support Center
National Hispanic University
255 East Fourteenth Street
Oakland, CA 94606

**California (Los Angeles, Santa Barbara,
Ventura Counties), Nevada**

Bilingual Education Multifunctional Support Center
California State University at Los Angeles
School of Education
5151 State University Drive
Los Angeles, CA 90032

Colorado, Kansas, Nebraska, New Mexico, Utah

BUENO Bilingual Education Multifunctional
Support Center
University of Colorado
Bueno Center of Multicultural Education
Campus Box 249
Boulder, CO 80309

**Commonwealth of Northern Mariana Islands,
Guam, Trust Territory of the Pacific Islands**

Project BEAM [Bilingual Education Assistance
in Micronesia]
University of Guam
College of Education
UOG Station,
Mangilao, GU 96923

Commonwealth of Puerto Rico, Virgin Islands

Bilingual Education Multifunctional Support Center
Colegio Universitario Metropolitano
P.O. Box CUM
Rio Piedras, PR 00928

**Connecticut, Maine, Massachusetts,
New Hampshire, Rhode Island, Vermont**

New England Bilingual Education Multifunctional
Center
Brown University, Weld Building
345 Blackstone Boulevard
Providence, RI 02906

**Delaware, District of Columbia, Maryland,
New Jersey, North Carolina, Ohio, Pennsylvania,
Virginia, West Virginia**

Georgetown University Bilingual Education
Service Center
Georgetown University
2139 Wisconsin Avenue, NW, Suite 100
Washington, DC 20007

**Illinois, Indiana, Iowa, Michigan, Minnesota,
Missouri, North Dakota, South Dakota, Wisconsin**

Midwest Bilingual Educational Multifunctional
Resource Center
2360 East Devon Avenue, Suite 3011
Campus Box 136
Des Plaines, IL 60018

New York

New York State Bilingual Education Multifunctional
  Support Center
Hunter College of CUNY
695 Park Avenue, Box 367
New York, NY 10021

Texas Education Service Center, Regions
I through IV, XX

Region Multifunctional Support Center
Texas A&I University
Kingsville, TX 78363
Native American Programs

Alaska, Arizona, California, Michigan, Minnesota, Montana, New Mexico, North Carolina, Oklahoma, South Dakota, Utah, Washington, Wyoming

National Indian Bilingual Center
Arizona State University
Community Services Building
Tempe, AZ 85287

Special-Needs Resources

Alexander Graham Bell Association for the Deaf
3417 Volta Place, NW
Washington, D.C. 20007

American Foundation for the Blind
15 West Sixteenth Street
New York, NY 10011

American Printing House for the Blind
1839 Frankforth Avenue, Box A
Louisville, KY 40206

American Speech, Language, and Hearing
  Association
10801 Rockville Pike
Rockville, MD 20852

Center for Multisensory Learning
University of California at Berkeley
Lawrence Hall of Science
Berkeley, CA 94720

Council for Exceptional Children
1920 Association Drive
Reston, VA 22091

ERIC Clearinghouse on Handicapped and
  Gifted Children
1920 Association Drive
Reston, VA 22091

The Lighthouse for the Blind and
  Visually Impaired
1155 Mission Street
San Francisco, CA 94103

National Technical Institute for the Deaf
One Lomb Memorial Drive
Rochester, NY 14623

The Project on the Handicapped in Science
American Association for the Advancement
  of Science
1776 Massachusetts Avenue, NW
Washington, DC 20036

Recording for the Blind
20 Roszel Road
Princeton, NJ 08540

Sensory Aids Foundation
399 Sherman Avenue
Palo Alto, CA 94304

Science Teachers Associations

The major association for teachers with an interest in science is the National Science Teachers Association (NSTA). For information on membership, write to this address:

National Science Teachers Association
1840 Wilson Boulevard
Arlington, VA 22201-3000

This affiliated organization may also be reached through the NSTA address:

Council for Elementary Science International

Other science-related associations that may be of interest include the following:

American Association of Physics Teachers
c/o American Institute of Physics
335 E. 45th Street
New York, NY 10017

American Chemical Society
1155 Sixteenth Street, NW
Washington, DC 20006

National Association of Biology Teachers
1420 N. Street, NW
Washington, DC 20005

National Earth Science Teachers Association
P.O. Box 2194
Liverpool, NY 13089-2194

School Science and Mathematics Association
16734 Hamilton Court
Strongsville, OH 44149-5701

NASA Teacher Resource Centers

NASA Teacher Resource Centers provide teachers with NASA-related materials for use in classrooms. Contact the center that serves your state for materials or additional information.

Alabama, Arkansas, Iowa, Louisiana, Missouri, Tennessee

NASA Marshall Space Flight Center
Teacher Resource Center at the U.S. Space and
   Rocket Center
P.O. Box 070015
Huntsville, AL 35807

Alaska, Arizona, California, Hawaii, Idaho, Montana, Nevada, Oregon, Utah, Washington, Wyoming

NASA Ames Research Center
Teacher Resource Center
Mail Stop 253-2
Moffett Field, CA 94035

California (cities near Dryden Flight Research Facility)

NASA Dryden Flight Research Facility
Teacher Resource Center
Lancaster, CA 93535

Colorado, Kansas, Nebraska, New Mexico, North Dakota, Oklahoma, South Dakota, Texas

NASA Johnson Space Center
Education Resource Center
1601 NASA Road #1
Houston, TX 77058

Connecticut, Delaware, District of Columbia, Maine, Maryland, Massachusetts, New Hampshire, New Jersey, New York, Pennsylvania, Rhode Island, Vermont

NASA Goddard Space Flight Center
Teacher Resource Laboratory
Mail Code 130.3
Greenbelt, MD 20771

Florida, Georgia, Puerto Rico, Virgin Islands

NASA Kennedy Space Center
Educators Resource Laboratory
Mail Code ERL
Kennedy Space Center, FL 32899

Kentucky, North Carolina, South Carolina, Virginia, West Virginia

NASA Langley Research Center
Teacher Resource Center at the Virginia Air and
   Space Center
600 Settlers Landing Road
Hampton, VA 23669

Illinois, Indiana, Michigan, Minnesota, Ohio, Wisconsin

NASA Lewis Research Center
Teacher Resource Center
21000 Brookpark Road
Mail Stop 8-1
Cleveland, OH 44135

Mississippi

NASA Stennis Space Center
Teacher Resource Center
Building 1200
Stennis Space Center, MS 39529-6000

Virginia and Maryland Eastern Shore

NASA Wallops Flight Facility
Education Complex-Visitor Center
Building J-17
Wallops Island, VA 23337

General inquiries related to space science and planetary exploration may be addressed to:

Jet Propulsion Laboratory
NASA Teacher Resource Center
Attn: JPL Educational Outreach
Mail Stop CS-530
Pasadena, CA 91109

For catalogue and order forms for audiovisual material, send request on school letterhead to:

NASA CORE
Lorain County Joint Vocational School
15181 Route 58 South
Oberlin, OH 44074

Index

Photo, Figure, and Text Credits